BOOKS SHOULD BE RETURNED ON OR BEFORE THE LAST DATE
SHOWN BELOW.   BOOKS NOT ALREADY REQUESTED BY OTHER
READERS MAY BE RENEWED BY PERSONAL APPLICATION, BY
WRITING, OR BY TELEPHONE. TO RENEW, GIVE THE DATE ꞈ   ND
THE NUMBER ON THE BARCODE LABEL.

FINES CHARGED FOR OVERDUE ⌐⌐   ᴤE
INCURRED IN RECOVERY. DⱯ   L
BE CHARGED TO THE BORROW

Leabharlanna
Dublin Pu
CENT

Leabharlann Ceoil
Music Library, Henry Street   Tel: 734333

DATE DUE	DATE DUE	DATE DUE
24. FEB 01	S / T	
27. SEP 01		

90

90

Books on Aviation by N. H. Birch and A. E. Bramson

Flight Briefing for Pilots series
(full details overleaf)

Flying the VOR
A Guide to Aircraft Ownership
The Tiger Moth Story
Captains and Kings
Radio Navigation for Pilots

By A. E. Bramson
Be a Better Pilot
Make Better Landings
Principles of Flight (Audio-visual trainer)

Flight Briefing for Pilots
by N. H. Birch and A. E. Bramson

Volume 1 **An Introductory Manual of Flying Training Complete with Air Instruction**

An elementary manual of flying training giving brief background information for the PPL. The air exercises contain detailed 'patter' for the flying instructor.

Volume 2 **An Advanced Manual of Flying Training Complete with Air Instruction**

An advanced manual of flying training which explains such exercises as Instrument Flying, Night Flying, Multi-engine Conversion, Aerobatics etc. – for pilots aiming for a professional licence and PPL holders wishing to improve their standards.

Volume 3 **Radio Aids to Air Navigation**

Radio navigation for the pilot training for the PPL or the professional Instrument Rating.

Volume 4 **Associated Ground Subjects**

A concise and readable ground-school book covering Airframes, Piston Engines, Airfield Performance, Weight and Balance, Meteorology, Navigation, Use of Radiotelephony and Air Law.

Volume 5 **Flight Emergency Procedures for Pilots**

Emergency situations illustrated, with examples of the results of pilot ignorance. Correct procedures are given, and reinforced with useful background information.

Volume 6 **Check pilot**

More than 250 multiple choice questions and answers, fully cross-referenced to the other volumes, on Navigation, Meteorology, Aviation Law, Principles of Flight, Engines and Propellers, Airframes, Instruments, Radio Navigation and Airfield Performance.

Volume 7 **The IMC Rating Manual**

Tailored to the needs of the Revised IMC Rating, this book is based on the CAA approved syllabus and covers the use of radio navigation and approach aids.

Volume 8 **The Instrument Rating**

Explains the requirements and privileges of an Instrument Rating, the flight test and the various reasons for failure. The technical examination is described, with examples of questions, and there is a section on flight panel readings.

Flight Briefing for Pilots

Volume 2

An advanced manual of flying training complete with air instruction

N. H. Birch MSc, MRAeS
Director, Hamilton-Birch Ltd. and
Liveryman of the Guild of Air Pilots and Air Navigators

and A. E. Bramson FRAeS
Chairman of the Panel of Examiners
Liveryman of the Guild of Air Pilots and Air Navigators

Illustrated by A. E. Bramson

FIFTH EDITION

PITMAN

PITMAN BOOKS LIMITED
128 Long Acre, London WC2E 9AN

Associated Companies
Pitman Publishing Pty Ltd, Melbourne
Pitman Publishing New Zealand Ltd, Wellington

© N. H. Birch and A. E. Bramson 1978

First published in Great Britain 1962
Reprinted 1964, 1966, 1967
Second edition 1968
Third edition 1970
Reprinted 1972
Fourth edition 1974
Reprinted 1976
Fifth edition 1978
Reprinted 1982

All rights reserved. No part of this publication may be reproduced,
stored in a retrieval system, or transmitted, in any form or by any
means, electronic, mechanical, photocopying, recording and/or otherwise
without the prior written permission of the publishers. This book may
not be lent, resold, hired out or otherwise disposed of by way of trade
in any form of binding or cover other than that in which it is published,
without the prior consent of the publishers. This book is sold subject
to the Standard Conditions of Sale of Net Books and may not be resold in
the UK below the net price.

ISBN: 0 273 01165 0

Text set in 10/11½ pt VIP Times, printed by photolithography and bound in
Great Britain at The Pitman Press, Bath

LEABHARLANNA ATHA CLIATH
HENRY STREET LIBRARY
ACC. NC.   0273 011650
COPY NC.   CC 1002
INV. NC.   1133
PRICE IR£   9.26
CLASS   629.13252.

Preface

Since Volume 2 in the *Flight Briefing for Pilots* series was first published it has constantly been up-dated to keep in step with the most rapidly changing activity in the developed world – aviation. Whereas Volume 1 is devoted to the needs of the private pilot and those seeking an Assistant Flying Instructor's Rating, this book continues the study process into more advanced areas of flying.

This new edition has been comprehensively revised. It embodies those exercises needed to complete the syllabus for the unrestricted Flying Instructor's Rating as approved by the Civil Aviation Authority. There are chapters devoted to aerobatics, instrument and night flying, multi-engine conversion and, for those interested in the art, formation flying. There is also an expanded chapter dealing with gas turbine engines, turbojets, turbofans and turboprops.

The exercises described in Chapters 5 to 10 will be of value to those studying for a Commercial Pilot's Licence or, for that matter, the private pilot wishing to broaden his knowledge and use his aircraft to better advantage. As in Volume 1, these exercises include suggested 'patter' as a guide to the flying instructor.

Previous editions of this book have benefited from the advice and criticism of the RAF Central Flying School and the Panel of Examiners. This advice is greatly valued by the authors.

There is little difficulty in filling a book of this size on flying. Rather the problem has been to decide what can be omitted without detracting from the value of the work. The aim has been to produce a book on aircraft handling with sufficient explanation of the background to each exercise to prevent the student pilot from asking 'why' too frequently.

There are now eight volumes in this series – details are given in the list at the beginning of the book.

NHB
AEB

Contents

	Preface	v
1	Fundamentals of Flight	1
2	Piston Engine Handling and Propellers	33
3	Introduction to Gas Turbines	58
4	Multi-engined Aircraft	80
5	Taxying (Twin-engined) [5]	87
6	Instrument Flying [19]	91
7	Night Flying [20]	156
8	Aerobatics [21]	176
9	Formation Flying [22]	212
10	Multi-engine Conversion [23]	234
11	Flying Instructors' Ratings	262
12	The IMC Rating	268

Note

The bold figures following chapters 5–10 refer to exercise numbers in the syllabus of the British Civil Aviation Authority. For ease of reference these numbers appear in **bold type** at the foot of each page in the relevant chapter.

1 Fundamentals of Flight

The principles governing flight are outlined in the simplest terms in *Flight Briefing for Pilots*, Volume 1, and the purpose of this chapter is to enlarge upon the various aerodynamic considerations which are likely to be of value to the pilot. Both volumes are essentially practical in character and it has been thought desirable to adhere to these terms of reference throughout the following pages.

To go deeper into the various explanations would involve mathematics, when the chapter would become of more academic than practical use.

Drag

Throughout Volume 1 drag has been considered as a single force opposing thrust under normal flight conditions. Such a force should really be called **Total Drag** since it is the sum total of air resistance caused by each part of the aircraft in a number of different ways. Total drags falls into two main categories—

1. *Profile drag:* that which results from resistance as the airflow passes around a shape such as an engine nacelle, the fuselage, the undercarriage, etc., and

2. *Induced drag:* which is a by-product of lift, inseparable from and a direct result of the wings function as a lift producer.

1. Profile Drag

Whenever a body is moved through air (or water) resistance will result from two sources—

(*a*) *Form drag* caused by the body as it disturbs the air through which it passes, and (*b*) *Skin friction* which is incurred as the air passes over and under the surface of the body.

Both of these aspects of profile drag are influenced by good design and manufacture and their reduction gives increased performance.

For practical purposes profile drag increases as the square of the indicated airspeed, e.g. twice the speed, four times the drag; three times the speed, nine times the drag, etc., and the following figures clearly illustrate the detrimental effect of this type of drag particularly as the airspeed increases.

Profile Drag for Aeroplane X

Indicated Airspeed	Profile Drag
100 kt	200 lb
200 kt	800 lb
300 kt	1,800 lb
400 kt	3,200 lb
500 kt	5,000 lb
600 kt	7,200 lb

Each pound of profile drag must be paid for in terms of equal thrust and during the design stage every effort is made to reduce both form drag and skin friction. For example a 10% reduction would mean a comparable saving in power at each airspeed. The designer could either decide upon a smaller engine with an attendant reduction in weight, or he could exploit the saving in drag and have a higher all-round performance with the engine originally selected. Indirectly a saving in drag represents fuel economy and this in turn influences the aircraft's range so that much time and effort is devoted to the reduction of profile drag. Because of its nature it is sometimes called **Parasite Drag** and some of the methods used to combat its two contributing factors are listed below.

Form Drag

Other things being equal, shape is all important since by definition this kind of drag results from the disturbance created by the body as it passes through the surrounding air. Minimize the disturbance by streamlining and form drag will be reduced. The effect of streamlining is shown in Fig. 1.

Most disturbance is caused when a flat plate is forced through the air in the manner shown in the diagram, but by correct streamlining its form drag can be reduced to one twentieth of the original value.

While a gradual change in the direction of airflow is conducive to low form drag, this entails long thin shapes of considerable surface area and in the more detailed explanation which

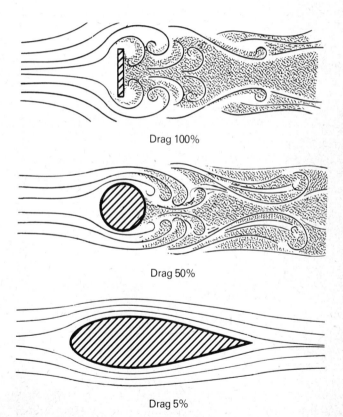

Drag 100%

Drag 50%

Drag 5%

Fig. 1. Reducing drag by streamlining.

follows it will be seen that area causes skin friction. Because of these conflicting requirements the ratio between the length and thickness of a streamlined body is important. This aspect of a streamlined body is called **Fineness Ratio** (Fig. 2).

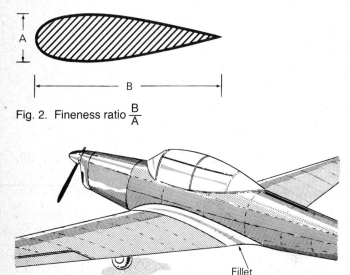

A

B

Fig. 2.   Fineness ratio $\dfrac{B}{A}$

Fillet

Fig. 3.   Reducing interference drag between wing and fuselage by incorporating a fillet.

When dealing with speeds up to 300 kt or so a fineness ratio of 4 is ideal, higher speed requiring a higher fineness ratio until supersonic speeds are reached when certain fundamental changes occur in aerodynamics. These are outlined briefly under 'Transonic and Supersonic Flight'.

While two components of an aircraft may in themselves be of low form drag, when they are joined the airflow over one part may react with the other to produce **Interference Drag.** This is really another type of form drag and a typical example would be the interference drag caused at the point where the wing joins the fuselage. By using **Fillets** one surface is made to flow into the other, thus reducing interference drag (Fig. 3).

Skin Friction

There are many examples of this kind of drag in everyday occurrence and their mention will contribute much towards an understanding of this form of resistance.

1. The resistance felt whilst shaving, which is reduced by the introduction of some form of lather.

2. The relative ease of operation when anything mechanical is lubricated.

3. The high speed of a toboggan on hard snow as opposed to its immobility on a road free from ice or snow.

4. Wind gradient or the slowing effect of the ground on those layers of moving air in contact with it.

All these examples are self-explanatory and to a large extent find an aerodynamic parallel in skin friction. Because of porosity or other irregularities in the finish of an aircraft the layer of air in immediate surface contact tends to adhere and become stationary relative to the airframe. This **Boundary Layer** extends for up to 5 mm from the surface, its thickness being determined by the degree of smoothness (or otherwise) of the aircraft's finish. While it is true to say that a well-polished surface reduces skin friction, it can never be completely eliminated and the boundary layer will always flow more slowly than those streams of air more removed from the aircraft. Provided the boundary layer can be maintained in a **Laminar** state, i.e. smooth flow, skin friction will be kept within reasonable limits. A poor surface will cause the boundary layer to break up into countless eddies and the resultant **Turbulent Boundary Layer** with thicken and incur an increase in skin friction. Skin friction is responsible for up to 35% of the total drag on a high-speed aircraft.

Over a considerable number of years experiments have been conducted into the possibility of **Boundary Layer Control.** The thought behind these experiments is that skin friction can be practically eliminated provided the boundary layer is kept moving. The experiments have been largely confined to the wing surfaces and areas have been made porous through which the boundary layer is removed by vacuum pumps. The results are said to promise worthwhile reductions in skin friction and boundary layer research continues.

Another and less complex method of controlling skin friction is by limiting the **Wetted Area** or total area of the aircraft in contact with the boundary layer. Similarly form drag can be reduced by keeping the **Frontal Area** of the aircraft as small as possible, e.g. the cross-section of the fuselage, the size of the windscreen, the use of a retractable undercarriage, etc. It therefore follows that profile drag (made up from form drag and skin friction) must be reduced by designing the aircraft with the smallest possible frontal and wetted area, the smoothest possible surface, the best streamlined shape and freedom from all unnecessary appendages during flight, such as undercarriage legs, nose or tail wheel.

Unfortunately these requirements often conflict with operational demands such as internal accommodation, pilot's view, directional and other stability and cost of manufacture so that most aircraft represent a compromise.

2. Induced Drag

While all parts of the aircraft, including the wings, are subjected to profile drag, an additional form of resistance is present in flight which, together with profile drag, makes up the total drag of the aircraft. This is induced drag to which reference has already been made at the beginning of the chapter. It is inseparable from the wing's function as a lift producer although steps can be taken to reduce its effects.

To understand induced drag it is necessary to refer back to basic principles when it will be remembered that in the process of producing lift, high pressure is caused under the wing and low pressure above. Figure 4 shows that in effect the high-pressure area is separated from the low-pressure area by the wing itself.

When a pneumatic tyre is punctured, air escapes into the atmosphere because it has been confined within the tyre at a higher pressure than the surrounding air. Unequal pressures cannot exist side by side unless they are separated by some means, and, unlike a serviceable tyre, a wing is an imperfect pressure separator. The diagram shows that, because of the

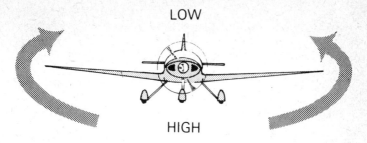

Fig. 4. Wingtip flow of air from high to low pressure.

difference in pressure, air from below the wings flows around the tips into the low-pressure area. The loss of pressure from below and the rise in pressure which results on the top surface has a damaging effect on the lift produced by the area of wing adjacent to the tips, although this complication is additional to the considerations of induced drag. As the air flows around the airfoil from leading to trailing edge, its path is influenced by the circulation (around the wing tips) from high to low pressure and the airstream on the top surface is deflected inwards towards the fuselage while an outward flow towards the wing tips occurs below. The net result amounts to a deviation from parallel flow and Fig. 5 shows that, as the upper and lower air streams meet at the trailing edge, their paths in relation to one another differ slightly setting up a number of rotating eddies, while a particularly large helix is caused at each wing tip. The **Wing-tip Vortices** in conjunction with the smaller **Trailing Edge Vortices** are the cause of induced drag and it follows that they will become more active as the pressure difference increases between upper and lower wing surfaces, i.e. at high angles of attack.

Should the angle of attack be reduced to the point when no lift is produced (usually a minus angle), the vortices will disappear and in consequence there will be no induced drag. Once the angle of attack is increased lift will occur and vortices develop causing induced drag, becoming more pronounced as the angle of attack is increased. As both angle of attack and induced drag increase the airspeed will decrease. In other words

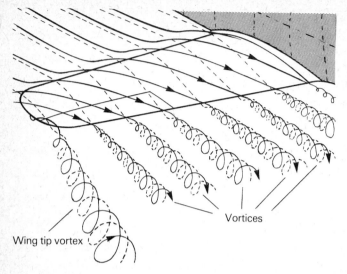

Fig. 5. Airflow over wings.
Solid lines depict airflow on top of the wings; the flow underneath is shown in broken lines.

induced drag becomes less as speed is increased, whereas the reverse is the case with profile drag.

Reducing Induced Drag

Induced drag may be reduced by efficient design particularly when related to the shape of the wing. Since the spillage of air around the wing tips, from high pressure to low, causes the vortices responsible for induced drag, it follows that any reduction in circulation around the tips will minimize the effects of induced drag. Assuming that a wing area of 200 square feet is required for a particular design, this could be obtained in a number of ways and three alternatives are illustrated in Fig. 6. The relationship between the span of the wing and its chord (or average chord when the wing is tapered) is called **Aspect Ratio,** wing A being an example of a low-aspect ratio wing, while wing C is of the high-aspect ratio type associated with high-efficiency sailplanes. For a given wing area, high-aspect ratio produces

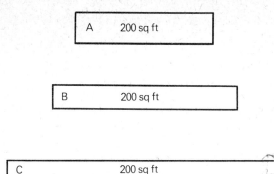

Fig. 6. Three wings of equal area.
A. Low-aspect ratio; B. Medium; and C. High.

more lift and less induced drag than a low-aspect ratio wing at the same speed and angle of attack, mainly because of the smaller wing tips which reduce the air spillage from high pressure to low. Unfortunately high-aspect ratio wings present structural problems, it being difficult to construct a wide-span narrow-chord wing of acceptable stiffness without incurring a severe penalty in weight.

Whereas sailplanes may have an aspect ratio of 30 or more, 8 to 10 is usual for transport aircraft and 5 or 6 for low performance light aircraft.

Stability

The stability of an aircraft is very much a design problem. Nevertheless a well-informed pilot should be conversant with the basic principles of stability. The subject received elementary treatment in Volume 1 and is dealt with in more detail here.

The Object of Stability

When, after a disturbance, an aeroplane returns to its original attitude without any corrective action on the part of the pilot, it is said to possess stability. For example, an aeroplane in straight and level flight may be deflected into a nose-down attitude during turbulent flying conditions. Were the nose to drop still further in a dive of increasing steepness the aeroplane would be unstable. Both stability and instability may be related to movement around all three axes and, while up to a point stability is a desirable characteristic in an aeroplane, instability can be dangerous and much research has gone into its elimination by good aerodynamic design.

Stability Characteristics

The tendency for an aeroplane to return towards its original trimmed condition of flight after it has been displaced is called **Static Stability.** This in itself is insufficient since in making the correction the aircraft follows an undulating path and behaves rather like a motor vehicle without shock absorbers.

The damping of these oscillations necessitates **Dynamic Stability** and the corrective behaviour of an aeroplane which is statically stable in the pitching plane is compared with a dynamically stable aircraft in Fig. 7.

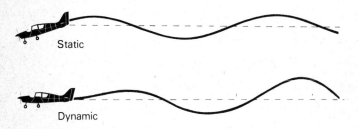

Fig. 7. Stability in the pitching plane.

In addition to these main characteristics, stability may vary in effectiveness from one type to another. A large transport aircraft will possess a high degree of stability whereas in a fighter aircraft this may be partially sacrificed in the interest of manoeuvrability and control.

Methods of Attaining Stability

So far only corrections in the pitching plane or longitudinal stability have been considered. A disturbance in the yawing plane is corrected with directional stability and when correc- tions take place in the rolling plane, lateral stability comes into play. Some of the design features incorporated in aircraft in attaining stability are explained under their relevant headings.

Longitudinal Stability

In Volume 1 it was explained that an airfoil is unstable since its centre of pressure moves forward as the angle of attack increases and vice versa. To overcome the out of balance **Couple** which occurs when lift and weight become out of alignment, a tailplane is fitted. The tailplane is usually of symmetrical airfoil section so that no lift is produced from its upper or lower surface until the disturbance raises or lowers the nose, when the resultant angle of attack causes the tailplane to produce a correcting force. The tailplane must correct the disturbance which was the prime cause of the change in attitude and the unstable movement of the centre of pressure.

After a disturbance the aircraft will, because of inertia, continue momentarily in a nose-up or nose-down attitude without changing its flight path. During the temporary change in attitude the tailplane assumes either a positive or negative angle of attack, so effecting a correction.

The degree of longitudinal stability is influenced by the following factors—

1. Movement of the Centre of Pressure

Modern airfoil sections are designed so that the centre of pressure remains within fairly close limits so reducing the magnitude of any nose up or down couple and improving longitudinal stability.

2. Area of Tailplane and Length of Fuselage

A large tailplane will exert more force than one of the smaller area so that corrective action will be more positive. A long fuselage provides the tailplane with extra leverage so that, tailplane size being equal, a long fuselage will assist longitudinal stability.

3. Position of the Centre of Gravity

This is an important factor since it is to some extent under the control of the pilot. In principle when the centre of gravity is well forward, longitudinal stability is at its best, although a point can be reached when elevator control becomes heavy and difficult, particularly at low speeds. As the centre of gravity is brought aft, longitudinal control improves at the expense of stability until a position is reached when instability occurs.

Centre of Gravity Limits are quoted in the Certificate of Airworthiness for all aircraft and it is the pilot's responsibility to ensure that these are not exceeded when loading the aircraft. Various methods are in use to determine the position of the centre of gravity and while little can go wrong with the loading of a small 2/4 seat aeroplane, the correct disposition of the load is of prime importance with larger types. Method of calculation will be shown in the Owner's/Flight/Operating Manual for the aircraft. This is explained in Chapter 7, Volume 4.

Lateral Stability

The close relationship which exists between lateral and directional control is clearly demonstrated in 'Further Effects of Aileron and Further Effects of Rudder'. Likewise there exists a close link between lateral and directional stability, although for the purpose of explanation these are considered separately.

Lateral stability is attained by using one or more of the following methods—

        1. High Wing
        2. Dihedral Angle
        3. Sweepback
        4. High Keel Surface

1. High Wing

By situating the wing on top of the fuselage well above the centre of gravity, there will exist a natural tendency for the aircraft to remain level rather like a plumb line. After lateral level has been disturbed the centre of gravity swings into alignment with the centre of lift so levelling the wings. This action is called **Pendulous Stability.**

2. Dihedral Angle

When the wing tips are raised the angle so formed between the wings and the horizontal is called dihedral (Fig. 8). When as a result of other design factors too much lateral stability exists to the detriment of lateral control, the wing tips are lowered below

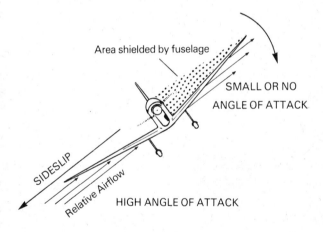

Fig. 8. Dihedral angle providing lateral stability.

the horizontal to form an **Anhedral Angle.** For its corrective action, dihedral angle is dependent upon the sideslip which occurs when a wing goes down for any reason not associated with yaw. The sideslip causes the relative airflow to change direction and, because of the dihedral, meet each wing at a different angle of attack. The illustration shows that lateral stability is achieved by –

(*a*) the larger angle of attack on the lower wing during the sideslip;

(*b*) loss of lift on the uppermost wing due to the partial shielding effect of the fuselage.

3. Sweepback

Like dihedral angle, sweepback is dependent for its effect upon the sideslip which follows a bank caused by a disturbance. The change in the direction of airflow during the sideslip has the effect of narrowing the chord on the lowered wing and increasing the effective span. The opposite occurs on the raised wing, these temporary changes being entirely due to the displaced airflow over the swept wing. Figure 9 shows that lift increases on the lower wing and provides lateral stability because –

(*a*) its aspect ratio is higher than the raised wings;

(*b*) its effective camber is greater because, while the chord is temporarily reduced, wing thickness remains the same.

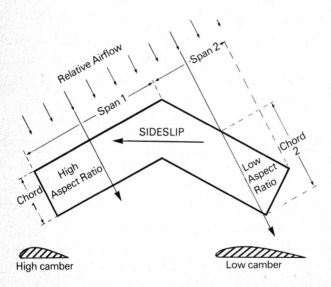

High camber   Low camber

Fig. 9. Sweepback and lateral stability when a dropped wing causes a sideslip to the left.

4. High Keel Surface

The term refers to all side area which is above the centre of gravity and once again sideslip provides the corrective airflow. When more keel area exists above the centre of gravity than below, there will be a levelling tendency during a sideslip (Fig. 10). A high fin contributes to the effects of keel area although undesirable complications may develop. These are outlined under 'Stability Interaction'.

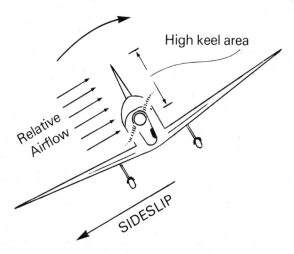

High keel area

Relative Airflow

SIDESLIP

Fig. 10. A high fin contributing to lateral stability.

Directional Stability

When the principles governing the behaviour of a weathercock are understood, directional stability as it applies to the aeroplane will need little explanation. The requirement for both weather vane and aeroplane is the same – more keel area behind the turning point than in front. In the weather vane, this turning point is represented by the pivot around which the indicator 'veers' or 'backs' according to the wind, whereas the turning point of an aircraft is its centre of gravity.

Although fuselage keel area is greater behind the centre of

gravity than in front in most (but not all) aircraft, to provide an acceptable degree of directional stability this is augmented by the addition of a fin. Like the tailplane and its contribution towards longitudinal stability, the fin is influenced by fuselage length, i.e., fin area being equal, a long fuselage behind the centre of gravity gives better directional stability than one of shorter length because of the increased leverage.

Stability Interaction

Because of the relationship already mentioned between directional and lateral control and stability, certain complications must be avoided by the designer in his quest for stability. The function of the sideslip in lateral stability may cause a strong turning motion towards the dropped wing, particularly when a large fin is used to promote directional stability. The turn causes the raised wing to gain lift because of its slightly greater speed and, when this is sufficient to overpower the effects of dihedral in levelling the wings, a spiral dive will develop which becomes progressively steeper. Such a condition is called **Spiral Instability** and its treatment is usually confined to reducing the fin area until its effects are at an acceptable level. It should be explained that most modern aircraft have a slight tendency towards spiral instability and, in fact, small amounts assist in turning.

Certain high-performance aircraft have exhibited an additional characteristic largely as a result of such design features as high wing loading and sweepback. The effect is more pronounced when flying at low airspeeds and is called **Oscillatory Instability.** For the purpose of this book it is sufficient to say that it is a combination of rolling and yawing which is difficult to control. The proportion of each movement may vary and is referred to as **Dutch Rolling** or **Snaking** according to the predominance of roll or yaw respectively. Automatic devices are fitted to some high-performance fighter and fast jet aircraft which are prone to oscillatory instability. This is most likely to occur at low airspeeds and high altitude.

Control

The great increase in aircraft performance has created severe problems in control design. Not only are control loads very considerable at high speeds, but the elevators, ailerons and rudder(s) must be capable of manoeuvring the aircraft throughout a much wider speed range than hitherto. While this would be confined within the limits of 45–200 kt in a light aeroplane, a modern transport aircraft can fly at any speed from 120–1,100 kt and high-performance fighters are capable of flight in excess of that maximum speed. At such speeds normal controls as applied to aircraft in the 150–300 kt category would be beyond the physical capabilities of the pilot. It may be suggested that in these cases the remedy is to reduce the size of each control surface, but the problem is one of providing adequate control throughout the speed range and small elevators, ailerons and rudders would be ineffective at low airspeeds.

Even at fairly modest airspeeds some form of assistance is required so that the pilot is relieved of at least part of the stick force required to move the controls. Up to certain speed limits this takes the form of **Aerodynamic Balance**. When the operating speeds go beyond these limits aircraft are fitted with **Power-assisted** control systems. At the highest speeds this is taken a stage further and the controls become fully **Power-operated**. The demarcation speeds are difficult to define since various other factors will influence the designer's choice such as the degree of manoeuvrability required, size of the aircraft, etc.

Aerodynamic Balanced Controls

The simple control surface devoid of any form of balance would be immovable at other than very low airspeeds and various means of assisting the pilot are in common use.

1. Horn Balance (Fig. 11)

This may be seen on both rudder and elevators on many aircraft. The shaded area in the illustration is added in front of

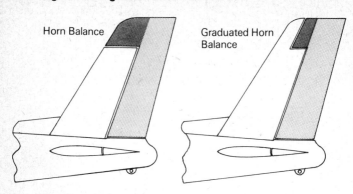

Fig. 11. Horn balance applied to the rudder surface.

the hinge line of the control surface, so balancing part of the load needed to move the control. Too much area before the hinge line would overbalance the control, so causing the pilot to **restrain the control from 'overbalance' when movement is made.** On occasion it is desirable to have no assistance during small control movements and a gradual introduction of balance as larger applications of control are made. Such an arrangement is called **Graduated Horn Balance** and incorporates a shield behind which the balance area is masked from the airflow until larger movements of the control bring it into action (Fig. 11).

2. Balance Tabs (Fig. 12)

Not to be confused with trim tabs, the sole function of balance tabs is to assist movement of the controls and they represent an alternative method to horn balance. By linking the balance tab to the related fixed surface (wing in the case of ailerons, fin for rudder, and tailplane for elevators) it will be made to move in the opposite direction when its associated control surface is moved by the pilot so relieving him of some of the load.

On occasion the linkage may be adjusted by the pilot through the trim controls when the tabs become of dual purpose – both trim and balance.

Aircraft with 'all moving' tailplanes are fitted with **Anti-balance tabs** for the purpose of preventing 'run away control'.

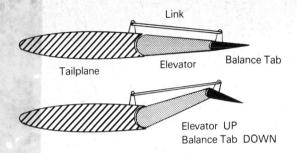

Fig. 12. Balance tab arranged to reduce elevator control loads.

Movement is in the same direction as the tailplane. The anti-balance tab is shown in Fig. 34, Volume 1, page 40.

3. Servo Tabs (Fig. 13)

In this interesting form of aerodynamic control assistance, the pilot's controls are linked to the servo tabs and movement of the stick and rudder bar on the ground produces movement of the relevant servo tab only and not the main control. The advantage of this system is that the pilot is merely called upon to move the small tabs which in turn actuate the main control surfaces. The arrangement is not satisfactory at low airspeeds since beyond certain angular limits the servo tabs stall and control is inadequate.

4. Spring Tabs (Fig. 14).

To overcome the shortcomings of servo tabs at low airspeeds the spring tab has been developed. The servo tab is connected to the rudder bar or stick as before but additionally the main control surface is linked via a spring which is of sufficient tension to move the elevators, aileron or rudder at low airspeeds when the servo tab is inadequate. As speed is increased to the point when a normal control surface would become too heavy (or even immovable), the spring gives and the servo tab only is moved by the pilot which in turn actuates the main control surface. Spring tabs have been used with success on large aircraft with cruising speeds of up to 400 kt.

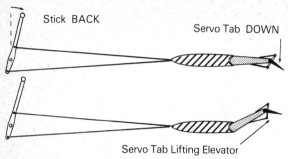

Fig. 13. Servo tab.
The control column is linked to the servo tab only.

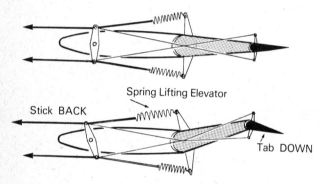

Fig. 14. The spring tab provides better low-speed control than the servo tab.

Powered Controls

This form of balance is dependent upon mechanical means as opposed to aerodynamic assistance and the degree of balance may vary between assistance (like the brakes on some motor vehicles) to controls which are entirely moved by power. The operation may be electrical but is usually hydraulic.

1. Power-assisted Controls

In this system movement of the control column or rudder pedals is transmitted to their related control in the usual manner. At the same time this movement causes a valve to open (in the case of an hydraulic system) when pressure is fed to a booster jack which assists the pilot in moving the required control surface. Should failure of the hydraulic system occur, it is possible to revert to manual control although the stick loads will be heavy until airspeed is reduced.

2. Power-operated Controls (Fig. 15)

In this system movement of the control column or of the rudder pedals operates an hydraulic valve, there being no direct linkage to the control surfaces. Taking the elevators as an example, the hydraulic valve would have three positions: elevators move down, elevators stationary and elevators move up. In the 'elevators stationary' position the valve closes off the flow of hydraulic fluid to the control jack when the control surface is locked in the position selected by the pilot on his control column. A 'follow up' linkage to the valve ensures that

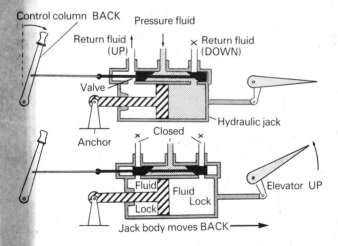

Fig. 15. Power-operated control.
In the top diagram the control column has been moved back, opening the valve admitting oil to the rear of the jack. The jack now moves back (lower diagram) until both valves close and lock the control.

it shuts off the hydraulic fluid at the correct angular setting of the elevators according to the position of the control column. Under these arrangements there is no aerodynamic load on the pilot's controls and some form of artificial 'feel' must be incorporated in the system to prevent the pilot from overstraining the airframe.

Because of the serious consequences of hydraulic failure, the systems are fully duplicated and in some cases arrangements are made for manual reversion.

Flutter (Fig. 16)

Modern materials have made possible the design and manufacture of extremely light airframe components of great strength. It is relatively simple to cater for the various stress requirements so that wings, fuselage, tailplane, etc., are strong enough to withstand loads in flight and landing but lightness means economy of material which is to the detriment of a further requirement – **Rigidity**.

Unless, for example, the wings possess rigidity, flexing may occur when the ailerons are operated, so twisting the wing and causing an adverse change in angle of attack on each wing when the function of the ailerons will be opposed or in extreme cases

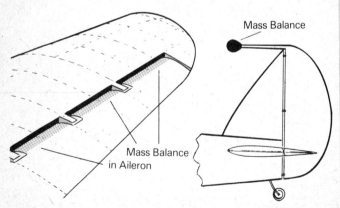

Fig. 16. Flutter corrected by mass balance. The aileron shown has inset hinges for aerodynamic balance.

overcome. Alternatively the flexing of the wing may set up a violent oscillation or vibration between wing and aileron which if allowed to continue would result within seconds in structural failure. Such behaviour is not confined to the ailerons and **Flutter** may occur with the rudder or the elevators. Its cure may on occasions necessitate stiffening the affected structure, but the method in common use is called **Mass Balancing** when a weight is attached to the control surface, ahead of its hinge line, usually within the horn balance. In some designs the weight is mounted on an arm which protrudes ahead of the control surface. In either case the amount of weight is carefully calculated and high-speed aircraft are particularly sensitive to changes in mass balance to the extent that an extra coat of paint on the rudder may provoke flutter. It was for this reason that the red, white and blue stripes were transferred from rudder to fin on RAF aircraft as their performance improved.

Aileron Drag

Particularly at low airspeeds, sudden application of aileron will cause a yaw in the opposite direction to bank. This is more noticeable on light aircraft of early design and, while the characteristic is less conspicuous on modern types, it is important in so far as the ailerons tend to oppose turning unless they are of good design. In the case of a bank to the left the nose will yaw to the right because of **Aileron Drag**. The explanation is that, in order to bank, the aileron on the rising wing must be depressed into high-pressure air, at the same time increasing its angle of attack. Conversely the aileron on the down-going wing will be raised into lower pressure and its angle of attack will decrease. In other words the aileron on the up-going wing will have more drag than that on the lower wing so causing the aircraft to yaw momentarily towards the raised wing until overcome by the weathercock stability of the aircraft which results from 'further effects of aileron'.

Drag can be more evenly balanced between the two ailerons by arranging the up-going one to move through a greater angle than the down-going surface. This is accomplished by simple geometric arrangement of the control linkage and aircraft fitted with the refinement are said to have **Differential Ailerons**.

An additional method is illustrated in Fig. 17 and this is often used in conjunction with differential ailerons. The hinge line is moved back behind the leading edge of the aileron and the hinge pins are carried on extensions from the wing so that the down-going aileron is in smooth continuance with the wings thus minimizing drag. Conversely, the up-going aileron protrudes its leading edge below the under-surface of the wing so causing additional drag on the inside of the turn. The leading edge of the aileron is often arranged to fit into a recess in the wing called a **shroud** and this still further increases the efficiency of this type of aileron which is named **Frise** after its designer (Fig. 17).

Frise ailerons have two further advantages –

1. The portion of the control surface forward of the hinge line may house the mass balancing weight (Fig. 16).

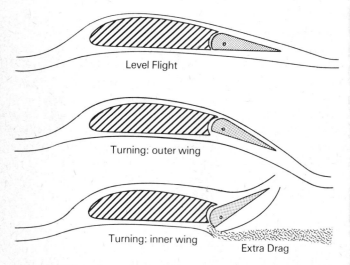

Fig. 17. Frise ailerons.
The centre and lower drawings show the ailerons during a turn to the left.

2. When unshrouded the area in front of the hinge line gives aerodynamic balance to assisting operation by the pilot.

Using both methods the results are very effective and the controls are then referred to as **Differential Frise Ailerons**. Unfortunately Frise ailerons are unsuitable for very high-speed aircraft because of the under-wing disturbance caused by the up-going surface.

On very fast aircraft lateral control may be assisted by **Spoilers** which extend above the wing on the inside of the turn, thus spoiling the lift and causing a roll in that direction. Spoilers have the additional advantage of providing drag on the inside of the turn.

Transonic and Supersonic Flight

With the rapid progress that has occurred throughout all branches of aviation within recent years, supersonic flight has become commonplace to the Service pilot and a reality for the travelling public. Because it seems likely that supersonic business or executive aircraft will be introduced within the foreseeable future this chapter is concluded with a very brief description of supersonic aerodynamics.

The Speed of Sound

Throughout the various aerodynamic explanations which have referred to subsonic flight, air has been considered as a fluid that flows around an airfoil and other parts of an airframe without becoming compressed. A wing moving at subsonic speed 'warns' the atmosphere of its approach and at some distance ahead of the leading edge the airflow changes direction in a manner which ensures that smooth contact is made with the airfoil. This interesting phenomenon can be convincingly demonstrated with a smoke tunnel and the 'warning' is in fact a pressure wave projected forward of the leading edge of the wing. The very act of speech creates pressure waves of this nature which are of course received on the ear drum as sound vibrations. These pressure waves travel at a speed which varies according to the temperature of the air. Under average sea-level conditions this is in the region of 660 kt. The warning pressure wave which precedes a moving wing is governed by the same limitations and its speed will be considerably less than 660 kt at high altitudes because of the reduced air temperature.

Assuming that a machine-gun bullet has a speed of 1,700 kt, when fired in the direction of flight from an aircraft flying at 450 kt, its total speed will be 2,150 kt. While the bullet has a velocity which is additional to the speed of the aircraft, the warning air pressure is limited to the speed of sound. Consequently when any part of the airflow exceeds the prevailing speed of sound, no warning will exist and an abrupt change in direction must occur when contact is made with the airframe. A **Shock Wave** will result accompanied by the now familiar 'sonic boom' which is heard on the ground (but not, incidentally, in the aircraft).

An airfoil section causes the airflow to increase speed as it passes over the top surface of the wing and this airstream can exceed the speed of sound when the aircraft is subsonic creating a shock wave at the point of fastest airflow. At this stage the airflow behind the shock wave will be subsonic and the pressure will be two to three times that which exists in front. As the aircraft's speed increases more of the wing will become supersonic and the shock wave will move back towards the trailing edge. At **Sonic** speed (speed of sound for the prevailing atmospheric conditions) the shock wave becomes attached to the trailing edge where it remains throughout supersonic flight. A small cushion of subsonic air will however remain in front of the wing when the airfoil has the usual rounded leading edge and a second shock wave or **Bow Wave** will occur at that point. The subsonic cushion disappears at higher speeds.

The foregoing explanation of the change from subsonic to supersonic flight is of the so-called **Transonic** stage and the various developments as they apply to a normal subsonic wing are illustrated in Fig. 18.

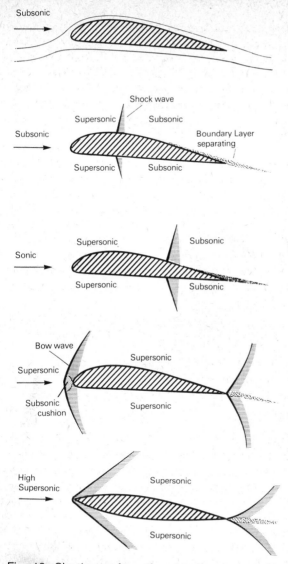

Fig. 18. Shockwave formation at various speeds.
Reading from the top: 1. Subsonic; 2. High subsonic; 3. Speed of
sound; 4. Supersonic; 5. A supersonic airfoil section.

During the transonic stage three important developments take place –

   1. A large increase in Drag.

   2. A large decrease in Lift.

   3. A considerable movement of the centre of pressure, in the early stages causing a strong 'pitch up' tendency followed by a powerful 'nose down' movement as sonic speed is approached.

These three factors seriously affected early high-speed aircraft and loss of control often occurred when shock waves developed on wing, fin and tailplane, causing their related control surfaces to operate in an area of turbulent air with no aerodynamic flow (Fig. 19).

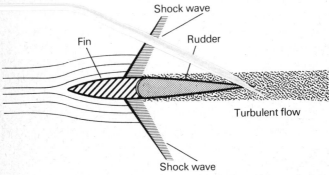

Fig. 19. Loss of rudder control due to shockwave formation.

On an airframe designed for subsonic flying, wing drag may increase more than five times during the transonic stage so that to attain supersonic speed a dive is required. Once the aircraft has accelerated through the transonic stage both lift and drag conditions improve to values not far removed from subsonic proportions. The aircraft will now be subject to the laws governing supersonic aerodynamics.

By now the significance of the speed of sound will be apparent. Because the speed of sound varies with atmospheric density the usual ASI is inadequate in itself and a further instrument is required which expresses the aircraft's speed in relation to the prevailing speed of sound. The instrument is calibrated in **Mach** numbers. Mach 1 represents the speed of sound whereas Mach 0.5 informs the pilot he is flying at half the prevailing speed of sound. The instrument is called a **Mach Meter** and may be additional to the usual Airspeed Indicator, although modern practice is to present the Mach Meter and the ASI in one instrument.

Supersonic Aerodynamics

When a wing moves at supersonic speed some of the usual laws of aerodynamics become reversed and in many ways the airstream behaves as would be expected by a newcomer to aerodynamics in that a restricted passage such as a venturi tube causes a deceleration coupled with an increase in pressure. Conversely when air passes through an expanding channel at supersonic speed, an acceleration occurs together with a decrease in pressure. When the shock wave develops and drag begins to increase because of compressibility, the aircraft is at its **Critical Mach Number**.

Perhaps the most important method employed to overcome the high drag increase during transonic flight is the adoption of thin airfoil sections with their maximum depth midway along the chord. The airfoil may be **Bi-Convex** or **Double-Wedge** shape and in many cases symmetrical (Fig. 20).

With either type the pressure distribution at supersonic airspeeds is quite dissimilar to the subsonic case and best L/D

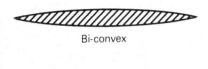

Bi-convex

Double-wedge

Fig. 20. Supersonic airfoil sections.

angle of attack is reached when the lower surface of the rear 'wedge' is parallel to the relative airflow. At angles of attack of this order only two half shock waves occur instead of the usual four (two full shock waves) and this arrangement together with the position of the centre of pressure and the distribution of pressure around the airfoil is shown in Fig. 21 in comparison with a subsonic airfoil.

When the aircraft accelerates from low subsonic flight through the transonic stage to supersonic speeds, a wide movement of the centre of pressure occurs with profound effect on longitudinal trim, and ordinary controls would be incapable of dealing with the forces involved. Powered controls have already been described in this chapter but the conventional

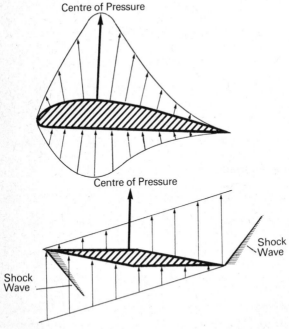

Fig. 21. Subsonic (top) and supersonic airfoils at their best L/D ratio angle of attack.

elevators are being replaced by the **All Moving** or **Flying Tail**. In this the entire tailplane is tilted by the powered controls so that a positive or negative angle of attack is assumed according to the load required for the particular speed or manoeuvre.

Sweepback

Under 'Stability' sweepback was discussed as a means of attaining lateral stability. The earlier generation of high-speed aircraft were conventional airframes with subsonic wings. Their behaviour during the transonic stage was a problem which had of necessity to be solved before the appearance of thin supersonic wings of the correct aerodynamic conception. These earlier designs often became uncontrollable during transonic flight owing to the effects of compressibility and, when the point was reached at which control deteriorated, the aircraft was said to be at its **Compressibility Mach Number**.

Before the advent of supersonic airfoil sections made it of no consequence, the compressibility Mach number was delayed by the introduction of sweepback which (*a*) causes the effective thickness of the airfoil section to be reduced when measured parallel to the airflow, and (*b*) because of the geometry of a swept wing the actual speed of flow from leading to trailing edge (which determines when the shock waves will occur) can be kept below the aircraft's speed. This second consideration is the more important and in the case of an aircraft flying at 660 kt, when the wings are swept at 45°, the speed over the actual chord would only be 470 kt, or in other words, subsonic.

Unfortunately both large amounts of sweepback and supersonic airfoil sections have an adverse effect on the low-speed characteristics of an aircraft. Furthermore both swept wings and those of thin supersonic airfoil section are a design problem in so far as structural rigidity is concerned. Whereas subsonic wings are usually constructed on a framework of spars and ribs to which is riveted a thin outer surface or **Stressed Skin**, modern supersonic practice is for wing surfaces to be machined from solid metal of proportions not hitherto associated with aeroplanes. In this way rigidity is obtained together with an airfoil of high accuracy and a surface finish of great perfection. This tendency towards thin, almost solid metal wings makes necessary the provision of other locations on the aircraft for fuel tanks and the stowage of the undercarriage when retracted.

The **Delta Wing**, so named because of its dart-like planform, offers certain structural and aerodynamic advantages over swept wings, in particular excellent stalling characteristics.

As speeds increase beyond Mach 2 the rise in airframe surface temperature as a result of skin friction is such that aluminium alloys are seriously weakened and other materials will be needed for future high-speed aircraft. Experiments have been conducted with an all stainless steel aeroplane, and titanium is gradually replacing traditional light alloys, but the problem exists to a lesser degree with present-day supersonic aircraft where the temperature rise is sufficient to justify the installation of special cooling equipment to maintain the pilot at a comfortable temperature.

2 Piston Engine Handling and Propellers

This chapter deals with certain mechanical aspects of a pilot's training and the effect of engine handling on aircraft performance. It is of course essential to have a good working knowledge of aircraft engine handling, and it is assumed that at this stage in his training the pilot has learned the elementary principles of piston engines as outlined in Chapter 1, Vol. 4.

The reader will understand that many books have been written on each subject contained in this chapter and, although by no means fully comprehensive, the following paragraphs will provide a foundation for further detailed study.

The Aircraft Supercharger

The efficiency of a piston engine is dependent upon the weight of combustible gas entering the cylinder. In a **normally aspirated** (unsupercharged) engine the mixture is induced into the cylinder by a fall in pressure within the cylinder as the piston moves down on the induction stroke. Assisting the charge to enter the cylinder is of course atmospheric pressure, although this reduces with altitude as the air becomes less dense. On the other hand certain factors restrict the air entering the cylinders, namely the throttle butterfly (unless fully open), and the carburettor choke or venturi. It follows therefore that as altitude is increased the weight of the 'charge' entering the cylinders is decreased and power decreases. The aircraft designer is able partially to off-set the fall in power by designing the air intake to face into the airflow so obtaining **ram effect** which is dependent upon the forward speed of the aircraft.

The **Supercharger** is a device which forces the mixture into the cylinder under pressure. Older designs featured an engine-driven blower usually installed between carburettor and induction manifold. The design was such that the centrifugal action of the blower caused a rise in pressure. The mixture then passed through **Diffusers**, i.e. diverging channels causing the pressure to increase still further (Fig. 22).

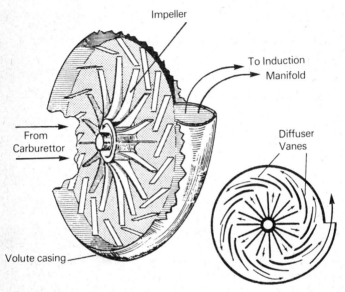

Fig. 22. The supercharger.

The mechanically driven supercharger is confined to engines of older design in so far as aircraft are concerned, and it is now the practice, certainly with piston engines within the 200–450HP range, to incorporate a **Turbo-supercharger** when power at height is required.

The Turbo-supercharger (Fig. 23)

One of the weaknesses of the piston engine is the relatively small use made of the available heat energy in fuel. Only a small proportion is converted into usable power and much potential energy is lost through the exhaust. To a considerable extent this

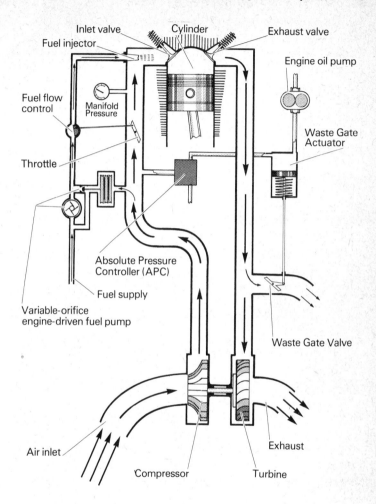

Fig. 23. Turbo-supercharger (simplified). Turbine speed is determined by the waste gate valve which is moved by the waste gate actuator. This in turn is controlled by the absolute pressure controller which senses 'upper deck' pressure (i.e. pressure between the compressor and the throttle). The manifold pressure gauge reads pressure *after* the throttle, like any normally aspirated engine.

energy is reclaimed by the turbo-supercharger.

In essence the turbo-supercharger (sometimes known as a **Turbocharger**) incorporates a turbine driven by the exhaust gases which in turn rotates a blower or supercharger. At lower levels, where the air is dense, there is considerable back pressure in the exhaust system. As the aircraft climbs it would normally lose power in proportion to the decrease in air density but when a turbocharger is fitted the decrease in density is made to assist the engine. There is a progressive decrease in back pressure with height so allowing the exhaust gases to flow at a higher rate and drive the turbine/supercharger assembly faster. The net result is an increase in fuel/air mixture over that inducted by a normally aspirated engine of the same type at the same height. The following figures relate to a well-known engine of 210 HP at sea level. They show the decline in power output with height for the normally aspirated version of the motor.

Altitude (ft)	Max. HP
20,000	99
15,000	122
10,000	148
5,000	177
Sea level	210

When the same engine is fitted with a turbocharger, maximum power increases during the climb from 210 HP at sea level to 215 HP at 12,000 feet, thus radically improving the rate of climb and cruise performance of the aircraft. Such an engine will maintain the usual 75% power for high speed cruising at altitudes of up to 20,000 ft.

While earlier turbocharged engines could be over-boosted at low levels it is now usual to incorporate a pressure relief valve to prevent this happening, particularly during take-off.

Manifold Pressure is measured in inches of mercury. In a normally aspirated engine maximum pressure would usually be 29.93″ at sea-level on a standard day, falling as altitude is gained. By employing a supercharger additional manifold pressure, and therefore power, may be available during take-off and this power may be maintained, depending upon the efficiency of the supercharger, to a considerable altitude. Highest power used for the take-off is limited to a maximum period which is usually five minutes. The highest power permitted for such purposes as climbing is called the **Rated Power**. This too may have a time limit which is not usually less than thirty minutes. Rated power can be maintained up to a height which is dependent upon the degree of supercharging; this is referred to as the **Rated Altitude**, and should the climb continue beyond this point it will no longer be possible to maintain rated power.

When a constant-speed propeller is fitted, manifold pressure at any height may be increased by selecting a finer pitch since the engine RPM will then increase causing the blower to turn at a higher speed. This procedure is of course restricted by considerations of fuel economy and the limits imposed by maximum continuous RPM for the engine type.

Flying for Range

An aircraft can only be operated efficiently when the correct power settings and most economical altitude have been selected by the pilot and these factors must be fully understood if the best is to be obtained from the aircraft.

Flying for range really means flying as many miles as possible on a fixed quantity of fuel which in light aircraft is invariably determined by fuel-tank capacity. The payload carried by a transport aircraft may limit the amount of fuel that can be carried.

The two principal considerations concern aerodynamic and engine/propeller efficiency, although these are by no means the only factors; others include (a) altitude related specifically to air density and temperature, (b) the load carried and its effect on aircraft performance, (c) the effect of wind, and (d) air-traffic requirements.

At first examination it may be supposed that, by flying relatively slowly using low power, fuel consumption would be improved, but this is not the case. In fact the lowest speed demands the greatest power (Ex. 6, 'Straight and Level Flight',

Vol. 1), because flight in the lower speed range requires a high angle of attack and in consequence a high induced drag factor. On the other hand near maximum speed also carries a penalty since drag increases as the square of the speed, once more demanding a high power setting.

Somewhere between these two extremes of the speed range is an optimum where the best lift/drag ratio can be obtained, i.e. at approximately 4° angle of attack. While this flight condition would usually produce best air miles/gallon fuel consumption, it is common practice for the Owner's/Flight/Operating Manual to recommend a slightly higher speed giving similar range performance at a more practical cruising speed. This speed must now be related to an economical power setting since it has already been stated that the two principal factors are aerodynamic and engine efficiencies.

Selection of the altitude at which to fly is to some extent a compromise between height required, operational considerations and air traffic instructions. At higher altitudes the TAS is higher for any IAS and, while this is an advantage, it is to some extent offset by the fuel required for the climb. Consequently, there is little, if anything, to be gained by operating an aircraft in this manner over short journeys. On the other hand as height is gained a weaker mixture can be selected and this presents a further economy.

To maintain the required IAS as economically as possible, the engine should be operated at high manifold pressure and lowest practical RPM below which detonation (knocking) and/or vibration would occur. High manifold pressure is preferable since this, in effect, results in improved mean effective pressure (the average pressure within the cylinders), while low RPM reduces fuel consumption. When flying for range the aircraft should cruise at **Full Throttle Altitude** for the power selected. At that altitude the throttle will be fully open and the engine will experience 'maximum breathing'. The carburettor heat control should wherever possible be in the 'cold air' position to provide maximum weight of charge.

In so far as transport aircraft are concerned, weight has a marked influence on range but the effect is small on light aircraft. It is worth mentioning, however, that on a long flight where range considerations are important, the IAS will tend to increase as fuel is consumed and this will permit power reductions during the course of the flight.

The effect of wind on range can be considerable in cases of high head or tail winds. In the former case a nominal increase in airspeed would be appropriate so that the head wind has less time to influence the ground speed, but this should seldom exceed 15 kt. A similar reduction in IAS may be made for a strong tail wind component so allowing it to contribute towards the ground speed. The exact changes in airspeed are dependent upon the wind strength and performance recommendations in the handling notes for the aircraft type.

In the case of aircraft which are not equipped with supercharged engines or variable pitch propellers the best range performance would be at a height of 8,000 to 10,000 ft. In a normally aspirated engine these conditions would correspond to 60–65% power with the throttle fully open and the mixture lean.

Where a variable pitch propeller is fitted to an unsupercharged engine the best settings for range are (*a*) the recommended economical cruising RPM and (*b*) manifold pressure maintained by manually opening the throttle up to the altitude where full throttle is applied. These conditions would probably result in an altitude of 9,000–12,000 ft at 45–50% power. These are of course general observations since much depends upon the aircraft/engine characteristics and specific fuel consumption. Full information can be obtained from the manufacturer's cruise performance tables.

In light aircraft with unsupercharged engines cruising speeds are usually relatively low and the effect of a 30–40 kt head wind at the required altitude could easily nullify the advantages of operating at full throttle height. With slower aircraft the main consideration will inevitably be the effect of wind and the selection of an altitude to fly will depend on the wind component. These factors will normally be calculated before the flight to achieve maximum range.

Carburettor Icing

Carburettor icing can be a hazard to the pilot who does not understand and recognize the conditions under which it may occur and the symptoms it produces. It can form under almost any conditions when the outside air temperature (OAT) is between −15° C and 30° C and not only in cloud as is sometimes erroneously supposed.

The two principal factors relating to carburettor icing are temperature and relative humidity of the air. Before considering the causes of carburettor icing, it should be understood that there is an airframe icing consideration which may affect the airflow into the carburettor, namely ice formation on the carburettor air intake. **Impact Ice** can occur when super-cooled droplets, hail or snow, freeze on impact progressively closing the intake, causing loss of power owing to the alteration in the fuel/air mixture relationship, disturbances of the air flow into the carburettor and loss of ram effect. It may be prevented by providing the engine installation with a wire-mesh icing guard slightly forward of the intake.

Icing within the carburettor is caused by cooling due to air expansion (**Adiabatic Cooling**) and cooling due to evaporation of fuel. In the former case when the intake air is passed through the throat or venturi of the carburettor, its pressure is reduced causing the temperature to fall and, if the outside temperature is within the icing range, ice will form to a degree dependent upon the relative humidity. These ice deposits (**Throttle Ice**) form in the throat of the carburettor in the vicinity of the throttle butterfly having the effect of disturbing the fuel/air ratio and further increasing the venturi effect to a point where rough running occurs followed by a **Rich Mixture Cut**. Heat required for the evaporation of fuel is taken from the indrawn air cooling it to a point where icing may occur (**Fuel Evaporation Ice**). Fuel evaporation is the major cause of temperature drop.

The first indication of carburettor icing in an aircraft with a normally aspirated engine will be a decrease in RPM. The pilot may then compensate this by increasing power and unless remedial action is taken this could continue until full throttle is applied. Rough running will follow and unless steps are taken to clear the ice a rich mixture cut will cause the engine to stop firing.

To prevent icing the carburettor may be heated by selecting 'hot air' when the supply of outside air will be ducted through a

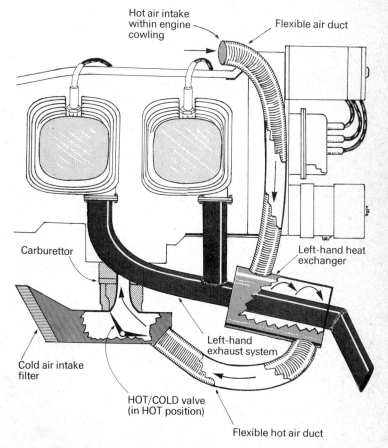

Fig. 24. Typical carburettor heat system. A similar heat exchanger is situated on the right-hand exhaust system.

heat exchanger fitted around the exhaust manifold (Fig. 24). Alternatively the carburettor butterfly may be heated by warm engine oil raising the temperature to a degree completely outside the range where icing could occur.

When the aircraft is fitted with a fixed pitch propeller application of carburettor heat will cause a small reduction in RPM as heated air of lower density enters the cylinders and decreases power. When carburettor ice has been allowed to build up to the point where a decrease in RPM has been followed by rough running, initial application of carburettor heat will provoke a further, at times quite serious, loss of power and even rougher running. This is caused by the reduction in air density already mentioned and the induction of water/melted ice. Pilots in this situation must resist the temptation of returning the carburettor heat control to the cold position before it has been allowed sufficient time to clear the build up of induction ice.

While flying in conditions where carburettor ice is likely to form pilots must at frequent intervals operate the carburettor heat control. When an initial drop in RPM is followed by an increase *before* returning the control to cold this is a certain indication that carburettor icing is occurring.

As a safeguard against accidental operation of the idle cut-off when practising those exercises requiring application of carburettor heat (e.g. stalling, spinning, gliding, etc.) the control should be moved to hot before closing the throttle. In this way the heat control may be tested for proper function and, should the mixture control have been pulled back in error, the engine will stop, thus warning the pilot of his mistake.

Under certain very cold OAT conditions, the temperature may be well below that at which ice can form in the carburettor. To select part heat under these extreme conditions would raise the temperature into the icing range. For this reason the pilot should be aware of the outside air temperature obtaining it either from the Met. Office or from the OAT gauge in the aircraft. Unless a **Carburettor Air Temperature Gauge** is fitted, pilots must operate the carburettor hot control on a basis of 'all or nothing' since, for the reason explained, part heat could be dangerous. Particularly when carburettor icing conditions are likely the hot-air system should be checked during the pre-take-off vital actions.

Fuel Injection

Partly as a means of overcoming most of the risks of carburettor icing but also because of fuel economy advantages many aero engines are these days fitted with a fuel injection unit in place of the carburettor. The earlier injectors were based upon those used in compression ignition engines and, as such, incorporated a number of accurately manufactured plungers, one for each cylinder. These meter the fuel to close tolerances before injecting it directly into the related cylinder. In this way fuel evaporation and adiabatic cooling within a choke tube no longer presents the risk of induction icing and at the same time fuel flow may be controlled more accurately than with a carburettor. Since there is no induction icing risk it is not necessary to fit a carburettor heat system, however, the possibility of impact ice on the air intake remains, and to safeguard against closure of the engine air supply an **Alternate Air** source is fitted. Usually this takes its air from within the engine bay.

Injectors of the plunger type must be machined to very close tolerances and are, in consequence, expensive to manufacture. There has, therefore, been a move towards multi-nozzle, rotary vane pumps of the continuous flow type which are simpler in design and cheaper to build than plunger pumps.

When starting fuel injected engines it is usual to use the electric primer with the mixture in 'rich'. The throttle is opened until a fuel flow is indicated on the combined manifold pressure/fuel flow meter. The pump may then be turned off. Some engines will start more easily with the mixture in idle cut-off. The starter may then be engaged and the mixture control advanced when the engine fires.

Use of the Mixture Control

These notes are for general guidance, fuller details being given in the Owner's/Flight/Operating Manual for the aircraft.

Carburettor Engines

At cruising level the mixture control should be leaned to the point where the RPM show a decrease. The control is then advanced sufficiently to restore RPM to their original value.

Fuel Injected Engines

It is usual to provide these engines with a data table giving percentage power required. Means of attaining the required power are listed against various altitudes, often with a choice of manifold pressure/RPM settings. For example at 7,000 ft the list may suggest a 75% power setting thus –

Engine RPM	2,200	2,300	2,400
Manifold pressure	24″	22.5″	21.75″

Against these settings will be given the **Fuel Flow** in gallons and using the fuel flow meter the mixture should be adjusted to attain the recommended setting.

The Fuel/Air Ratio Meter

An aid to achieving best fuel economy, one that can be fitted to any aircraft, is the **Fuel/Air Ratio Meter**, sometimes known as the **Engine Gas Temperature** gauge. In effect it analyses the exhaust gases and presents a single finger display. The mixture control should be leaned until the finger moves from its stop to the maximum position when further leaning will cause it to reverse direction. At that point the mixture should be enriched to the point where peak reading is indicated, then the needle may be retarded slightly further to guard against possible damage to the engine due to running on too lean a mixture. Usually these meters have an adjustable datum which may be set at the optimum position for future use.

Propellers

The theory of the propeller and its application to the problem of providing thrust is a complex subject which can involve

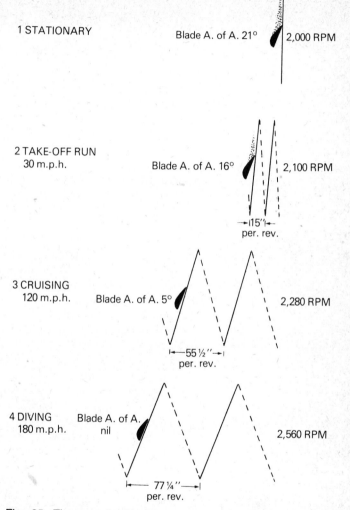

Fig. 25. The propeller blade.
Solid lines denote path of blade near observer, while broken lines are on the opposite side of the helix. Note partially stalled blade in first two diagrams.

advanced mathematics. This section deals with propellers in practical terms only, giving information useful to the pilot.

The propeller is a means of converting engine power into thrust. Whereas the gas turbine produces thrust by accelerating a small diameter of air to a high velocity, the propeller differs in that a large diameter of relatively low-speed air is displaced rearwards.

An aircraft propeller consists of two or more blades of airfoil section which, like a wing, produce lift and drag. When these forces apply to a propeller they are referred to as **Thrust** and **Torque Reaction** respectively.

The angle of the blade is greatest at the hub decreasing progressively towards the tip, thus compensating for the increase in radial speed towards the maximum diameter of the propeller. For example the tip speed of an 8-ft diameter propeller at 2,100 RPM would be 600 MPH, reducing to approximately 75 MPH where the blade enters the spinner.

The propeller's efficiency is dependent upon the amount of engine power converted into thrust and this is largely determined by the blade lift/drag ratio. In the case of a **Fixed-pitch** propeller best lift/drag ratio can only occur under certain flight conditions. The distance a screw will penetrate into wood for one turn will depend upon the pitch of its thread: a fine thread will give a small penetration per turn while a coarse thread will result in a greater advance per revolution. Obviously a propeller has far less adhesion in air than a screw in wood. For this reason were its blades at a large angle (**Coarse Pitch**) the propeller would be fully or partly stalled during take-off since the aeroplane would be incapable of moving fast enough to correspond with the 'advance per revolution' for which the blade angle has been set. Looking at the problem in another way, each part of a propeller blade travels on a circular path while the aircraft is stationary. As the aeroplane moves forward this circular path changes to one that is helical and a visible trace left by the point on the blade under consideration would have the appearance of a very large coil spring. As airspeed is increased so the coils of the spring become more stretched and this has the effect of altering the angle of attack of the propeller blade (Fig. 25).

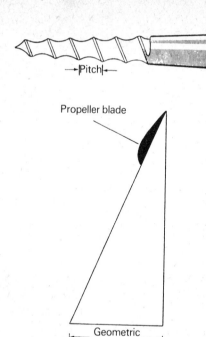

Fig. 26. Geometric pitch.
In this comparison the wood screw rotates in the opposite direction to the propeller while moving forward.

During take-off there is considerable blade slip and loss of efficiency and in the early stages the blades are often stalled. For take-off it therefore follows that a **Fine Pitch** is desirable but this would be unsuitable at higher speeds when in all probability the propeller would be incapable of absorbing the available engine power.

These conflicting requirements illustrate the shortcomings of the fixed-pitch propeller.

The distance a propeller would move forward for each revolution assuming there to be no blade slip is called the **Geometric Pitch** and this corresponds to the penetration per turn of the wood screw which was mentioned earlier (Fig. 26).

Due to propeller slip the aircraft will move forward a smaller distance for each revolution than that represented by the geometric pitch.

To overcome the problem of providing an ideal pitch for each condition of flight it is necessary to provide means of adjusting the blade angle in the air and this is achieved by the **Variable-pitch Propeller**. In the early stages these were of the 'two pitch' variety and control from the cockpit was confined to two settings, 'coarse' and 'fine'.

While the two-pitch airscrew represented a major advance over the fixed-pitch propeller, it was obvious that the problem of efficient pitch over a wide range of flight conditions was only partly met and a propeller with blades infinitely variable over a wide range was later developed.

The pitch-change mechanism is housed in the hub of the propeller. It is hydraulically operated. In some propellers engine oil is boosted in pressure to some 200 PSI for the purpose and this is fed via a valve to either side of an hydraulic piston according to the desired pitch change, 'fine' or 'coarse'. It was soon realized that, if the valve controlling the pitch change could be made to function automatically according to load demands on the propeller, the engine would remain at a constant speed while the pitch would always present itself at a pre-determined angle at any power setting within the normal Cruise to Maximum Power Range.

The automatic device is called a **Constant-speed Unit** and propellers so equipped are called **Constant-speed Propellers**.

The constant-speed unit is built around a governor which is similar in function to that found in the older type of gramophone motor. Bob weights are made to rotate by the engine and under centrifugal reaction these fly outwards against the load of a spring as RPM increase. Should the RPM decrease for any reason the spring will overcome the centrifugal action of the weights and the arms of the governor will then move inwards. The bob weights are arranged to move the pitch-changing valve via a simple linkage, and when the arms of the governor are upright the valve is in a neutral position blocking both 'fine' and 'coarse' pitch oil passages, locking the propeller

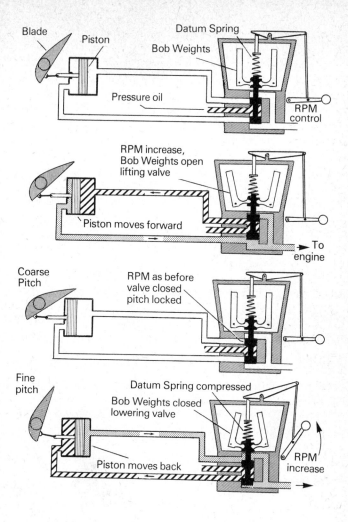

Fig. 27. Constant-speed propeller (diagrammatic).
The hydraulic leads to the propeller are in fact drillings in the propeller shaft. The first three drawings refer to the sequence described in the text. In the last illustration, higher RPM have been selected.

in whatever pitch it has at the time. By altering the tension on the spring this neutral position can be made to occur at whatever engine speed is required provided this is within the capabilities of the engine. The propeller control is linked to the constant-speed unit so that tension on the governor spring may be altered by the pilot, so determining the engine RPM at which the unit will 'constant speed'. In reality, movement of the propeller control alters the governor datum and any subsequent variation in engine speed will then cause the pitch valve to operate in one direction or the other accordingly.

Taking a specific case, suppose 2,100 RPM has been selected by the pilot on the propeller control during steady cruising. Were the nose depressed into a shallow dive the airspeed would increase, causing the spiral blade path to elongate (Fig. 25), reducing the angle of attack of the blade. Blade drag would decrease in consequence and this would manifest itself in reduced torque reaction. In other words the load on the propeller would decrease and the engine would have less work to perform. The net result would be an increase in RPM. This would cause the governor in the constant-speed unit likewise to speed up and the bob weights would fly outwards overcoming the spring pressure and causing the pitch-changing valve to open. Pressure oil would then enter the hub of the propeller and increase the pitch of the blades. The pitch would continue to increase until the blade angle of attack was such that the propeller could absorb sufficient power to slow down the engine to the original RPM. At this point the bob weights in the constant-speed unit would once more return to neutral, closing the valve and locking the propeller in its new pitch.

The foregoing sequence is illustrated in Fig. 27.

When an additional load on the propeller decreases engine speed, the constant-speed unit will operate the pitch-changing valve in the opposite direction causing a change to a finer pitch which will allow the engine to maintain the pre-determined RPM.

In comparison with a fixed-pitch airscrew the constant-speed airscrew has these advantages –

1. Engine speed remains constant at the level selected by the pilot.

2. Since it is a function of RPM power remains constant at any given manifold pressure.

3. Propeller efficiency is improved throughout all conditions of flight.

4. A shorter take-off results from the greater power available from the engine since the blades are unstalled and in fine pitch at the commencement of the take-off run, progressively coarsening as the aircraft accelerates.

5. As height is gained compensation for the decreased density occurs automatically as the pitch is increased by the constant-speed unit.

As engines have become more and more powerful the problem of converting horse-power into thrust has grown acute. Various alternatives are at the disposal of the designer.

(*a*) Propellers of larger diameter. This method is limited by the necessity to keep the tip speed of the blades below the speed of sound and, with ground clearance in mind, the need to keep the undercarriage length within reasonable proportions.

(*b*) Increasing the thickness of the blade airfoil section. This is inefficient at higher speeds.

(*c*) Increasing the **Solidity**, i.e. the blade area in relation to the disc area of the rotating propeller. This is the usual method adopted and it can be accomplished in three ways –

(i) Increasing the blade chord. This is the simplest procedure but, as in the case of a wing, aspect ratio must be taken into account if efficiency is to be maintained.

(ii) Increasing the number of blades. This is the more efficient approach towards solidity although five blades represents a limit which is dictated by blade interference. Most of the larger modern propellers have four blades.

(iii) **Counter Rotating Propellers.** When piston-engined fighters reached their highest stage of development, two propellers were arranged to rotate in opposite direction, one behind the other, thus providing great solidity and absorbing considerable engine power without subjecting the aircraft to torque effect. This complex arrangement has been overtaken by the advent of jet propulsion.

The range of pitch selection is limited by stops which are incorporated in the design of the propeller. The angular movement of the blades from 'fine' to 'coarse' pitch is sufficient to cater for more flight conditions, but there are two additional refinements which are to be found on many of the modern aircraft: **Feathering** and **Reversible Pitch.**

Feathering Propellers

The procedure to be followed when an engine fails in flight on a twin- or multi-engined aircraft is explained in some detail in Exercise 23 'Multi-engine Conversion'. Briefly there are two main considerations when this situation occurs –

1. The reduction of drag from the windmilling propeller.

2. When the failure is a mechanical one, the prevention of further damage to the engine, by stopping rotation. Additionally in more advanced aircraft it is essential to stop rotation when fire occurs in the engine. (*See* Emergency Exercise 1: 'Action in the Event of Fire', Vol. 1.)

The reduction of drag and the prevention of rotation are attained by arranging for the pitch to go past the 'fully coarse' position so that the blades are presented to the airflow 'edge on'. The twist of the blades from root to tip must be taken into account and when the propeller is 'feathered' the average angle along the length of the blade is such that

(*a*) minimum drag exists,

(*b*) no windmilling force occurs.

The feathering procedure is quite simple and forms part of the multi-engine pilot's training practice. The engine to be stopped is throttled back completely. The propeller control is then moved through the coarse pitch gate to the feathering position when the pitch will go past 'fully coarse' and continue towards the 'fully feathered' position. With the engine stationary no oil pressure will be available to complete the feathering or to un-feather when the engine is to be re-started, and a separate electrically driven hydraulic feathering pump may be installed for the purpose. The electro-hydraulic pump is operated by a **Feathering Button** which is prominently marked as such in the cockpit and usually protected by a red-hinged flap to prevent accidental use. Feathering is completed with this button. Its function when re-starting the engine is as follows –

1. Switches 'on', fuel 'on' and mixture 'rich'.
2. Throttle open to starting position for engine type.
3. Propeller control to minimum RPM position.
4. Press the feathering button bringing into use the feathering pump which will proceed to un-feather the propeller. Usually the airflow will windmill the propeller as the pitch changes when the engine will start and the feathering button should be held in until rotation commences. It can then be released since the engine-driven pump will take over. Should the engine resist rotation the starter should be used.
5. Allow the engine to warm up, then synchronize with the other engine(s).

Note – Most light multi-engined aircraft dispense with the feathering button, the action being controlled on the pitch lever, which operates a compressed air spring within the propeller hub.

Reversible Pitch Propellers

Notwithstanding the remarkable advance in braking efficiency brought about by the advent of anti-skid and disc brakes and the fact that the tricycle undercarriage permits full use to be made of this braking power, landing distance has remained a problem with large heavy transport aircraft. Additionally the rapid tyre wear which results from heavy application of brakes is an embarrassment to the airline operator. Both of these difficulties are sometimes alleviated by arranging for the propellers to reverse pitch after the landing, when the application of power causes thrust to act in the opposite direction and materially assist in the stopping of the aircraft. Not only is wear on the tyres and brakes minimized but the landing run is considerably shortened even when snow or ice on the runway prevents full use being made of the brakes.

It is universal practice to fit reversible pitch propellers to turbo-propeller engines and their operation is described on page 67.

Constant-speed Propeller Faults

1. Overspeeding

In the event of the constant-speed unit becoming unserviceable or possibly as a result of loss of oil pressure the propeller may go into fully fine pitch when the RPM will then exceed maximum permissible. When this happens the following remedial actions should be taken –

1. Close the throttle on the affected engine.

2. Immediately raise the nose and reduce the airspeed.

3. When efforts to bring the propeller under control prove impossible, an attempt should be made to feather.

2. Failure of the Constant-speed Unit

This may be occasioned by a temporary blockage of the oil feed and can often be cleared by exercising the propeller control. The pitch valve will move and may dislodge whatever is causing the blockage. When the fault persists the pitch will lock in a position appropriate to the flight condition at the time of failure and the various effects on the aircraft are as follows –

(*a*) *In Level Flight*. Pitch will be suitable for normal cruising speeds but may be too coarse should it be necessary to go round again after a faulty landing. The higher the IAS at the time of failure the coarser the pitch when the propeller locks.

(*b*) *Failure During a Climb*. The propeller will be in a fine pitch which should be suitable for level flight although care must be exercised to prevent overspeeding the engine, by limiting both throttle opening and airspeed.

The Propeller During Take-off

In converting engine HP into thrust the propeller produces certain undesirable side effects which are most apparent during the early stages of take-off when a tendency to swing occurs.

This results from four independent causes, all attributed to the propeller.

1. Slipstream Effect

As the slipstream travels back along the aircraft it describes a helical path around the fuselage. The slipstream is able to pass freely around the undersurface of the rear fuselage but, because of its helical path, it must eventually strike one side of the fin and rudder, causing the aircraft to swing. When the propeller rotates in an anti-clockwise direction (as seen from behind) the fin will be pushed to the left and a swing to the right will result. (The diagram on page 52, *Flight Briefing for Pilots*, Vol. 1, will explain further.)

2. Torque Effect

Because of torque reaction there is a tendency for the aircraft to rotate in the opposite direction to the propeller. This may best be understood by holding a rubber driven model aircraft by the propeller and letting the airframe rotate freely under the power of twisted rubber bands. On light aircraft of low power this effect is not very pronounced during take-off although the rolling tendency assumes considerable importance on high-performance single-engined Service types prior to the jet engine. In resisting the rolling tendency during the early stages of the take-off, one wheel must support more weight than the other causing additional resistance to wheel rotation on one side of the aircraft. When the propeller rotates as before, the right wheel will be called upon to resist torque reaction and a swing to the right will result.

3. Gyroscopic Effect (Tailwheel aircraft only)

When the propeller rotates it assumes the properties of a flywheel and is subject to gyroscopic characteristics. These are described more fully in 'Instrument Flying' (page 103). When an attempt is made to alter its plane of rotation, a gyroscope reacts at 90° to the applied force. As the tail is lifted during the take-off this has the effect of tilting the propeller disc forward as though a forward force had been applied at the top of the circle described by the propeller. The applied force travels through 90° in the direction of rotation (in this case anti-clockwise seen from behind) and the reaction will emerge as a force pushing forward the left-hand edge of the propeller disc. This will cause a swing to the right (Fig. 28).

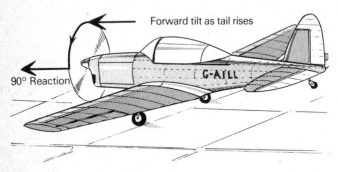

Fig. 28. Gyroscopic effect causing a swing on take-off as the tail is raised.

Gyroscopic effect is only active as the tail is raised during take-off although it may be experienced to a lesser degree during turns when a 90° reaction causes the nose to rise or drop according to the direction of the turn.

4. Asymmetric Blade Effect (Tailwheel aircraft only)

Not to be confused with the multi-engined exercise to be described later, asymmetric thrust occurs during the early stages of the take-off run whilst the tail is still on the ground. In the tail-down attitude the propeller shaft is inclined upwards causing the blades to follow a tilted plane of rotation. As the aircraft moves forward the propeller blades will follow a helical path (Fig. 25, No. 2) when, because of the inclined propeller shaft, the blades will have an increased angle of attack as they enter the 'down-going' side of the propeller disc. Conversely, blade angle of attack decreases as the 'up-going' sector is entered, so causing more thrust on one side of the aircraft than the other. After the tail is raised, blade angle of attack is constant

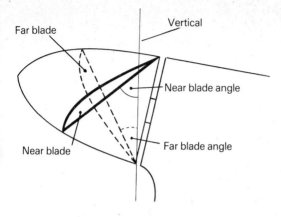

Fig. 29. Asymmetric blade effect.
Note the larger angle of attack on the near blade caused by the inclined propeller axis.

throughout its rotation and Asymmetric Blade Effect disappears. Figure 29 shows that, with the anti-clockwise rotation used throughout these explanations, as the blade enters the left half of the propeller disc its angle of attack will increase causing a swing to the right. For simplicity the illustration shows the helical blade path as a vertical line.

It will be noted that all these effects produce a swing to the right when the propeller rotates anti-clockwise. Opposite rotation, as adopted for the majority of modern engines, would cause a swing to the left. Since both Gyroscopic Effect and Asymmetric Blade Effect result from the tail-down attitude or its change to the level flight position, neither effect will occur on aircraft with tricycle undercarriages.

3   Introduction to Gas Turbines

Turbojet and Fanjet Engines

The idea of jet propulsion is not a new one and early literature shows that the ancient Greeks knew of the principle and had a toy steam engine based on jet propulsion. The ancient Chinese civilization used rockets, yet another application of the principle of jet propulsion. To understand these principles it is necessary to consider Newton's third law which states that every action has an equal and opposite reaction. This can be seen in hundreds of everyday examples – the kick when a gun is fired, a rowing boat moving forward when the water is displaced rearwards by the oars, etc. If a balloon is inflated and then released the escaping air will drive it in the opposite direction. Movement results from the reaction to the jet of air issuing rearwards and the balloon is not propelled because the jet pushes against the outside atmosphere.

Methods of aircraft propulsion, both jet and propeller, provide thrust by displacing a mass of air rearwards, the basic difference between the two types being the nature of the rearward airstream. In the case of the propeller a large diameter of air is displaced at a relatively slow speed whereas the jet engine accelerates a much smaller diameter of air to a very high speed. The amount of reaction, i.e. thrust, could however be the same in each case as this is a product of weight of air displaced multiplied by the acceleration.

A four-stroke piston engine produces a power stroke once in every two revolutions. The gas-turbine engine however operates on a continuous cycle in which the four strokes (induction, compression, power and exhaust) are carried on at the same time but in different parts of the engine, and the power output is continuous. This cycle, together with the absence of reciprocating parts, explains the smooth vibration-free operation of the gas-turbine engine.

Whereas the processes of induction, compression, power and exhaust take place in the cylinders of a piston engine, these separate phases occur in four distinct parts of the gas turbine. These are the **Intake, Compressor, Combustion Chambers** and **Exhaust Nozzle** respectively. At this stage it should be explained that the high power needed to drive the compressor is taken from the gas stream by a turbine situated after the combustion chambers.

The compressor may be one of two basic types, **Centrifugal** or **Axial Flow**. The former was developed from piston-engine

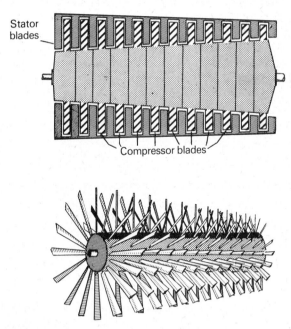

Stator blades

Compressor blades

12 Stage Axial Compressor

Fig. 30. Axial compressor (diagrammatic).

superchargers, one of these being illustrated in Fig. 22 on page 34. The intake is fed into the centre of an impeller revolving at high speed causing a rapid rise in pressure as the air is flung outwards into diffuser vanes. Sometimes this high-pressure air is fed into a second impeller and the process repeated to gain a further rise in pressure. This is of great benefit as the higher the air pressure before combustion, the lower the fuel consumption of the engine relative to its power.

This need for high compression led to the introduction of the axial flow compressor. With this type a gradual increase in pressure is obtained by a series of rotating discs fitted with blades of airfoil section. These are made to rotate between sets of fixed blades causing a small increase in pressure; each set of fixed and rotating blades being called a **Stage**. By incorporating up to fifteen or more stages a very high final pressure is obtained and this type of compressor is found in most modern gas-turbine engines (Fig. 30).

By now the air from the compressor may have reached a temperature in excess of 250° C due solely to compression in much the same way as a bicycle pump connection becomes warm while inflating a tyre (i.e. adiabatic heating). This air is led from the compressor assembly to the combustion chambers which in many ways resemble blow lamps. The number of combustion chambers varies according to the design of the engine but each assembly, or **Flame Tube** as it is sometimes called, has a fuel burner at the forward end which is designed to atomize kerosene, the fuel commonly used. In most engines combustion takes place in a single annular type burner.

When the engine is started fuel pumps cause a fine spray to emerge from the burners and this is ignited by a powerful electric spark. Once the engine is running, combustion is continuous rather like a workshop blow lamp, and the ignitor switches off.

The design of the flame tubes is very complex as approximately five tons of air are passed through an average engine every minute at temperatures in the region of 2,000° C at the hottest point. Some of the air from the compressor by-passes the burning fuel and is used to mix with the hot gases from the

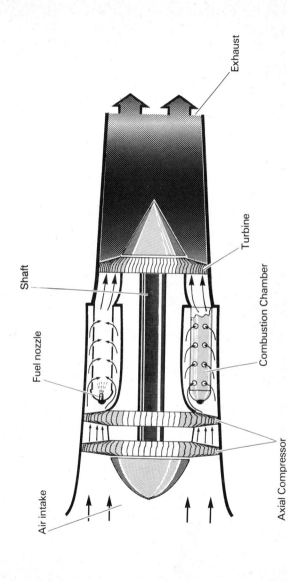

Exhaust

Shaft

Turbine

Fuel nozzle

Combustion Chamber

Axial Compressor

Air intake

Fig. 31. Basic turbojet engine. This simple power unit based upon a single rotating assembly. Fixed guide vanes between compressor stages have been omitted for clarity.

flame tube, so lowering the temperature to below 1,000° C before impinging on the turbine. The original very high temperature would cause damage to that part of the engine.

Burning the fuel at a high rate (more than 1,000 gallons per hour in a big engine) puts immense energy into the gas in the form of heat, pressure and velocity. The gas is then passed through carefully shaped guide vanes to the turbine blades which rotate the turbine disc at very high speed. In the process, energy is taken out of the gas stream and the power from the turbine is transmitted via a shaft to the compressor. Some engines employ a series of turbine wheels (**multistage**) so that high power is produced while turbine diameter is kept to a minimum.

The power taken from the gas stream and used by the turbine to drive the compressor may amount to some 20,000 HP. The remaining energy in the gas stream is converted into a high-speed jet by the exhaust nozzle at the rear of the engine and it is the forward reaction, inside the engine, to this jet of high-speed gas which creates thrust. The complete cycle of the **Turbojet** is shown in Fig. 31.

Engine power is a factor of temperature and mass flow, i.e. the greater the temperature the higher the power output for any given mass flow. Power is also affected by the compression ratio of the engine. In attaining this aim the compressor is assisted by the ram effect of the air entering the intake, and this contribution to the power of the engine increases with airspeed.

Whereas piston engine output is measured in horsepower, jet engine power is expressed in pounds thrust. The approximate relationship is: –

At 250 kt 1 lb of thrust = 1 HP
At 500 kt 1 lb of thrust = 3 HP

In the operation of gas turbines and in particular turbojets, fuel consumption is of great importance since this tends to be high in relation to piston engines. These engines work efficiently at high altitudes where the air density and airframe drag are reduced and it is usual for turbojet aircraft to operate at the highest altitude that the flight stage allows.

Control of the engine is simple. Engine speed is controlled by a 'power lever' which in reality adjusts the fuel flow according to the desired engine speed. An automatic fuel system keeps the RPM constant regardless of airspeed or altitude.

Engine instruments consist basically of an RPM indicator, turbine inlet temperature gauge, oil-pressure gauge and a fuel-flow meter.

Some turbojet power plants are equipped with **Thrust-reversal** which enables the jet stream to be directed forwards by means of shutters in the exhaust nozzle, so reversing the direction of thrust during the landing run. The equipment shortens the landing run and substantially reduces wear and tear on the brakes and tyres.

The Fanjet

The basic turbojet so far described does have certain disadvantages, in that fuel consumption is high and noise levels have caused an understandable reaction from the public, particularly from those living near major airports.

A development of the basic turbojet, one that powers most modern subsonic aircraft, is the **Fanjet,** so called because a considerable portion of the power generated by the gases is used to rotate a fan of relatively large diameter at the front of the engine. The fan, which turns within a duct, creates a tube of slower moving air which is discharged around the high velocity efflux from the turbine jet pipe. The arrangement has an insulating effect on jet noise caused by the high speed discharge from the jet pipe.

So that the fan and the **Gas Generator** may be allowed to operate at their most efficient speeds it is usual to arrange for the compressor stages to be driven by one turbine while an additional turbine drives the fan via a separate shaft. Such engines (illustrated in Fig. 32) are known as **two-shaft** power

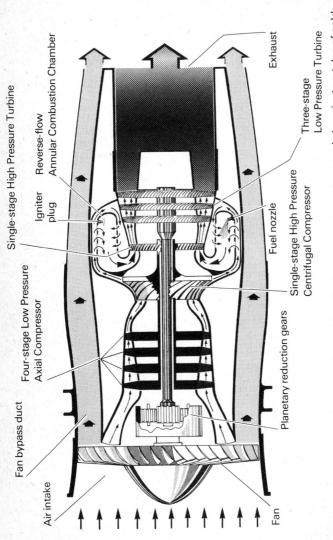

Fig. 32. Fanjet engine. The fan, which acts as the first compressor stage and also ejects a tube of cold, low-velocity air, is coupled to the three-stage low pressure turbine via a shaft which runs through the tubular gas generator shaft. The guide vanes, which are fixed between the compressor stages and also the turbine stages, have been omitted for clarity.

Single-stage High Pressure Turbine

Reverse-flow Annular Combustion Chamber

Igniter plug

Three-stage Low Pressure Turbine

Exhaust

Fuel nozzle

Single-stage High Pressure Centrifugal Compressor

Four-stage Low Pressure Axial Compressor

Fan bypass duct

Planetary reduction gears

Air intake

Fan

units and they are provided with two RPM indicators (reading in percentage maximum RPM), one relating to the fan (known as N1 RPM) and the other reading gas generator speeds (N2 RPM).

A further refinement offering still more attractive fuel economy is the **three-shaft** engine, an example being the Rolls Royce RB211 shown in Fig. 33.

Turbo-propeller Engines

Background

Early turbojet engines suffered from a number of shortcomings. Engine acceleration was slow and the throttle had to be moved slowly otherwise surging, a breakdown in gas flow that sounded like a machine gun, would occur and, if allowed to continue, could cause turbine damage. At low levels these early engines were particularly uneconomical and even at, say, 30,000 feet with the advantage of an enhanced TAS for the IAS achieved, fuel economy could not approach that of contemporary piston engines. Since at low levels the early jet aircraft offered only moderate improvements in cruising speed over the best piston engine designs of the day, it followed that to obtain the best performance from a turbojet it had to be operated at high altitude. **Specific Fuel Consumption**, i.e. fuel economy expressed in terms of lbs fuel burned/HP/hour, has greatly improved over the years but the need to fly high for best performance remains. Furthermore, the power output of a turbojet is to a considerable extent dependent upon forward speed in obtaining sufficient airflow for best fuel/power performance, so that a turbojet, or fanjet aircraft, has to be capable of flying both high and fast if it is to be economical.

Such requirements, as outlined above, are bound to be costly and therefore unsuited to the needs of some air transport/freight operations, particularly those calling for relatively short ranges at moderate speeds, or when heavy loads are to be lifted out of small airstrips. Early in the development of the gas turbine engine it was realized that to cater for these require-

Fig. 33. Rolls Royce RB211-524 Three-shaft fanjet engine. Note the large diameter fan and the relatively small gas generator and jet pipe. These high by-pass ratio engines (4.4:1) return outstanding fuel economy. *Photo courtesy of Rolls Royce.*

ments better **Propulsive Efficiency** at lower speeds could be obtained from the gas turbine engine by using most of its power to drive a propeller. Thus, on 20 September, 1945, Gloster Meteor EE227 became the first turbo-propeller aircraft to fly when it took off on the power of two Rolls Royce RB50 Trent engines driving five-blade Rotol propellers.

While the turbo-propeller, or as it is commonly known, **Turboprop** engine is no longer favoured for long distance passenger aircraft, some very successful military turboprop freighters of outstanding short field performance continue in widespread use. Within civil aviation the turboprop engine has for some years powered transport aircraft in the 20–100 seat category and it is now finding growing acceptance as a power plant for light twin-engine designs as well as commuter aircraft providing 18–30 seats.

The Turbo-propeller Engine

The turbine in a turbojet engine is confined to driving the compressor, thus leaving much of the gas energy to provide maximum propulsion by ejecting a high velocity jet. However, the turbine in a turboprop engine is designed to absorb the greater proportion of gas energy for use in driving the compressor and the propeller, leaving a small amount of residual thrust to be ejected in a manner similar to a turbojet. The following figures relate to some modern low-powered turboprop engines in common use. They show the proportion between **Shaft HP** (as delivered to the propeller), **Residual Thrust** and **Equivalent Shaft HP (ESHP)** which represents the total power of the engine. Also shown is the amount of fuel burned to develop one HP for one hour (Specific Fuel Consumption).

Shaft HP	Thrust	ESHP	SFC lb/HP/hr
575	75 lb	605	·665
715	102 lb	755	·626
1,040	115 lb	1,086	·558

Most low-powered turboprop engines offer a **Time Between Overhauls (TBO)** of 3,000–4,000 hours which is twice the life of a piston engine, although considerably less than that achieved by a good turbojet or turbofan engine. However, unlike a piston engine, which can accelerate quickly from idling at, say, 600 RPM to its maximum 3,000 RPM, small gas turbines rotate at some 42,000 RPM. Although idling speed might be a relatively high 25,000 RPM, the engine must nevertheless accelerate through 17,000 RPM when power is applied for take-off or to initiate a missed approach.

In many piston engines the carburettor is fitted with an accelerator pump to ensure good throttle response. Such an arrangement would not work on a turboprop engine and the methods of providing the pilot with good power response will be explained later in this section.

Obviously an engine rotating at 42,000 RPM cannot be directly coupled to a propeller and a gearbox must be provided offering a speed reduction in excess of 20:1. A pick-up point measuring the twisting force (**Torque**) between the engine and the reduction gears presents the information on a **Torque Meter** situated with the other engine instruments. Often these Torque Meters are calibrated in horsepower. At low levels it is possible to **Over Torque** a propjet engine and Torque Meters are 'red lined' to indicate the limit of power that may be applied. This is of particular relevance during take-off. Some engines are protected against over torquing by an automatic **Torque Limiter**.

While high gas temperature is a prerequisite of high power, limits are imposed by the ability of the 'hot' section of the engine (turbine, flame tubes, etc.) to withstand such heat. To guard against the possibility of exceeding the temperature limits of the engine an **Interstage Turbine Temperature Gauge (ITT)** is provided for the pilot. Turboprop engines are more likely to exceed their temperature limits during a faulty starting procedure, or while flying at height, and some engines are equipped with a temperature limiter governing the amount of fuel flow to the engine by sensing the ITT. Other engine instruments are –

Propeller RPM (in percentage maximum)

Fuel Flow (in lb/hr)
Oil Pressure/Oil Temperature Gauge

Engine Controls

The power output of a piston engine fitted with a constant speed propeller is controlled by adjusting manifold pressure and propeller RPM while optimum fuel economy is attained by using the mixture control. Turboprop management is somewhat different. There is the wide range of engine RPM from idling to cruising power already mentioned and the added facility of reverse thrust for aerodynamic braking which has become a normal requirement with this type of engine. Furthermore because of the high minimum turbine RPM needed to sustain these engines, propeller idling speeds are likewise higher than is usual with piston engines, consequently even in fine pitch there would be excessive thrust while taxying. Propellers fitted to gas turbine engines must, therefore, be more versatile than those driven by piston engines and a typical pitch range would be $-10°$ to $+60°$. They are capable of being adjusted from fine to fully coarse pitch in the constant speed range and from fine through zero thrust to reverse thrust in the manually controlled or **Beta Range**. The following control arrangements have now become more or less standard for turbo-propeller engines.

Power Lever

In its operating arc between 'idle' (i.e. back against the idle stop) and fully open the power lever performs a similar function to that of the throttle on a piston engine. Whereas throttle setting is monitored on the manifold pressure gauge (piston engines) power levers for turboprop engines are adjusted to attain a required torque/HP (Torque Meter), temperature (ITT gauge) and fuel flow (Fuel Flow Meter). To avoid the need for excessive use of the brakes while taxying (the result of high levels of thrust even when the power levers are back against the idle stops) provision is made to lift the levers and move them rearwards (or in some cases lift latches which allow the levers to move behind their stops), so placing the propeller in the manually operated Beta Range. First movement adjusts the blades to a finer setting than idle followed by zero thrust. Further backward movement selects reverse pitch at the same time adding power. Maximum reverse thrust occurs when the power lever is fully back. Warning lights on the flight panel inform the pilot when the propellers have entered the Beta Range.

While reverse thrust allows the pilot to taxi backwards the practice is not to be encouraged. It is not usually possible to see behind the aircraft and there is always the danger of striking an obstruction. Furthermore unless the brakes are applied very gently there is a tendency for aircraft taxying backwards to pitch back on their tail bumpers.

Propeller Control

This lever controls propeller RPM via the constant speed unit in much the same manner as with a piston engine. The propeller may be feathered by moving the control to the coarse pitch stop, lifting it and then bringing back the lever to the feathering position.

Condition Lever

Incorporating a **High Pressure Cock**, which is similar in purpose to the idle cut-off function of a piston engine mixture control, this lever also selects the correct setting for the fuel governor according to phase of flight, e.g. taxying, take-off, cruise, etc.

It has become the practice to combine the propeller function with the condition lever, thus simplifying engine management. Under this arrangement the condition lever quadrant may be marked HIGH RPM (fully forward position), LOW RPM (back to the stop) and ENGINE STOP EMERGENCY FEATHER (condition lever lifted and brought fully back), when the high pressure cock will close, thus starving the engine of fuel, and the propeller will move into the feathered position.

Negative Torque Sensing

Mention has already been made of the very high turbine speeds attained in small gas turbine engines and the consequent need of a 20:1 gear reduction before the power may be coupled to a propeller. However in the event of power failure for any reason (fuel starvation, flame-out, etc.) the windmilling propeller would continue to drive the turbine/compressor assembly through the gearbox reversing transmission loads through a gear *increase* of 20:1. Such loads on the propeller, gears and drive shaft resulting from the windmill energy needed to drive the engine at 42,000 RPM, are bound to create excessive drag and severe asymmetric problems could occur while the pilot identifies the failed engine, tries to determine the cause of failure, and carries out feather action.

To guard against further damage to the engine, and as a means of reducing asymmetric flight problems during the first phase of engine failure, turboprop engines are fitted with a **Negative Torque Sensing** device which is activated when at any time the propeller drives the engine following power loss. When negative torque is sensed the propeller is automatically moved to the fully coarse position, so minimizing drag, at the same time placing the blades at a setting that will ensure speedy feather action when the condition lever is brought fully back to the feather position.

Engine Starting

Details of engine starting vary slightly from one power plant to another. In most cases the sequence is automatic, or semi-automatic, requiring little of the pilot other than the need to switch off the generator, an action that converts it to a starter motor. An ignition plug, provided for starting and as a safeguard against flame-out during take-off and landing, is switched on, then the starter is engaged. When the RPM have stabilized (about 10% to 15% RPM will show on the propeller speed indicator) the condition lever is brought out of the shut down gate, thus opening the high pressure cock and allowing fuel to enter the engine. 'Light up' should be confirmed by an immediate rise in temperature on the ITT gauge. It will most likely go up to 600°C and then fall by 100° or so, but if during starting there is a tendency for the ITT to approach the red line the engine must be shut down immediately. When idling RPM have been attained the engine will be self-sustaining and the ignition may be switched off, the generator turned ON (starter OFF) and the procedure will then be repeated for the other engine(s). However, electric current requirements for starting are very considerable and when the aircraft batteries are used rather than an external source the voltmeter must be checked for power recovery (i.e. voltage build-up) before the next engine is started.

Cabin Pressure and Anti-icing

An altitude of 10,000 ft is generally regarded as the maximum for flying without oxygen. Higher cruising levels bring with them the dangers of oxygen starvation and discomfort from pressure build-up which must accompany the eventual descent. Certain turbo-propeller powered aircraft are intended for use at relatively low levels but the usual light twin designed for company executives will normally be required to cruise at flight levels between 200 and 300, well above the altitude where oxygen masks would have to be worn. To cater for both the need for adequate oxygen and a near constant cabin altitude at all flight levels, aircraft are pressurized. This entails stressing the cabin area to withstand internal pressures of between 5 and 8 lb/sq/in in the case of small turboprop and turbojet designs. Pressure is taken from the compressors for the purpose, in some cases direct to the cabin, while many installations feature an air conditioning system.

To guard against ice formation on the engine air intake warm air from the compressor may also be directed to the intake casing. Like the cabin pressurization intake heating is under the control of the pilot.

Turbo-propeller Engine Types

There are two main types of turboprop engines –

Fixed Shaft Engines
Free Turbine Engines

Each has its advantages and disadvantages. The following brief description is only intended as an introduction to the subject and full operating procedures will be found in the manufacturers' instructions or the aircraft Owner's/Flight/Operating Manual.

Fixed Shaft Engines

The advantage of this type of engine is its simplicity, there being only one main rotating assembly and a propeller reduction gear from which accessory drives are taken for such services as starter/generator, RPM indicator, hydraulic pump, instrument vacuum, etc. Figure 34 is a simplified illustration of the Garrett AiResearch fixed shaft turboprop engine and reference to it shows that air is drawn through a forward-facing intake. This is directed to a two-stage centrifugal compressor and then blown at increased pressure and temperature (through adiabatic heating) to an annular combustion chamber which encircles the 'hot' end of the engine. In it the flow of pressure air reverses before entering an inner burner chamber which carries a number of fuel nozzles and a single ignition plug. Air from the compressor is mixed with fuel, ignited and, following a considerable rise in temperature, greatly expanded. These gases, by now possessed of great energy, eject forward from the combustion chamber, turn through 180° and then impinge on a three-stage turbine which extracts most of the gas energy, using the power to drive the compressor and the propeller to which it is coupled via the reduction gearbox. Residual gas flow is ejected as a jet from the rear of the engine. The advantage of reversing flow through the combustion chamber is two-fold –

(*a*) the arrangement allows for a shorter engine than would otherwise be possible in a front to rear flow;

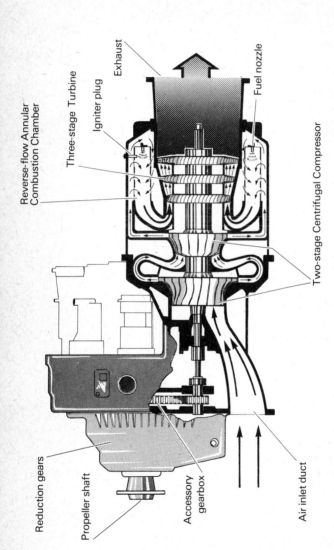

Fig. 34. Fixed Shaft Turboprop Engine. The two-stage centrifugal compressor and the three-stage turbine which drives it are mounted on a common shaft and this is the only moving assembly in the engine. The reduction gears convert 48,000 turbine RPM into a propeller speed of approximately 1,900 RPM. Fixed guide vanes within the turbine section have been omitted for clarity.

(*b*) the swirl effect of reversing flow ensures adequate mixing of the fuel and air, so avoiding smoke and aiding fuel economy.

Such engines overcome the problem of power lever response by running at a constant speed irrespective of power lever position, so that movement of the lever produces an instant change in power and no time is required to speed up or slow down the turbine/compressor assembly. Power increases at constant RPM are simply affected by advancing the power lever, when more fuel will enter the engine, the propeller blades coarsening to absorb the additional power. Likewise when the power lever is brought back fuel delivery is reduced, power is reduced and the propeller goes into a finer pitch, reducing thrust while maintaining the engine at a constant speed.

Power is transmitted to the reduction gearbox by a 24-in. long spring steel shaft which is only some $\frac{3}{8}$-in. in diameter. Twist in the shaft is proportional to the engine power being developed and this is measured by a sensitive device which is coupled to the pilot's Torque Meter while opposite twist (that would be present in the event of engine failure) activates the Negative Torque Sensing device causing the propeller to move into coarse pitch.

Other than a tendency to be noisy while idling on the ground, these simple engines have proved both easy to handle and very reliable in operation.

During starting, the engine is rotated until RPM stabilize, then the HP cock is opened to allow fuel flow and ignition. To prevent feathering of the propeller, which would add unnecessary load to the electric starter at this stage, the propeller is fitted with a **Fine Pitch Lock**. This holds the blades in fine pitch when the engine is shut down making it ready for the next start. Fine pitch locks are released after starting by lifting and bringing back the power lever until the Beta light comes on, when the propeller will be free to operate throughout its range of blade angles.

Free Turbine Engines

Unlike fixed shaft designs free turbine engines utilize two separate, but interdependent turbines. One drives the compressor

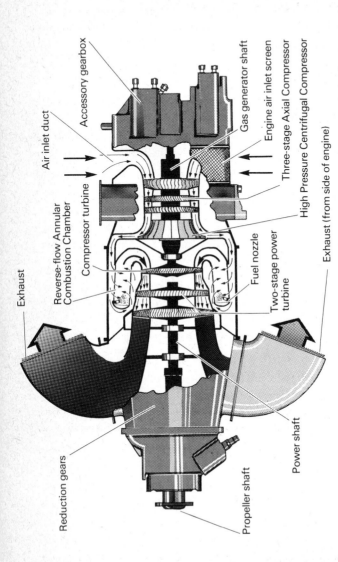

Fig. 35. Free turbine turboprop engine (seen from above). The three-stage axial and single stage centrifugal compressors, along with their driving turbine, are mounted on the rear shaft which also drives the accessories. A separate shaft, which rotates in the opposite direction, carries the two-stage power turbine which is coupled to the propeller through suitable reduction gearing. Guide vanes between the turbine and compressor stages have been omitted for clarity.

Labels (clockwise from top):
- Air inlet duct
- Accessory gearbox
- Gas generator shaft
- Engine air inlet screen
- Three-stage Axial Compressor
- High Pressure Centrifugal Compressor
- Exhaust (from side of engine)
- Fuel nozzle
- Two-stage power turbine
- Power shaft
- Propeller shaft
- Reduction gears
- Exhaust
- Reverse-flow Annular Combustion Chamber
- Compressor turbine

to which it is linked, and the assembly is known as a gas generator (already mentioned on page 63). A second, **Power Turbine**, is connected to the propeller via a reduction gear. The advantage of this kind of engine is that the gas generator and the power turbine may be designed to rotate at optimum RPM. Such an engine is the Pratt & Whitney Aircraft of Canada Ltd PT6 and a simplified illustration is provided for reference while reading the following text (Fig. 35).

For the purpose of directing moisture, ice or other debris away from the engine the air intake incorporates an inertial vane and a rear by-pass door. Ice or other potentially damaging foreign matter, being heavier than air, is free to enter the front of the nacelle and flow out of the rear. These vanes are electrically controlled through a temperature sensor. There is also a manual override. Air entering the inlet passage is sucked upwards into a wire mesh protected annular air inlet, which encases the rear of the engine. From here it flows forward through the three axial compressors and their related fixed or stator vanes, each stage raising the pressure of the air. From the third stage it flows to a centrifugal compressor which directs the air through 90° before it resumes forward flow and enters an annular casing surrounding the combustion chamber. At this stage the air is at high pressure. Holes in the combustion chamber are positioned to ensure thorough mixing of air and fuel, which is pumped under pressure through 14 nozzles or flame tubes. Two igniter plugs are provided for starting and the prevention of flame-out at a critical stage of flight.

The flame tubes heat the compressed air, expanding it and directing the high temperature gas forward on to the compressor turbine which is directly coupled to the compressor. 100% RPM for the assembly (N_1 or gas generator) is 37,500 while maximum continuous N_1 speed is 38,100 RPM (101.5%). Gas generator speeds are indicated on the N_1 tachometer which is adjacent to the other engine instruments.

Forward of the N_1 turbine is a two-stage power turbine which is mounted on a separate shaft running forward to the propeller reduction gear. Gas flow from the N_1 turbine moves forward through guide vanes rotating the two-stage power turbine in the opposite direction to the gas generator. By now most of the energy has been removed from the gas which flows into an annular exhaust plenum for ejection to the atmosphere through two large diameter exhaust ports situated left and right of the engine. Propeller RPM are monitored on a separate indicator. When the propeller is rotating at 2,000 RPM the power turbine will be turning at 30,000 RPM.

While engine installations vary the PT6 is usually controlled through a power lever (offering the lift up and pull back Beta/Reverse Thrust facility already explained), a propeller lever with feathering selection by moving back the control past the coarse pitch stop, and a condition lever marked as follows –

> FUEL CUT-OFF (fully back)
> LOW IDLE (lever on rear stop)
> HIGH IDLE (lever fully forward)

In 'Low Idle' fuel is governed to provide idling at 52% RPM (N_1) for taxying, while 'High Idle' gives an N_1 idling speed of 70% RPM.

Other than a fine pitch limit there are no stops fitted in the propeller hub and the pitch change is free to move from reverse thrust through maximum coarse to feather. Oil pressure moves the blades towards fine pitch and centrifugal counterweights assisted by a spring alter pitch in the reverse direction, consequently during engine shutdown the blades feather. While idling in confined spaces with the gas generator running at its 'Low Idle' 52% RPM N_1, *feather* may be selected on the propeller control, when the airscrew will drift slowly around without causing unwanted slipstream which could inconvenience others on the ground.

The PT6 is fitted with a torque sensor pick-up point at the first stage reduction gear housing. This measures the force being applied by the power turbine, then transmits the reading to the pilot's torque meter which is calibrated in ft/lb. Negative torque following power loss automatically feathers the propeller. **Autofeather** is intended for use during take-off and landing only and it cannot operate unless the power lever is set to at least 90% N_1 RPM. Being a free turbine engine, power failure does not require the propeller to drive the compressor through high gearing, therefore autofeather should be switched off during the cruise.

The air intake is kept free of ice by heat from the exhaust. This type of engine is available in versions offering from 550 HP to more than 1,000 HP.

Turbo-propeller Engines in the Landing Phase

With the condition lever/propeller lever in the correct position for landing and the power lever back against the idle stop, turboprop engines are adjusted to provide sufficient thrust to ensure a low rate of sink during the hold-off phase. After touch-down the power lever(s) should be moved back through the Beta range and into reverse thrust, brake being applied as required to still further shorten the post-landing rolling distance.

4 Multi-engined Aircraft

In the early days of flying when engines were of very limited power it soon became apparent that aeroplanes were becoming too large for one engine. Largely as a result of the First World War, twin-engined aircraft were developed to meet military requirements and during the early twenties these bombers were to be seen as civil passenger aircraft on the London–Paris and other routes.

When loaded the early twins were incapable of maintaining height on one engine, a shortcoming which will cause no surprise when it is realized that these large aircraft had an all-up weight of 12,000–13,000 lb, were of a design encumbered with a high drag factor yet flew on engines of little more than 200 HP each. Indeed the installation of two engines was motivated by a desire for more power rather than an attempt at twin-engine security. This requirement was to come later in the development of the aeroplane and as engines became more powerful and, what is of equal importance, weighed less per horse-power, so the twin-engined aeroplane was looked upon as a minimum requirement for passenger flying.

It was to be many years before all but the smaller twins reached the stage where really acceptable single-engine performance was attained and it was not long before three engines were adopted by most of the aeroplane-designing countries since this layout provided better 'engine out' characteristics than the twins of that time. The three-engine or 'tri-motor' aeroplane retained its popularity in Italy until 1944, although thoughts had long since turned towards four engines for large passenger aircraft, while two engines were adopted for small/medium designs.

The tendency for aeroplanes to outgrow the engines available at the time was perhaps best illustrated during the early thirties when the German Dornier Do-X, a large flying boat weighing over 50 tons, appeared with no fewer than twelve engines, this being the only means of providing 7,200 HP at the time.

Since 1946 very stringent requirements have come into force, particularly with regard to public transport operations, and the single-engine performance of modern twins is now very different from that considered acceptable before. Substantial improvements in both reliability and power output have made possible the fulfilment of these requirements, and whereas the aircraft designer of the past has on occasions been forced to resort to the complication of installing many engines of low power, the advent of the gas turbine has seen the reverse situation, and in recent years engines of undreamed-of power have awaited suitable airframes.

Because of the availability of such engines the twin-engine layout is no longer confined to the medium-size aircraft and such designs as the BAC 111 (100,000 lb), the Russian TU 104 (160,000 lb) and the A300 Airbus (349,000 lb) spring to mind as examples of large twin-engined aircraft with excellent single-engine performance.

Current thinking has turned once more to three engines and history repeats itself on this occasion in the form of three turbojets installed in the rear fuselage. Once more four engines are reserved for the largest types. The method of installing gas-turbine engines is still the subject of divided opinion amongst designers. They may be buried within the wings (Comet and TU 104) while American opinion has favoured suspending them in 'Pods' below the wings (Boeing 707 and Douglas DC 8). Although the French were the first to situate the turbojet at the rear of the aircraft (Caravelle) other designs with this feature have emerged from British manufacturers in the Hawker Siddeley Trident (three turbojets), BAC 111 (two turbojets) and the much larger VC 10 (four turbojets).

In a book of this kind, with flying training the primary object, the previous paragraphs should be regarded as purely background information since at this stage the reader will be concerned with the transition from an elementary or advanced single-engined type to a twin-engined aeroplane.

The Handling of Twin-engined Aircraft

The conversion from single- to twin-engined aircraft will present little difficulty: the major differences in handling procedure are largely confined to taxying and the actions to be taken when an engine fails during one of the various conditions of flight. Both 'Taxying' and 'Multi-engine Conversion' are dealt with in detail under those headings.

At this point it is opportune to list some features of twin-engined aircraft that are likely to be unfamiliar to the single-engine pilot.

Fuel Systems

It is usual for each engine to have its own fuel system consisting of one or more tanks. When several tanks are employed for each engine their management may entail individual fuel cocks or, alternatively, there may only be one to each engine with certain fuel tanks piped to drain into others as they are emptied by their respective engines.

It is normal practice to arrange a **Crossfeed** so that, when it is necessary to fly on one engine, full advantage can be taken of all tanks by opening the crossfeed cock after closing the one normally relating to the live engine. Since mismanagement can provoke an 'airlock' the correct operation of the fuel system should be learned and fully understood.

Fuel contents may be indicated by one gauge controlled with a multi-position switch so that the contents of any tank may be selected or alternatively each fuel tank may have an individual gauge. Sometimes a single gauge reads total fuel in all tanks. On the types of aircraft likely to be flown by the pilot making his first transition from singles to twins, the fuel gauge will usually receive its information from a tank unit very similar to the type used in a motor vehicle, i.e. a float which alters the setting of a potentiometer (variable resistance).

Such an arrangement has the disadvantage that an accurate reading will only occur when the aircraft (or vehicle) is level.

More advanced aircraft are normally equipped with an

ingenious fuel-gauge system which is without any moving parts other than the finger of the gauge itself. This type is able to give continuous and accurate readings provided the aircraft has no more than 15° of roll or pitch. These are called **Pacitor** fuel gauges. To simplify weight and balance calculations, the fuel gauges in some modern aircraft are calibrated in pounds or kilogrammes.

Engine Controls

In view of the wide diversity in aircraft design it is necessary once more to talk in general terms and the arrangements for engine control will be influenced, like so many things mechanical, by the age of the design and the country of origin.

While each engine will have its separate throttle, mixture may be controlled by one of the following methods –

1. Separate control for each engine.
2. One control for both engines.
3. No control lever, the mixture being linked to the throttles so that selection is mechanical.

When the mixture is controlled by a separate lever to the throttle its function will depend on whether the engine has automatic mixture or not. More detailed information will be found in Chapter 2.

When variable-pitch propellers are incorporated their constant-speed controls will be mounted near the throttles, usually on a central pedestal between the first and second pilots' seats. Feathering is usually accomplished by bringing back the pitch levers to their full extent, although some aircraft incorporate a feathering button. This is explained on p. 52.

Starting Systems

Priming of carburettor-type engines on simpler twins is normally by plunger-type pump and there may be one for each engine or a single priming pump with a three-position cock marked **Port – Off – Stbd** so that each engine receives prestarting attention in turn. Fuel injected engines are electrically primed (page 43). The ignition switches to each engine may be either tumbler or multi-position rotary type. The starter buttons are usually protected by a small hinged flap to prevent accidental operation.

On most aircraft it is possible to start either on the aircraft's own battery or with the aid of an external accumulator mounted on a trolley. A two-position **Ground-Flight Switch** (isolator switch) provides selection and when it is required to start on internal sources of supply the pilot selects 'Flight'. Should it be preferable to use the starting trolley, 'Ground' will be selected, thus isolating the aircraft's battery. The starting trolley will be plugged into the aircraft when first one and then the other engine can be started.

The first pilot is usually unable to see if the propeller is free from obstruction on the starboard engine so that it is practice to start this side first after making sure that it is safe to turn the engine over by shouting 'Clear Starboard'. The port engine will be in full view from the first pilot's seat and its starting is preceded by the usual 'thumbs up' sign to the ground crew.

When both engines are running the isolator switch is turned to the 'Flight' position so that the aircraft's own generator(s) and accumulator may supply the various services such as radio, instruments, navigation lights, etc., after the starter trolley has been removed.

Primary Controls

While duplication of the engine controls and trimmers is usually avoided by arranging them on a central pedestal together with flap and undercarriage selectors, most but not all twin-engined aircraft are equipped with two sets of primary controls for the use of the first and second pilots. The control column is replaced by a wheel, although in practice this is more likely to resemble a pair of spectacles or a figure eight on its side. Unless the pilot has been accustomed to American single-engined aeroplanes, the control wheel will at first seem strange after the familiar stick. Nevertheless the pilot will be surprised how quickly he will feel at ease with this arrangement.

Control in the pitching plane is exercised by moving the wheel back and forth in the same sense as the control column on singles while the ailerons are actuated by turning the wheel in the desired direction of bank. Possibly 'tilting' would be a better description since, unlike the steering wheel of a car, movement on the control wheel is restricted to some 45° rotation left or right. The wheel feels natural in the left hand while the throttles are manipulated with the right. The rudder arrangements represent no change from single-engine practice.

Control loads in flight can be fairly heavy on larger twins and full use must be made of the trimmers.

The Trim Controls

There will be a rudder trim in addition to the usual one for the elevators. On larger aircraft with multi-tank fuel systems an aileron trimmer will be provided for the pilot so that lateral level can be maintained without having to hold on aileron when, as a result of single-engine flight, more fuel is consumed from the tanks in one wing than the other.

Synchronizing the Engines

During climb, cruising flight and powered descent, power from the two engines will be matched by controlling the RPM on pitch controls while the manifold pressure is selected on the throttles. Although the engine-speed indicators provide an accurate guide to RPM it will not be possible to match the speeds of both engines to perfection with reference to them alone and, although the difference may only amount to a small number of revolutions per minute, one engine note will beat against the other. Unless the engines are synchronized unnecessary vibration will result together with a distracting throbbing that can be unpleasant for the occupants. An instrument called a **Synchroscope** is included on the panel of more advanced aircraft and in some cases an automatic device takes care of synchronization, but neither refinement is likely to be found on smaller twins. Nevertheless it is not difficult to synchronize the engines without the help of a special instrument. After the required manifold pressure and RPM have been set with reference to the manifold pressure gauges and engine-speed indicators, the engine 'beat' can be removed by altering the position of either pitch control slightly. If the beat quickens, the control is being moved in the wrong direction. When the engine throb becomes slower the pitch control should be moved still further in the same direction until the throb ceases and both engine notes merge into one. One pitch control only should be moved since in that way a finer adjustment can be made than would be possible were both levers to be moved towards or away from one another. When there is a big difference in speed between the two engines no definite beat will be heard, so that it is important to set the engines accurately on the engine-speed indicators before finally synchronizing.

5 Taxying (twin-engined aircraft)

The aim of this exercise is to teach the pilot to control and manoeuvre a twin-engined aircraft on the ground.

An aircraft is controlled and manoeuvred on the ground by the use of power, rudder and brakes, either independently or interrelated. Most modern aircraft are fitted with tricycle undercarriages, when taxying is simplified by nosewheel control. This simplicity must not lead to over-confidence. Fast taxying is perhaps the greatest cause of accidents on the ground for which there is invariably no excuse. Speed should therefore always be kept low to give the pilot adequate time to see, think and manoeuvre the aircraft. While the view ahead is usually better than on single-engined aircraft, it is sometimes difficult to see the wing tips on larger twin- and multi-engined aircraft and great care must be taken when moving into and out of confined spaces.

Use of Power

The amount of power to be used depends upon the surface of the ground. More power is required to taxi an aircraft on grass than on concrete. Likewise more power is needed to overcome inertia and move the aircraft from rest than to maintain a constant speed, which should seldom be faster than a brisk walking pace.

Airfields are by no means flat areas; many runways and perimeter tracks have undulations which may cause an aircraft to continue rolling further than was anticipated and/or at a speed higher than required. Since the inertia of a twin-engined aircraft is much greater than that of a small training aircraft this point should be watched and the danger avoided.

The propellers should be in 'Fine' pitch and the throttle friction slackened since easy movement of the throttles is essential while taxying. Although modern engines do not tend to overheat, temperatures should be watched during prolonged taxying. An overheated engine must be stopped and allowed to cool; otherwise loss of power during take-off will result.

Turning

Most turns are made using nosewheel steering in the usual way, although while manoeuvring in confined areas radius of turn may be reduced by a combination of braking (on the inside of the turn) and **Differential Throttle**, i.e. reducing power on the inside engine and, if necessary, opening up power on the engine which is on the outside of the turn. As with single-engine aircraft, care must be exercised not to lock the wheel being braked and it is good practice to ensure that the nosewheel is straightened before the aircraft stops rolling. The outer engines (Nos. 1 and 4) are used on multis for directional control on the ground.

The amount of power/brake/rudder used for a turn varies from one aircraft type to another. When taxying on concrete the application of additional power to provide the correct turning moment may also increase the speed and it is sometimes better to leave the power constant and, when necessary, assist nose-wheel steering with gentle use of brake.

Use of Brakes

Similar considerations apply to the use of brakes on twin-engined aircraft as on single-engined machines. Prolonged braking should be avoided since this will heat up the brakes and increase wear on the tyres.

Disc brakes are fitted on most twins and multis, sometimes with the added refinement of a **Maxaret** anti-skid device which permits the brakes to be fully applied on a wet or slippery surface, producing maximum braking without actually locking the wheels.

5

Taxying Checks

The usual full rudder and instrument function checks apply to multi-engined aircraft.

Nosewheel-undercarriage Handling

Whereas the centre of gravity is behind the main wheels on a tailwheel aircraft, the reverse is the case with nosewheel undercarriages. With the former a swing will develop when left uncontrolled while the tricycle undercarriage is by nature directionally stable. Furthermore it possesses the important advantage that harsh application of brake will not cause the aircraft to nose over.

The advantages of a nosewheel undercarriage are not confined to taxying and some of the improvements in handling during other manoeuvres, which apply equally to single and multi-engine aircraft, are as follows –

During Take-off
1. During the early stages of the take-off run the nosewheel-undercarriage aircraft is already in flying position allowing good acceleration because of the low drag.

2. Because (*a*) the tail does not have to be raised and (*b*) the thrust line is level throughout, two of the causes of swing on take-off are eliminated (Gyroscopic Effect, page 55, and Asymmetric Blade Effect, page 56).

During Landing
Since the centre of gravity is forward of the main wheels, the natural tendency is for the aircraft to pitch forward on to its nosewheel on touch-down, causing the angle of attack to decrease. There is in consequence less tendency to bounce, even during an imperfect landing.

During Loading
The level floor is usually to the advantage of both passengers and freight handling on the ground.

While nosewheel undercarriages are in general some ten per cent heavier than comparable tailwheel installations, in view of the foregoing advantages they are fitted to modern aircraft practically without exception.

Ground Practice

Taxying

a)   Exercise all the usual precautions and adopt the normal procedure when moving away from a standstill. Test the brakes and while taxying check the gyro instruments for serviceability.

b)   When turning in confined areas unlock the nosewheel (if applicable to the type) and turn using differential throttle assisted by brake and rudder as necessary. For turns of normal radius steer the aircraft with the nosewheel. Do not turn on a locked wheel.

c)   When taxying along a line follow the required path by steering the aircraft through the nosewheel. Maintain a steady speed on the throttles and brakes. Keep a sharp lookout for obstacles and other aircraft.

d)   Remember the size of the aircraft and make allowance for this when passing close to structures, etc.

Emergencies (Ex. 5E)

Should the brakes fail during taxying –

a)   Close the throttles.

b)   Turn away from obstacles and allow the aircraft to roll to a halt.

c)   If necessary increase rolling friction by turning on to the grass.

d)   If the aircraft continues to roll and a danger of collision exists operate the idle cut-offs, turn off the fuel and switch off the ignition and master switch.

6 Instrument Flying

The aim of this exercise is to teach the pilot to fly the aircraft accurately, solely by reference to the instruments in the absence of outside visual cues.

Human ability to maintain a sense of balance is achieved by a combination of three senses –

1. Vision.
2. Muscle sense.
3. The balancing function of the inner ear.

These senses contribute towards man's estimation of attitude and under normal conditions vision is most important. This is equally true when applied to flying under visual conditions when the attitude of the aircraft is controlled by the pilot with reference to the horizon or other prominent features. Should these outside references be obscured by cloud or poor visibility, the sense of balance afforded by the inner ear has then to be relied on for appreciation of attitude, aided by muscular sense. Under the effects of aircraft acceleration in the three planes of movement, the inner ear tends to give a misleading impression of attitude which may be quite the reverse of what is actually happening to the aircraft at the time, and various **Flight Instruments** have been designed to indicate attitude and provide other information when outside references are obscured.

The standard **Flight Panel** consists of six instruments which for many years were grouped as shown in Fig. 36. Still to be seen in aircraft of older design this layout has been replaced by the **Basic 'T'** flight panel (Fig. 37). On more advanced modern transport and Service aircraft many of these instruments have been replaced by others which provide more complex information, but such a panel is unlikely to be met with during the early

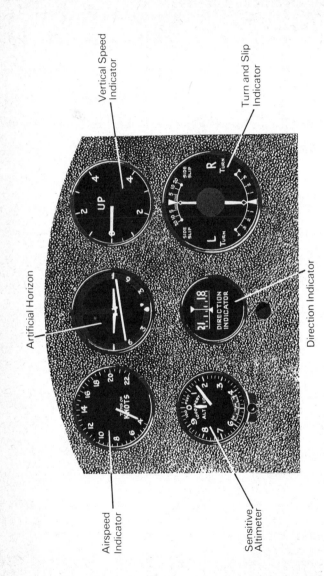

Vertical Speed Indicator

Turn and Slip Indicator

Artificial Horizon

Direction Indicator

Airspeed Indicator

Sensitive Altimeter

Fig. 36. Flight panel (old layout).

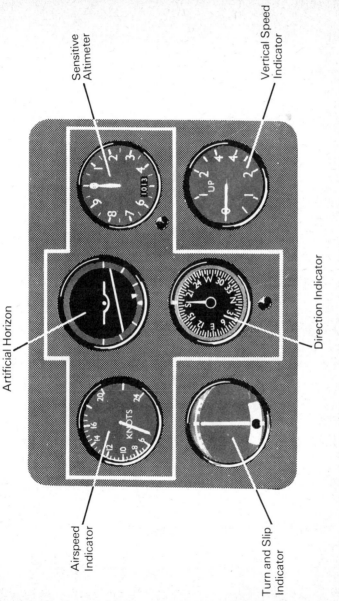

Sensitive Altimeter

Vertical Speed Indicator

Artificial Horizon

Direction Indicator

Airspeed Indicator

Turn and Slip Indicator

Fig. 37. 'Basic T' flight panel.

19

stages of instrument flying.

Most of the instruments will by now be familiar to the pilot, but at this stage of his training a more detailed knowledge of their method of operation and limitations is desirable. Basically they may be considered under two categories –

1. Pressure-operated instruments.
2. Gyro-operated instruments.

Pressure-operated Instruments

The Airspeed Indicator

This instrument may be calibrated in miles per hour, knots (or kilometres per hour in some countries). Two samples of air are fed into the ASI, one from an open-ended or **Pitot Tube** which samples moving air at existing static pressure plus the dynamic pressure caused by forward movement of the aircraft. The other sample may come from a **Static Tube** blocked at the forward end with small holes drilled along the sides or one or more small inlets situated on another part of the aircraft well away from the pitot tube. Such an arrangement, called a **Static Vent**, gives a more accurate reading. When both pitot and static tubes are arranged together (sometimes concentric with one another) the assembly is called a **Pressure Head**. Pitot tubes, pressure heads and static vents are usually electrically heated to prevent the formation of ice under relevant conditions. A water trap is sometimes provided to prevent the pipe lines becoming blocked by moisture. The instrument itself measures the pressure difference between these two sources by employing a diaphragm or a capsule. When the aircraft is stationary both tubes transmit static pressure, but during forward movement, dynamic pressure is built up through the open-ended pitot tube and the diaphragm will distend accordingly. In effect the instrument measures the pressure difference between the two samples, the dial being calibrated in units of speed instead of pressure. Fig. 38 illustrates the complete installation.

19

Errors

While there is no lag in the instrument itself, an aeroplane, like any other vehicle, takes time to change from one speed to another so that an alteration in attitude will not produce an immediate change in airspeed. This important fact is sometimes forgotten, resulting in airspeed chasing during instrument flying. The positioning of the pressure head is critical and even in the best installations errors are caused which are due to airflow disturbances. This **Position Error** is taken into account along with **Instrument Error** (inaccuracies in the instrument itself)

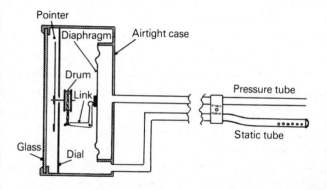

Fig. 38. Airspeed indicator and pressure head (diagrammatic).

when converting IAS to RAS. A correction card will be found adjacent to the instrument except when the position and instrument error is small. For practical purposes IAS is often treated as RAS while flying training aircraft.

Of more importance is the effect of varying air density which in turn is dependent upon height (pressure) and temperature. The difference between RAS and TAS resulting from these factors can be very considerable and the following examples will illustrate the importance of calculating TAS for navigational purposes.

19

Height	Outside Air Temp. (°C)	RAS	TAS
2,000 ft	20°	140 kt	146 kt
5,000 ft	14°	140 kt	153 kt
10,000 ft	4°	140 kt	165 kt
20,000 ft	−16°	140 kt	192 kt
30,000 ft	−34°	140 kt	230 kt

The Airtour and other computers will calculate a TAS when height and outside air temperature are set against the appropriate scales.

The serious consequences of taking off in instrument meteorological conditions without first removing the pressure head cover are very obvious.

The Altimeter

The purpose of the altimeter is to indicate vertical distance accurately above a pre-set datum which may on occasions be airfield level or a standard datum used by all aircraft flying in the area (see Chapter 4, Vol. 4). In its simplest form the instrument consists of an airtight box which is connected to the static line so that the interior of the altimeter is at the pressure of the surrounding air. An **Aneroid Capsule**, partially evacuated, is situated in the box. The capsule is prevented from collapse by a powerful leaf spring. As height is gained the air pressure in the box decreases allowing the spring to expand the capsule. A linkage system magnifies this movement conveying it to a dial. In reality the instrument is an aneroid barometer with its scale calibrated in units of height instead of pressure. To compensate for the errors induced by expansion and contraction of the mechanism due to temperature changes, a bi-metal strip is incorporated in the linkage which distorts in a corrective sense according to the temperature. The simple instrument described is calibrated at intervals of 200 ft and the dial may be moved by a setting knob so that airfield or mean sea-level may be set before take-off. The principles of the instrument are illustrated in Fig. 39.

19

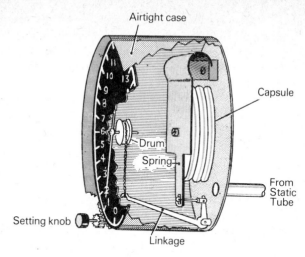

Fig. 39. Altimeter (simple type).

The Sensitive Altimeter

Most aircraft are fitted with this development of the simple altimeter. The instrument incorporates several capsules and is manufactured to very high standards. A much greater degree of magnification makes possible a large finger which completes one sweep of the dial every 1,000 ft. The dial is numbered from 0 to 9 and each main division is subdivided into five smaller ones. In so far as the larger pointer is concerned, each small division represents 20 ft and the main numbered divisions hundreds of feet. A second smaller finger moves at one tenth the rate of the 'hundred foot' pointer indicating thousands of feet, while a third still smaller finger reads in tens of thousands.

As it is a pressure instrument subject to changes in barometric pressure, provision is made for re-setting the datum of the altimeter. This may be accomplished by turning the setting knob until the instrument indicates zero or airfield level as the case may be, or alternatively an altimeter setting can be passed to the pilot from airfield control which is set on a

19

small subsidiary scale on the instrument. When the altimeter is required to indicate airfield level the airfield QNH should be requested while a QFE will cause it to read zero on landing.

The subsidiary scale is calibrated in millibars or, on American aircraft, inches of mercury. The setting knob alters the reading on the subsidiary scale while at the same time moving the fingers.

Because serious errors have resulted from misreading three finger instruments, modern altimeters in aircraft capable of high cruising levels (say 25,000–40,000 ft) tend towards digital-type (**drum**) presentation of thousands of feet, a single finger being retained for tens and hundreds of feet only.

Errors

The instrument is subject to a number of errors and these are –

(a) instrument error　　　　(d) temperature error
(b) pressure error　　　　　(e) lag error
(c) barometric error

In practice the pilot need not concern himself with all these discrepancies although the following should be understood.

(c) Barometric Error

The instrument is designed to function in accordance with set conditions (ICAN Law) which stipulate a barometric pressure of 1,013.2 millibars at mean sea-level and a temperature of plus 15° C. It follows that when, as is so often the case, these average conditions do not exist, the altimeter will fail to give a correct reading. For example, were the pilot to set his altimeter to zero while on the ground when the pressure is 1,010 mb, a pressure rise to say 1,015 mb would cause the instrument to read 150 ft below zero while a decrease in pressure to 1,000 mb would make the altimeter indicate 300 ft above sea level. Furthermore, since barometric pressure varies, sometimes considerably, from one area to another it is not uncommon to fly from a high-pressure region to a low when the altimeter will over-read (or under-read when flying from 'low' to 'high'). Caution must be exercised particularly when flying into lower pressure particularly under instrument flight conditions.

Altimeter setting procedure is explained in Chapter 1 of Volume 3 in this series and the subject is further amplified in Volume 4 ('The Altimeter' Chapter 4).

(d) Temperature Error

Instrument inaccuracies due to temperature changes are largely compensated for by the bi-metal link, but temperature also affects the atmosphere which provides pressure for the instrument. Under the ICAN standards which form the basis of the sensitive altimeter's calibration, a certain temperature **Lapse Rate** (temperature change per 1,000 ft) is assumed. When the MSL temperature departs from 15° C and/or when the lapse rate differs from the ICAN standard atmosphere, air density will likewise alter. Cold air, being heavier than warm, produces greater pressure at any given height and vice versa. For example at 10,000 ft the temperature is assumed to be −5° C under the ICAN Law, but should the outside temperature be −10° C when the reading is taken at that height the resultant higher pressure will cause the altimeter to read 10,000 ft when the aircraft is at 9,800 ft. Temperature corrections to height are calculated by applying the reading from an outside air temperature (**OAT**) thermometer to an Airtour or other computer.

(e) Lag Error

Unlike the airspeed indicator and largely owing to the very high degree of magnification involved, the altimeter reading will lag particularly when rapid changes of altitude take place. At rates of climb within the capabilities of most light aircraft, this will not be noticeable, although a prolonged steep descent will cause the altimeter to over-read on levelling out by up to several hundred feet until the instrument has time to settle to the correct reading.

19

Accuracy

While the instrument is sufficiently sensitive to register changes in height of 20 ft or less its accuracy, owing to instrument errors, is not of that order. An average instrument should be within +30 ft to −45 ft at sea-level, the error increasing to ±350 ft at 30,000 ft.

The Vertical-speed Indicator

The VSI measures rate of climb or descent and during a let-down procedure assists the pilot to maintain a constant known rate of descent and of course accurate rates of climb.

The operation of the instrument is in many respects similar to the altimeter in so far as it consists of a capsule inside an airtight case together with suitable magnifying linkage between the capsule and the indicating finger. The VSI is connected to the static line which leads from the pressure head to the altimeter and the airspeed indicator. Inside the instrument the static line is coupled to the capsule so that its internal pressure is the same as that of the surrounding air at whatever height the aircraft may be flying. Air at static pressure is also led into the case of the instrument via a small choke which is finely calibrated so that pressure can change at a constant known rate.

When the aircraft is flown at a steady height, pressure will be the same both within and outside the capsule and the instrument will read zero. Should a climb or descent occur, pressure inside the capsule will change accordingly, whereas the restricted choke will cause the pressure outside the capsule to alter at a slower rate. The capsule will contract (climbing) or expand (descending) until level flight is resumed when the restricted choke will allow the pressure within the instrument case to equal that inside the capsule. It will then return to its normal shape causing the instrument to indicate zero once more.

Because the restricted choke is calibrated to leak at a steady rate, a quick gain or loss of height will produce a correspondingly greater difference in pressure between the inside and outside of the capsule causing it to expand or contract more extensively when a high rate of climb or descent will be indicated. A setting screw is incorporated to adjust the capsule so that when static pressure is steady a zero indication is given.

The restricted choke is compensated for changes in air density which occur with height and which would otherwise affect the rate of flow through the orifice. Temperature changes resulting from a climb or descent distort a bi-metal strip to which is attached a small conical projection which alters the size of the choke (Fig. 40).

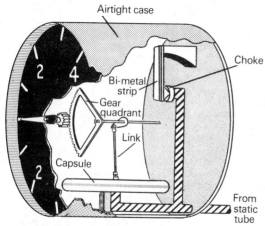

Fig. 40. Vertical-speed indicator.

Errors

The instrument is affected by position error but this is of little consequence unless the aircraft's ASI is subject to a considerable error when high degrees of acceleration or deceleration will cause the instrument to give a false reading.

There is a little lag with the instrument but this is only noticeable when a sudden climb or descent occurs and then the lag is confined to one or two seconds.

Should the static line become blocked owing to an obstruction or ice, the instrument will fail to indicate any changes in

19

height. Breaking the instrument's glass will allow the VSI to function, when it will provide reversed readings.

Accuracy is within ±200 ft per minute unless the outside air temperature is above 50°C or less than −20°C when errors are in the region of ±300 ft per minute.

Before take-off the pilot should check that the instrument indicates zero.

The pressure instruments so far described give an incomplete picture to the pilot flying without visual reference, their information being confined to –

1. Airspeed (ASI).
2. Height (Altimeter).
3. Rate of height change (VSI).

Certain important factors are missing in the readings provided by the pressure instruments and these are –

1. Heading.
2. Attitude in the lateral plane.
3. Slip or skid.
4. Rate of turn.
5. Attitude in the pitching plane.

In view of the relationship between pitch attitude and airspeed, to some extent the last requirement is catered for by the airspeed indicator while requirement 1 (Heading) may be obtained from the magnetic compass. The turn and slip indicator will provide items 2, 3 and 4 and this instrument will be described in detail later. An aircraft fitted with a turn and slip indicator together with an altimeter, airspeed indicator and magnetic compass is said to have a **Limited Panel** and, while instrument flying is practicable in an aeroplane so equipped, the demands made on the pilot are somewhat fatiguing.

The vertical-speed indicator does not normally form part of the limited panel but its addition, together with an artificial horizon and a direction indicator, brings the flight panel up to the standard illustrated in Fig. 37. The flight instruments are built to very fine limits and the panel is mounted on rubber attachment points to prevent damage from shock or vibration.

19

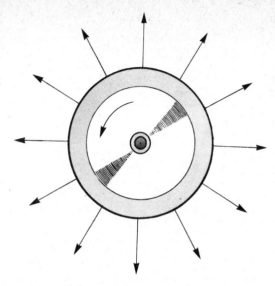

Fig. 41. Rigidity in a spinning wheel.
Arrows show outward component of force.

Gyroscopic Instruments

Before the gyro-operated instruments are explained in detail, the behaviour of a gyroscope should be understood. When a wheel of any kind is rotated there is a tendency for the material of which it is made to fly outwards as a result of centrifugal reaction (Fig. 41).

Because the resultant lines of force emanate radially around its circumference, the wheel tends to remain in its plane of rotation and will resist attempts to alter its position. This property is called **Rigidity** and its magnitude depends upon the speed of rotation and the mass of the wheel or other object (this is equally applicable to an airscrew or a child's top). Rigidity in a gyroscope is used to provide attitude information when no natural visual references exist.

The second important property of a gyroscope is called **19**

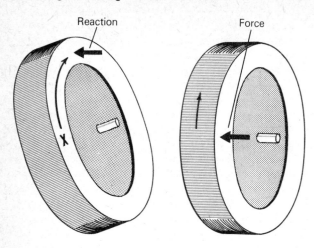

Fig. 42. Precession

Precession. When an attempt is made to disturb its position the gyroscope will resist the force at its point of application, but a reaction will occur as though the pressure had been applied at a point around the circumference of the wheel which is 90° to the actual disturbance (Fig. 42).

The 90° shift from the point of disturbance to the reaction is always in the direction of rotation. Here again precession is not confined to a flywheel or gyroscope and Fig. 28 (page 56) illustrates the principle as it applies to a propeller causing an aircraft to swing as the tail is raised during take-off. The rate at which a gyro precesses is dependent upon the rate of the disturbing movement, and this principle is employed to provide information about the rate at which an aircraft changes heading.

Using the properties of rigidity and precession, gyroscopes are mounted in instruments according to the information required. The gyroscope may be free to move in one plane only or arrangements may be made to allow freedom around all axes. This is accomplished by suspending the gyro in one or more **Gimbal Rings** (Fig. 43).

The gyro illustrated is driven by air which is directed via jets into notches or **Buckets** indented around the outside edge of the

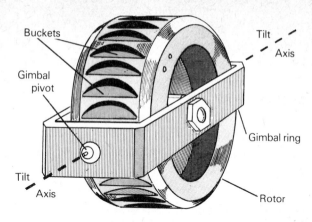

Fig. 43. Gyroscope mounted in a single gimbal ring.

gyro. In practice air is drawn out of the instrument by a venturi tube or an engine-driven vacuum pump. Replacement air flows into the instrument after passing through a suitable filter and finally discharges through jets, rotating the gyro at some 9,000–12,000 RPM according to the type of instrument. Because the jets of air must be directed constantly on the periphery of the gyro and as a result of certain other mechanical difficulties, angular movement of the gimbal rings is limited in instruments of earlier design by stops. Should the aircraft take up a flight attitude outside the limits of these instruments both artificial horizon and direction indicator will **Topple**, i.e. the gyro will cease to hold itself rigid thus causing the instrument to fluctuate violently until it has been re-set. More modern instruments have complete freedom of movement.

Electrically rotated gyroscopes are now in common use, some of their advantages being –

1. Simpler design of the gimbal rings allows the instrument to register more extreme flight attitudes before toppling (or freedom from toppling).

2. Higher rotational speeds are possible with the attendant greater rigidity of the gyro.

19

3. Whereas the efficiency of air-driven gyros decreases at high altitudes because of reduced atmospheric density, electrical gyros are not similarly affected.

4. Electrical instruments may be completely sealed and have no contact with fine dust particles and moisture as is the case with air-operated instruments, however well filtered.

When the flight instruments are vacuum operated it has become common practice to fit an electric turn and slip indicator as an insurance against complete loss of gyro instruments in the event of vacuum pump failure.

The Turn and Slip Indicator

Function

The turn and slip indicator is used by the pilot to complete turns at a required rate without slip or skid. It is also the primary reference for balanced flight.

When used as a primary instrument on a limited panel (page 102) lateral level and direction are maintained on this instrument during straight flight.

Principle

The turn and slip indicator is in fact two entirely separate instruments which, in view of their close relationship, are mounted within one casing. The earlier design illustrated in Fig. 36 incorporated two needles but in the type of instrument referred to throughout this chapter, the ball indicates slip or skid while the needle shows rate of turn to the left or right.

Turn Indicator

This consists of a gyro which, apart from its own rotation, is free to move in one plane only. The gyro is suspended in a single gimbal ring so that rotation is in the vertical plane. When the complete assembly is turned to the left or right the gyro is made to alter its position as if a force had been applied to one side. Precession causes the gyro to tilt along with its gimbal ring

19

which is restrained by two springs. The gimbal ring ceases to increase its tilt when the force of precession is equalled by the pull of the spring under tension. Should the rate of turn increase, the gyro will precess more powerfully causing the gimbal ring to tilt at a greater angle until spring tension becomes powerful enough to balance the gyro at its steeper angle.

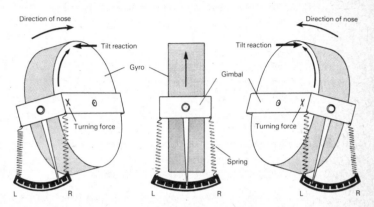

Fig. 44. Turn indicator (diagrammatic).
From left to right: turning right; straight flight; turning left.

When the turn stops, precession ceases allowing the springs to level the gimbal ring and return the gyro to the vertical position. A pointer is attached to the gimbal indicating rates of turn to the left or right and movement of the assembly is damped by a small piston and cylinder to prevent erratic indications (Fig. 44).

The springs are adjusted so that when the instrument indicates **Rate 1**, the aircraft is changing heading at 3° per second or 180° in one minute. For practical purposes this rate of turn is important since it is used for most instrument procedures. The dial is usually calibrated up to Rate 3 or 4.

Slip Indicator

Many of the two-needle instruments are still in use. In these a pendulum, suitably damped to prevent undesirable fluctuation,

19

is linked to the slip or balance needle of the instrument. During straight flight the pendulum hangs vertically. The lowering of a wing carries the instrument case with the aircraft causing the linkage to deflect the top needle in the direction of bank. The position of the needle is dependent upon the angle of bank but the linkage is such that small angular movements in the rolling plane produce magnified indications on the instrument. In most modern instruments the slip indicator takes the form of a ball in a glass tube.

When turning, the slip indicator ceases to show lateral attitude, the ball being influenced by centrifugal reaction in addition to gravity. In a correctly executed turn the ball will line up with the normal axis of the aircraft so indicating neither slip nor skid.

A turn with insufficient bank or too much rudder pulls the ball towards the outside of the turn, indicating a skid, while insufficient rudder or too much bank cause the ball to move towards the centre of the turn, indicating a slip.

Errors

Provided the vacuum supply to the instrument is within the limits laid down (a suction of $2\frac{1}{2}$ in of mercury), no errors occur during normal flight and because the gyro is free to pivot in one plane only toppling cannot occur. Reliability is of a high order.

Under conditions of 'g', exaggerated turning indications are given when yaw is present; for instance during the early stages of a loop the needle may indicate a Rate 4 turn and care must be exercised when practising 'Recovery from Unusual Attitudes' (page 134) not to misunderstand the instrument when the manoeuvre involves abnormal loading.

Before flight the pilot may check the instrument for correct function by watching its behaviour during turns on the ground. The turn needle should indicate a turn in the correct direction whilst a skid in the opposite direction will be shown by the ball. Alternatively the instrument panel may be moved slightly on its rubber mountings with the same results. When the aircraft is stationary and standing level, both needle and ball should be central.

19

Operation in Flight

The instrument is of great value provided the correct handling technique is employed. This will depend upon the manoeuvre.

Straight and Level Flight, Climbing and Descending

With the high degree of directional stability associated with modern aircraft, even small amounts of bank will produce a turn. It is therefore the practice to consider a movement of the turn needle as an indication of bank. When for example the turn needle swings to the right, left aileron is applied to raise the right wing and remove the cause of the unwanted right turn.

To maintain balanced flight the ball (or slip needle) is kept in the centre with rudder used in the appropriate direction as outlined under 'Turns'.

Turns

Bearing in mind that rate of turn is largely dependent upon angle of bank, the turn on instruments is initiated by applying aileron in the desired direction until the turn needle indicates the required rate. Rudder is used in the normal manner and correct balance during the turn is achieved by following the ball which is kept in the centre by applying rudder in the direction shown.

As an illustration of this rule of thumb method, assume that during an instrument turn to the right the ball points to the right, indicating a slip. Application of rudder in the direction of the ball, i.e. right, will bring the turn into correct balance. Conversely, should the ball displace to the left a skid would be indicated. Left rudder in this case would reduce the excessive amount of right rudder which is causing the skid and so balance the turn.

During these corrections rate of turn must be maintained with angle of bank. Rate of turn may be increased or decreased by altering the angle of bank accordingly while maintaining the ball in the centre with correct use of rudder.

With a full panel, angle of bank is established on the artificial horizon using the turn and slip indicator as a means of confirma-

19

tion and to ensure that correct rate of turn is being maintained. Other than timing the number of degrees turned, the turn and slip indicator is the only instrument giving rate of turn information.

Spinning on Instruments

Because a yaw induced by rudder at low airspeed is the cause of a spin, during this manoeuvre the turn needle is controlled with rudder. When autorotation stops the turn and slip indicator is controlled as before (see 'Recovery from a Spin', page 138).

The Direction Indicator

Function

The direction indicator enables the pilot to fly on any heading and to execute turns without acceleration or other errors associated with the magnetic compass. Furthermore the instrument gives an immediate indication when there is a change in direction. Unlike the compass it has no means of seeking magnetic north so that it must be synchronized with the aircraft's compass before use.

Principle

A gyro mounted so that it rotates on a horizontal axis is attached to an inner gimbal ring. This assembly is suspended in an outer gimbal which allows the gyro and its inner ring to rotate through 360° in the horizontal plane. Air is fed to the rotor buckets via a double jet, its purpose being to make the gyro maintain its horizontal axis should a tilt occur over a period of time. To the outer gimbal is attached a scale usually graduated at 5° intervals although some instruments indicate every degree (Fig. 45).

The gyro with its inner and outer gimbal rings is suspended in an airtight case incorporating a window which allows the scale to be seen against a lubber line. In modern instruments this takes the form of a compass rose as shown in Figs. 37 and 50 to 56. Although the aircraft is banked during turns, the gyro is free to maintain its upright position because of the inner gimbal in

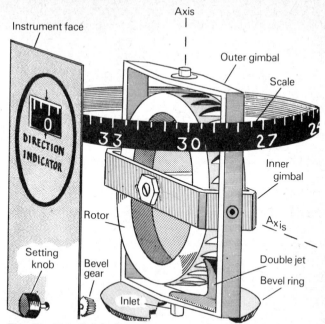

Fig. 45. Direction Indicator.
For simplicity the locking mechanism which cages the gyro has been omitted in this example, which uses an older instrument to illustrate the principle.

one plane and its axis in the other. In instruments of older design a bank or pitch in excess of 55° will cause the inner gimbal ring to come up against stops, when the gyro will topple causing the complete assembly with its indicating scale to rotate quickly. Although for practical purposes the toppling limits of the instrument are 55° in pitch or bank, complete freedom of movement exists when the gyro is positioned so that the manoeuvre takes place around its axis, e.g. when the aircraft heads so that the axis of the gyro runs from nose to tail, a roll through 360° could take place without toppling the gyro. Many modern instruments are topple free.

The front of the instrument carries a setting knob which is normally disengaged from the assembly within. When the

19

setting knob is pressed in, (*a*) the inner gimbal ring is moved into the upright position and locked preventing the gyro from tilting in relation to the aircraft, and (*b*) a bevel gear engages with a bevel ring so that rotation of the setting knob causes the complete assembly to revolve allowing the pilot to synchronize the DI with the magnetic compass. The instrument is inoperative until the setting knob is pulled out enabling the gyro system to remain in its plane of rotation whilst the aircraft changes heading around it. In modern instruments the knob is spring loaded in the 'out' position.

Errors

Over a period of time the DI will fail to agree with the reading shown on the magnetic compass, the difference becoming larger as time advances. This drift from the correct setting emanates from two sources, **Mechanical Drift, Apparent Drift** and **Transport Error.**

(a) Mechanical Drift

Although the DI is manufactured to high standards, bearing friction, imperfect balance of the gimbal rings and severe turbulence in flight will cause the gyro to precess. Furthermore the erecting action of the double jet supplying the rotor tends to displace the outer gimbal ring so that up to 4° drift may occur in a 15-minute period.

(b) Apparent Drift

Apparent drift is non-existent at the equator. In the extreme case of an aircraft flying over the North or South Pole, the scale of the DI will remain rigid while the earth rotates at its rate of 15° per hour and the DI will appear to have wandered off setting by that amount. As an aircraft flies towards the equator, apparent drift decreases accordingly and in proportion to the latitude. The instrument is compensated by employing a **Drift Nut** which applies a precessing force to the inner gimbal ring so balancing apparent drift. The drift nut completely balances apparent drift at one latitude only and when an aircraft moves to another base some distance north or south of original, the

19

instrument should be adjusted. This is of particular importance when a change is made from the northern to the southern hemisphere or vice versa since apparent drift is the reverse in each case.

(c) Transport Error

Yet another error results from convergence of the meridians towards the poles. In northerly or southerly latitudes an aircraft flying in a straight line on an easterly or westerly heading would cut successive meridians at different angles. This is because they converge towards the poles and are therefore not parallel. In consequence there will be a changing relationship between magnetic north as indicated on the compass and DI reading which remains fixed in space. This is known as **Transport Error**; it is at its maximum at the poles and does not exist at the equator where, for practical purposes, the meridians run parallel to one another.

The mechanical limitations imposed by the inner and outer gimbal system cause the scale to rotate past the lubber line at an uneven rate when the aircraft is banked, but as the wings become level the gimbal system aligns itself and the correct heading will be indicated. While this **Turning Error** is noticeable at fairly steep angles of bank, it is of little importance in instrument flying when turns are limited to a Rate 1 or less.

Vacuum supply at 4–5 in. of mercury is required by the instrument for two minutes before use. The pilot may check the DI for serviceability by seeing that an immediate change in heading is indicated during turns on the ground. There should be a resistance felt when the caging knob is engaged and turned.

Operation in Flight

When a manoeuvre likely to exceed the toppling limits is contemplated, some DIs may be caged by pressing in the setting knob. The gyro will then be protected from shocks which would result from the inner gimbal coming up against its stops. Normally the instrument should be free to operate in the uncaged position.

19

Great care must be exercised while synchronizing the DI with the magnetic compass; it is essential that the wings are level and the airspeed constant during the process. It is good practice to turn the DI to the approximate heading and leave it caged while the magnetic compass needle settles. It may then be adjusted and uncaged when it is certain that the aircraft is steady and the compass is reading correctly. So that it indicates magnetic heading allowance should be made for deviation when setting the DI against the magnetic compass. After setting the knob should be rotated to ensure complete disengagement with the outer gimbal systems; otherwise some time may elapse before it is realized that the instrument is not working, by which time the aircraft may be off heading.

If for any reason the instrument topples, it should be caged and re-set with the magnetic compass.

Because of mechanical and apparent drift the DI must be checked against the magnetic compass every fifteen minutes or less and if necessary re-set.

Heading Indicators

On medium-size and large aircraft the Direction Indicator previously described is replaced by an instrument possessed of the advantages offered by the DI but embodying automatic synchronization with magnetic north. There are various types of these instruments available, examples being the Distant Reading Compass and the Gyro-Magnetic Compass. In the latter case principle of operation is as follows –

The instrument is based upon a heading gyro which is linked to the pilot's compass card and such repeater units as are required by other crew members. Situated in a remote part of the aircraft, away from magnetic interference is the Detector Unit, an assembly of three coils spaced at 120° to each other. The Detector Unit is sensitive to the earth's magnetic field, minute electric current being generated in the three coils, their relative strengths being dependent upon the alignment of the unit to Magnetic North. These minute currents are fed to a Signal Selsyn which is constructed around the drive shaft between the heading gyro and the compass card. Should at any time the heading gyro fail to synchronize with the information from the Detector Unit (i.e. magnetic headings) a small electric current is generated by the Selsyn which is amplified and passed to a Precession Coil surrounding the Heading Gyro. In effect the gyro is locked onto Magnetic North by the Detector Unit.

Some Gyro-Magnetic Compasses have one or possibly two needles superimposed on the dial which may by linked to the ADF and/or VOR receivers, so giving the pilot QDMs between the aircraft and the ground facility (NDB). Such instruments are known as **Radio Magnetic Indicators** and they are explained in Chapter 5 of Volume 3.

Another development of the slaved gyro features a VOR display which rotates with the compass card, so presenting the LEFT/RIGHT deviation needle in true angular relationship with the aircraft, which itself is depicted in plan form in the centre of the instrument glass. These instruments, which usually form part of an Integrated Flight System, are called **Horizontal Situation Indicators**.

The Artificial Horizon

Function

The artificial horizon is essentially an attitude instrument giving the pilot indication of pitch and roll when no natural features can be seen. The information is shown pictorially by employing a small aircraft symbol together with a horizon bar. Additionally a pointer denotes angle of bank so that when the relationship between bank and rate of turn is known, turns may be executed on this instrument alone, always remembering that the angle of bank for a given rate of turn will depend upon airspeed.

Because of the very wide range of information provided by the artificial horizon, this instrument is of great importance to the pilot.

Principle

A small aircraft symbol is suspended within the face of the instrument representing the actual aircraft as seen from behind.

19

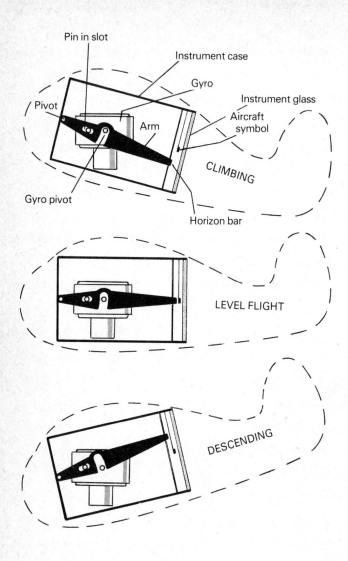

Pin in slot

Instrument case

Gyro

Instrument glass

Pivot

Aircraft symbol

Arm

CLIMBING

Gyro pivot

Horizon bar

LEVEL FLIGHT

DESCENDING

Fig. 46. Artificial horizon.
Method of indicating movement in the pitching plane showing reversal mechanism.

Because it is fastened to the instrument case the symbol will move with the aircraft. A gyro-controlled horizon bar is positioned behind the aircraft symbol and when the instrument is in operation a pitch or roll will cause the small aircraft in the instrument to move accordingly in relation to the horizon bar which is held rigidly by its gyro so that it conforms to the real horizon. This description is in fact an over-simplification since, although correct when applied to movement in the rolling plane, it is necessary to introduce a reversal mechanism for pitch indications; otherwise a dive would be shown during a climb and vice versa.

Mechanically the instrument utilizes a gyroscope rotating on a vertical axis. The gyroscope spins within a case which acts as an inner gimbal. The rotor case/inner gimbal is suspended in an outer gimbal, and movement between the two actuates the horizon bar in the pitching plane via a simple reversal mechanism which is shown in Fig. 46. The outer gimbal is free to tilt in the rolling plane so that the aircraft may bank while the gyro (and horizon bar) remains level. A pointer is attached to the outer gimbal indicating angles of bank against a scale on the instrument face (Fig. 47).

There are various artificial horizons in use and, while earlier instruments have toppling limits of 110° in bank and 60° in pitch, later designs allow complete freedom in roll and 85° in pitch. Others have complete freedom in both axes.

When toppling occurs the instrument will re-set automatically although some ten to fifteen minutes is required for full recovery. During the re-setting period the horizon bar will move random fashion across the face of the instrument, the oscillations becoming less as the automatic re-setting device brings the gyro under control. Automatic erection of the gyro is accomplished by a valve suspended below the rotor called the **Pendulous Unit**. The pendulous unit also maintains the rotor in its correct position when for any reason it has become displaced.

A vacuum of $3\frac{1}{2}$ in. of mercury is applied to the instrument case. Replacement air enters through a filter at the back of the instrument and is led through the rear pivot of the outer gimbal.

19

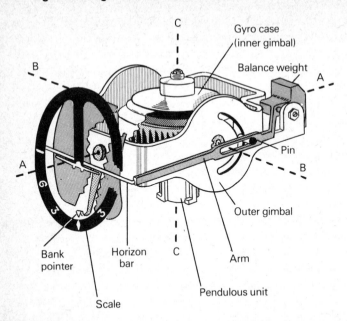

Fig. 47. Artificial horizon.
Showing the complete mechanism. AA—Roll axis; BB—Pitch axis;
CC—Gyro axis.

A passage in the outer gimbal transmits the air through the
pivot of the rotor case/inner gimbal where it discharges via two
jets which are directed towards the rotor buckets. Having spun
the rotor the air is drawn down through the pendulous unit
which is in effect an extension of the rotor case. Air leaves the
unit through four holes that are partly covered by hanging vanes
or pendulums. When the gyro is level the four vanes hang
perpendicularly allowing air to escape evenly through the four
holes (Fig. 48). Should the rotor take up a permanent tilt in one
plane, two of the vanes will be displaced so that one hole is fully
open while that opposite is covered by its vane causing one of
the four air jets to cease and its opposite number to increase.
The air jets will now be out of balance and the rotor will precess

in a corrective sense.

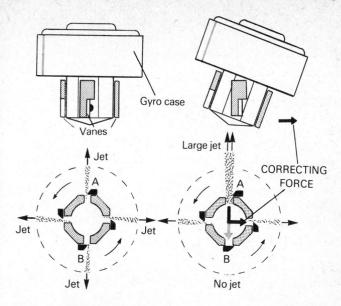

Fig. 48. Pendulous unit.
Illustration on left shows gyro level. When tilted (right) vane A opens and B is closed causing a reaction in the direction of the shaded arrow (i.e. towards B). The 90° effect precesses and corrects the gyro returning it to level position.

The action described is limited in precessing power requiring some appreciable time to effect a correction so that displacement of the vanes during turbulent flight will not cause the rotor to shift its axis. Air from the pendulous unit is extracted from the instrument case by an engine-driven vacuum pump.

Errors

In flight, accelerations in the fore-and-and-aft and lateral planes will displace the pendulous vanes so producing a 90° precessing effect on the gyro axis when the horizon bar will fail to correspond with the true horizon. Furthermore the pendulous unit is suspended below the tilting axis of the gyro so that any **19** tendency for the assembly to swing under the influence of acceleration or deceleration will cause the gyro to precess through 90° and as a result to give an incorrect indication.

(a) Acceleration

While the effect is of less importance in light aircraft or those of moderate performance, serious displacement of the horizon bar can occur during take-off with a high-speed aircraft capable of more vivid acceleration. The combined effect of vane displacement and pendulous unit inertia during take-off will cause the instrument to indicate a climbing turn to starboard (or, in the case of electric instruments, a climbing turn to port) and while the indication is small an attempt to correct would result in a descending turn in the opposite direction. This error would be most likely to occur with a high-performance aircraft when it would be particularly dangerous. It can be overcome by monitoring the artificial horizon with the turn and slip indicator and ASI during the early stages of the take-off and climb away.

(b) Deceleration

The effects of deceleration are the reverse to acceleration causing the instrument to show a gentle descending turn to port, although it is emphasized that such indications will only occur when a high-speed aircraft reduces airspeed over a lengthy period.

(c) Turning Errors

During a turn, centrifugal reaction will displace the two pendulous vanes which pivot on a fore-and-aft axis causing the rotor to precess through 90° in the rolling plane. Additionally the pendulous unit will be subjected to centrifugal reaction causing rotor precession in the pitching plane.

The combined effect of both displacements during a prolonged turn results in errors which increase until the aircraft has changed heading through 180°. Continuation of the turn beyond 180° has the effect of progressively cancelling these errors until 360° is completed when accurate indications will be given again. These inaccuracies, which are not of great mag-

19

nitude, show themselves as incorrect nose up or down indications coupled with too large or too small a degree of bank, according to the direction of turn and the number of degrees change of heading. The errors are partly compensated for by arranging the gyro to run at a slight angle so that during a rate 1 turn errors are very small, increasing slightly when heading changes are made above or below that rate.

Full rotor speed is reached after the correct suction has been applied to the instrument for four minutes although it will operate satisfactorily within half that time.

While on the ground, the artificial horizon may be checked for serviceability by noting that the horizon bar is steady and in the correct position relative to the aircraft symbol. Turns during taxying must not disturb the horizon bar. The glass should be free from cracks.

In flight the instrument must indicate immediately any attitude changes in the pitching or rolling planes.

With instruments which may be caged for aerobatic manoeuvres it is important that the knob is set in the 'un-caged' position four or five minutes before take-off so that the horizon bar is able to adopt its correct level in relation to the true horizon. On later electrically operated instruments a **Fast Erection Button** re-sets the instrument quickly when the need arises.

Operation in Flight

The artificial horizon is the only instrument providing attitude information pictorially and during instrument flying this unique facility should be used to the full. This does not mean that the other instruments are to be ignored since they too have an important function to perform: the art of reading the complete panel is explained later in the chapter.

The pilot should become conversant with the position of the aircraft symbol in relation to the horizon bar during straight and level and other flight conditions.

The angle of bank pointer may be used to establish a desired rate of turn and correct angle of bank for a **Rate 1** turn may be

19

determined by taking the IAS in knots, removing the last figure and adding 7, e.g.

$$80 \text{ kt} = 8 + 7 = 15°$$
$$100 \text{ kt} = 10 + 7 = 17°$$
$$250 \text{ kt} = 25 + 7 = 32°$$

(for MPH use the same procedure but add 5).

It should be remembered that because of the miniaturized presentation, small changes in pitch attitude are difficult to recognize on the instrument so that it must be monitored by the ASI.

The Magnetic Compass

The instruments described form the complete flight panel. This on its own would be incomplete without the magnetic compass which is the only instrument indicating magnetic north (after correction for deviation). The magnetic compass and its use in the air is fully described in Ex. 9, Vol. 1, and at this stage of his training the pilot should be conversant with its operation.

The Flight Panel

The standard flight panel forming the basis of this chapter has, in one form or another, been in use for a considerable number of years. Major developments have taken place which link the instruments with certain radio navigational and landing systems so that the combined information is fed into a computer when the results are depicted on a single instrument called a **Flight Director** which is used in conjunction with the Horizontal Situation Indicator mentioned on page 115. This complex equipment represents a very significant improvement over the standard flight panel. Nevertheless instrument flying tuition will almost invariably be given in aircraft equipped with the type of panel described throughout these pages until a later stage when, subject to the type of aircraft to be flown, training will continue on a **Flight System** or other advanced equipment.

General Considerations

If certain prerequisites are understood a pilot may considerably reduce the time required to become competent in instrument flying.

In all aspects of flying co-ordination is of prime importance and its development, in so far as instrument flying is concerned, may be enhanced by taking advantage of **Simulator** facilities when these are available.

When flying under visual conditions the pilot should make a mental note of the various power settings used to attain a particular condition of flight together with the associated position of the artificial horizon and other instruments, e.g. power settings and instrument indications during a climb or descent.

It is also important to remember that under instrument flight conditions human senses often give false impressions with regard to the aircraft's attitude.

Reading the Instrument Panel

The technique of reading the flight panel must be developed in the course of training, since initially the pilot will usually concentrate on one aspect of control at the expense of others. Practice will overcome this difficulty. The subject is not a straightforward one because the importance of the various instruments varies according to the mode or phase of flight. Generally the Artificial Horizon, which is the only instrument to provide a pictorial representation of attitude in pitch and roll, is regarded as the 'Master Instrument', in so far as the readings of the supporting instruments are used to supplement it under most conditions of flight. How these instruments are integrated with readings from the Artificial Horizon, or **Attitude Indicator** as it is often called, will depend on the manoeuvre being flown. For example, when cruising at a particular speed the AH will be used to establish attitude then the ASI will be scanned to provide accurate adjustment of power/attitude/trim. To ensure that height is being maintained the pilot will, at intervals, look at the VSI and Altimeter, while occasionally, heading will be

19

checked on the DI. On the other hand, when turning on to a particular heading more time will be devoted to holding the correct bank angle (AH), checking the rate of turn (turn needle), balance (ball or balance needle) and watching for the required reading to be approached on the DI. From this it will be realized that the eyes must move from Artificial Horizon to the other instruments in a pattern that varies according to the information required. This technique is known as **Selective Radial Scan** and it is based upon using the Artificial Horizon as the main reference instrument while the eyes move from each relevant instrument and back to the AH according to the manoeuvre being flown. It is a technique that, with practice, can be used without fatigue or strain over quite lengthy periods of flight.

Instrument flying practices are normally carried out 'in the clear' when instrument conditions may be simulated by one of the following methods.

1. Screens

The pilot's view is obscured by the use of approved screens on his side of the cabin. A small aperture opens to permit a visual take-off, but this is closed to simulate entry into cloud. Vision for the examiner/safety pilot is unobstructed. This is the principal method.

2. Visors

A simpler method consists of a visor worn by the pilot under instruction which confines his vision to the flight panel

In each case the instructor or safety pilot has a clear view out of the aircraft.

Instrument Flying Techniques

Reduced to simple terms the performance of an aircraft is dependent upon the amount of power applied together with the attitude. Application of power is a straightforward matter of handling the engine in accordance with the controls at the disposal of the pilot (manifold pressure, RPM, mixture). Attitude is attained in the usual way with reference to the flight panel, and the following basic examples form the foundation for more complex manoeuvre.

Fore and Aft Level

The correct sequence of events follows a pattern that is common to other manoeuvres during instrument flight.

1. Decide upon the required airspeed and condition of flight (e.g. climb, level flight or descent).

2. Apply power applicable to the required flight condition and using the artificial horizon place the aircraft in an attitude likely to produce the desired results.

3. Allow the aircraft to settle while the new attitude is held on the artificial horizon. Use the trim control to assist in holding the aircraft steady.

4. Cross-reference the artificial horizon with the airspeed indicator and vertical-speed indicator/altimeter and make any necessary adjustments to power and attitude.

5. Finally trim the aircraft so that the required performance occurs in correct balance (Fig. 49).

Lateral Level and Direction

The foregoing procedure has referred to climb, level flight and descent. While these flight conditions are being attained and during their execution lateral level is maintained with reference to the artificial horizon. Because of the close relationship between roll and yaw the wings must be kept level if direction is to be maintained so that the artificial horizon is read in conjunction with the direction indicator and the turn needle of the turn and slip indicator (Fig. 50). Balance is attained by applying rudder in the direction of ball displacement.

19

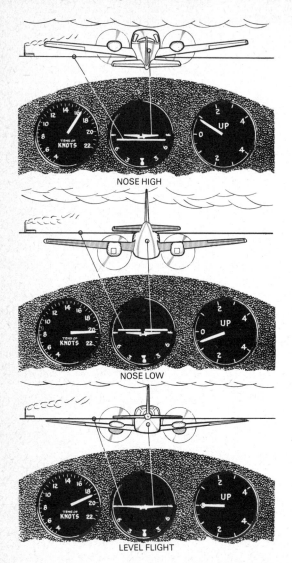

NOSE HIGH

NOSE LOW

LEVEL FLIGHT

Fig. 49. Interpretation of fore and aft level.
19 The ASI and VSI are read in conjunction with the artificial horizon.

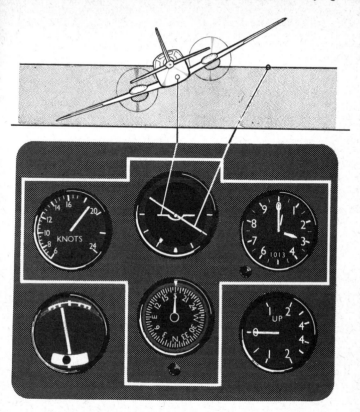

Fig. 50. Interpretation of lateral level.
The turn and slip indicator confirms the reading on the AH.

Turning

During instrument flying, turns are usually executed as part of a procedure which may be a controlled descent towards the runway or a holding pattern designed to keep the aircraft clear of other traffic. These turns are of a precise nature in regard to rate and position and a Rate 1 (3° per sec) is most commonly

19

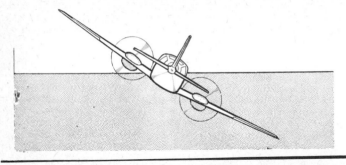

Fig. 51. Medium level turn to the right.

used although there may be occasions when the pilot will be required to decrease his rate of turn.

Turns are initiated in the usual way, referring to the artificial horizon so that the correct angle of bank is assumed according to the airspeed at the time (see pages 121/122).

During the turn, balance is attained by controlling the rudder in accordance with the indications of the ball (turn and slip indicator), although on modern aircraft very little rudder will be

Fig. 52. Climbing turn to the right.

required during the gentle turns associated with instrument flight.

While rate of turn may be attained by taking up the correct angle of bank on the artificial horizon, this should be cross-referenced with the turn indicator. For precision turns rate of heading change is checked against the stopwatch.

The extent of the turn will be shown on the direction indicator and throughout the manoeuvre both VSI and altimeter should be checked to ensure that –

(*a*) height is being maintained during a level turn (Fig. 51); **19** (*b*) height is being gained at the desired rate during a climbing turn (Fig. 52);

(*c*) height is being lost at the required rate during a descending turn (Fig. 53).

Taking Off

While a take-off solely with reference to the instruments is rarely made in civil flying, it is nevertheless a practical proposition and during training the exercise demonstrates the accuracy of modern flight instruments. Additionally the instrument take-off promotes confidence in instrument flying. Practice must be carried out with a safety pilot.

The technique to be adopted is largely dictated by conditions and aircraft type. Provided visibility is sufficient to reveal at least part of the runway ahead a white centre line will assist the pilot to keep straight in the early stages when attention can be transferred to the flight panel at a stage of the take-off which will depend upon the weather conditions at the time. Clearly any natural visual references will assist the pilot during a bad-weather take-off.

Irrespective of the degree of reliance upon the flight panel, when a full or partial instrument take-off is contemplated it is most essential while taxying to carry out the function checks outlined in the previous pages which describe the instruments individually.

When visibility is such that it is deemed necessary to carry out a full instrument take-off procedure is as follows –

1. While taxying to the holding point make the usual instrument serviceability checks. Maintain sufficient RPM to ensure a vacuum supply to the gyro instruments which should have been spinning for four to five minutes prior to the actual take-off. Ensure that the pitot heater is on.

2. Position the aircraft on the centre of the runway and line up with it accurately. Set the altimeter to read airfield level (QNH) and check the DI with the compass. Some pilots prefer

19

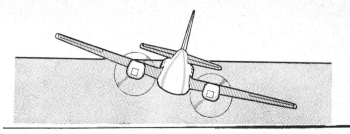

Fig. 53. Descending turn to the right.

to adjust the DI to the nearest 5° mark since direction is maintained on this instrument during the take-off.

3. During the early stages open the throttle slowly and concentrate upon the DI. Correct any swing immediately and should one develop at any time close the throttle and start again.

4. When it is certain that the aircraft is running straight open the throttle smoothly and fully in the usual way. Hold the ailerons neutral (Fig. 54). (On tailwheel aircraft, ease the stick

19

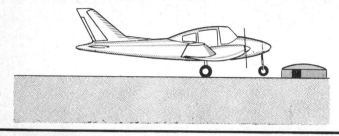

Fig. 54. Take-off (early stage).
With the tricycle undercarriage the raising of the tail mentioned in the text is unnecessary.

forward until the aircraft symbol is just above the horizon bar.)
Check that full power is being developed.

5. When a safe take-off speed has been reached, lift the aircraft off the ground and using the artificial horizon adopt an attitude so that the aircraft symbol is slightly above the horizon bar. A positive rate of climb should be established. Once **19** the aircraft is off the ground, attitude in the lateral plane must

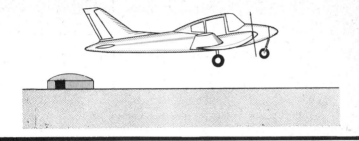

Fig. 55. Take-off (later stage).
The undercarriage is not retracted until the altimeter shows a positive reading.

be watched, with reference to the artificial horizon and turn and slip indicator (Fig. 55).

6. When climbing speed has been reached, adopt the climbing attitude (AH), check the climbing speed (ASI) re-trim if necessary. At a safe height reduce power (manifold pressure and RPM) and retract the undercarriage.

19

Throughout the procedure the aircraft must be kept straight with reference to the DI and in common with all manoeuvres on instruments, the radial scan must be adopted except during the early stages of the take-off run when in an effort to keep perfectly straight the attention should be focused on the DI. The exercise is much simpler when the aircraft has a nosewheel undercarriage, there being little or no tendency to swing and no necessity to raise the tail. The aircraft is simply steered with reference to the DI and lifted off the ground when the ASI reads the appropriate take-off speed.

Flight on a Limited Panel

For a variety of reasons it is possible to lose the use of the artificial horizon and direction indicator. For example, if the DI is not caged prior to aerobatics it will topple along with the artificial horizon. It is usual to mask both AH and DI when limited panel practice is to take place in a fully equipped aircraft, and while for the purpose of limited panel of flying it is possible to cage the DI and intentionally topple the AH (assuming these instruments do not have full freedom of movement), the behaviour of the latter instrument as it re-erects can be very distracting.

Control in the Pitching Plane is effected primarily with reference to the ASI using the altimeter and, when available, the VSI to cross refer. While the ASI is a most accurate indicator of pitch attitude, presentation is not pictorial nor is it instantaneous since the aircraft requires time to settle to a different airspeed when a new pitch attitude is adopted. All changes of attitude should be small and gradual during instrument flying and this precaution is particularly important when flying on the limited panel. Full use of the trim controls is essential.

When levelling out from a climb or descent the altimeter assumes great importance although it must be read in conjunction with the ASI to prevent over-correction.

Lateral Level and Direction are maintained with reference to the turn and slip indicator using the techniques outlined in the section dealing with that instrument.

Turning on the limited panel involves controlling the rate of turn with bank while the ball should be kept central with correct use of rudder in the usual manner.

The altimeter should be checked during a level turn to prevent gain or, what is more usual, loss of height. During a correctly executed turn the airspeed will decrease slightly by an amount dependent upon the angle of bank (rate of turn) since this influences the degree of backward stick pressure needed to prevent loss of height.

Turns through a specific number of degrees can be made with reference to the magnetic compass, although many pilots prefer an alternative method, which is based upon the fact that, at a steady Rate 1, an aircraft changes heading at 3° per second. Assuming a change from 045° to 075° a right turn through 30° would be required, or in other words 10 seconds at Rate 1. To attain the new heading a Rate 1 turn is commenced which would be timed with a suitable watch. The ability to count accurately at second intervals dispenses with the need to refer to a watch.

At the end of the ten-second period the aircraft is rolled out of the turn. The magnetic compass is allowed to settle when minor adjustments to the heading can be made if necessary. Provided the count starts as the aircraft rolls into the turn no allowance need be made for the roll-out which must commence at the end of the count. In this way the 'roll in' period will compensate for the 'roll out'.

Climbing and descending turns are executed in a similar manner with suitable power adjustments at the correct airspeed. In the absence of a VSI, rate of climb or descent may be gauged using a watch in conjunction with the altimeter. The introduction of a watch into these procedures will at first prove a complication but with practice its use will become quite natural.

Taking Off can be accomplished on the limited panel with surprisingly good results although obviously the absence of a full panel makes heavier demands on the pilot. There is now no requirement for such an exercise.

19

Recovery from Unusual Attitudes

When practising this exercise it is usual for the instructor to put the aircraft into a steep climb or dive, with and without turn. The ability to recognize the aircraft's attitude immediately from the limited instruments rather than the sense is vital, since for example a steep turn followed by a stall turn and a spiral dive will certainly leave a most confusing trail of impressions on the pilot, bearing no relation to the actual movement of the aircraft. Here again the exercise will promote confidence and equip the pilot to deal with the most extreme contingency likely to be met in instrument flying.

Broadly speaking the behaviour of the ASI is the main source of information during extreme flight attitudes. A rapidly decreasing airspeed denotes a high 'nose-up' attitude, while a steep 'nose-down' position will cause a rapid increase in air-speed.

Whether or not the ASI indicates a steep 'nose-up' or 'nose-down' attitude, lateral level must be regained as a first action. When the turn and slip indicator confirms that lateral level has been resumed, the stick should be moved in the appropriate direction to regain normal airspeed. In any attitude associated with an extreme 'nose-down' position, power should be reduced to minimize loss of height. The method of regaining fore and aft level is important and the stick must be moved in the appropriate direction to the point where the rapid increase or decrease in airspeed is checked. Immediately the airspeed moves towards cruising speed the aircraft will be in the approximate level attitude and the stick should be held in its existing position while the aircraft settles again into level flight. Over a period of time the altimeter will confirm if the correct attitude/power combination has been applied to produce the required performance. The importance of the trim control cannot be over-stressed and only by allowing the aircraft to settle into a trimmed attitude will the pilot avoid 'chasing the airspeed'.

These remarks deal in general terms with the problem of regaining normal flight from an extreme attitude when the AH and DI may have toppled. Additionally two cases of a more specific nature should be understood.

The Stall on the Limited Panel will be recognized by decreasing airspeed and, on some types, diminishing effectiveness of controls. Again dependent upon the aircraft type, buffeting may occur shortly before the actual stall. The recovery is effected in the usual manner but, as the stick is moved forward and power added, the turn and slip indicator is kept in balance with rudder only, so preventing the onset of a spin should a wing drop and yaw develop. Only when the airspeed has increased above stalling speed may the ailerons be used in answer to indications on the turn and slip indicator.

The Spin on the Limited Panel must not be confused with a spiral dive where the airspeed is high and increasing and all the controls are operative. In a spin the ASI will give a low reading while the turn and slip indicator will show the direction of autorotation, at the same time indicating some skid. The altimeter will show a rapid decrease in height (Fig. 56).

To recover from the spin first close the throttle to minimize loss of height, apply full rudder in the opposite direction to that shown on the turn indicator and progressively ease the stick forward. When autorotation stops the turn indicator will suddenly flick in the opposite direction and then centralize when the rudder should likewise be centralized. Using the ASI as a guide the aircraft is then eased out of the dive until the airspeed begins to decrease when the approximate level attitude will have been regained and power is applied for level flight. The recovery from the dive must be gradual, any violent backward movement of the stick being liable to cause unnecessary loading and the risk of a stall. Additionally the turn indicator may give a false reading under conditions of abnormal loading.

It is of particular importance during spin recovery to ignore the senses. Many pilots have the impression that spinning is continuing in the opposite direction after the recovery has in fact taken place.

19

19　Fig. 56. Spiral dive (top drawing) and the spin on instruments.

Instrument Flying – Multi-engined Aircraft

The principles outlined in this chapter are applicable to twin- and multi-engined aircraft, and in most cases larger types are less fatiguing during flight on instruments because of their stability, which is usually of a higher order than that of single-engined aeroplanes of light weight. Differences are largely confined to aircraft handling characteristics related to such parameters as inertia, performance, etc., but the interpretation of the flight panel remains the same.

Throughout this section the term 'twin-engined' can be taken to include 'multi-engined,' the considerations being very similar in each case.

While no special problems are associated with twin-engined instrument flying in general, the actions to be taken in the event of an engine failure must be fully understood. It is therefore advisable to study Ex. 23, Part II, 'Asymmetric Power Flight' (page 234), before proceeding with the remainder of this chapter.

When an engine fails during instrument flight on a four-engined aircraft in particular, it is often surprisingly difficult to identify the faulty engine. While the ASI will show a lower airspeed and the turn indicator a turn towards the dead engine, the ball a skid away from the failed engine RPM will remain constant on the failed power plant, its propeller continuing to windmill in fine pitch. Oil pressure will also remain constant unless the fault is associated with mechanical failure when the operation of the constant-speed unit with its attendant influence on the propeller will very likely be affected.

After a short period the failed engine can be identified by its oil temperature and/or cylinder-head temperature gauge(s), either or both indicating a decrease in temperature. In the early stages it may therefore only be possible to determine whether a left-hand or right-hand engine has failed. The yaw which provides the indication determines without doubt which engine has failed on a twin. In either case when an engine fails the resultant yaw will produce a roll towards the inoperative

19

engine. The yaw will be shown on the turn needle coupled with a heading change on the direction indicator. The associated roll will be depicted on the artificial horizon. Because of the power loss, a lower airspeed will be indicated on the ASI. Engine failure procedure is outlined in Ex. 23 Part II, 'Asymmetric Power Flight,' and the sequence of actions described in that chapter is followed, controlling the yaw with reference to the turn needle and the roll with regard to the artificial horizon. When power on the live engine has been adjusted so that height is maintained the supply to the instruments must be ensured.

Vacuum supply may usually be obtained from both or all pumps on a twin- or multi-engined aircraft. When engine failure occurs, vacuum gauge must be checked, since without vacuum supply the gyro instruments will cease to provide accurate information after two minutes.

While single-engine handling characteristics are good on modern twin-engined aircraft, certain older types may not be so simple to control. Should directional and lateral control become difficult at any time, power on the live engine should be decreased and only returned to that necessary for level flight when full control has been regained with reference to the instruments.

When all is settled it will be necessary to revise the Flight Plan and inform ATC.

General Conclusions

The foregoing sections have explained the workings and limitations of the instruments together with their use when applied to certain basic flight manoeuvres. No mention has been made of instrument landings since the systems required are confined to more complex aircraft. However, landing on instruments by automatic control under conditions which preclude visual references nevertheless requires the pilot to monitor the flight panel throughout the procedure. Without **Auto Land** equipment instrument flight is continued through to the final approach when, at a point determined by such factors as airport limitations, aircraft type, pilot's ability and operator's instructions, the landing is completed visually. When the aircraft is equipped with high grade avionics and a good autopilot/flight system **Coupled Approaches** on the ILS are possible down to a **Decision Height** of 100 ft.

Modern flying has demanded the integration of the flight panel with various radio aids, both navigational and approach. Fully explained in Volume 3 these form a study which is essential for the pilot contemplating instrument flight. This book is confined to matters of aircraft handling, and the various basic manoeuvres on instruments are explained step by step in the Flight Practices that follow.

Flight Practice

COCKPIT CHECKS

Check the instruments for serviceability before take-off.
Arrange screens or visors.

OUTSIDE CHECKS

a) Altitude: Sufficient for practice. Climb into smooth air when possible.
b) Location: Not over towns, airfields or in controlled airspace.
c) Position: Check in relation to a known landmark.

AIR EXERCISE

Note: While the following exercises must be taught by a suitably qualified flying instructor, they may be practised with a non-instructor safety pilot.

1. The Instruments

In the Open

a) Adopt the level flight attitude and compare the position of the nose **19** in relation to the horizon with the symbol and horizon bar on the artificial horizon.

Alter the pitch attitude and notice that the indications on the artificial horizon follow the movement of the aircraft in relation to the real horizon. Large pitch changes produce small indications on the instrument.

Now bank the aircraft and compare the position of the wings in relation to the horizon with the indications which are given on the artificial horizon. The angle of bank is reproduced correctly and the number of degrees is indicated by the roll needle.

b) Turn the attention to the direction indicator. Before use, the instrument must be synchronized with the magnetic compass. To do this fly at a steady speed with the wings level and without yaw. Use the artificial horizon and direction indicator to attain steady level flight.

When the compass has settled read the heading and set this on the direction indicator by pressing in the setting knob and rotating until the correct heading appears on the instrument. Before uncaging the instrument ensure that the wings are level, that airspeed is steady and that the compass reading has remained unchanged.

When uncaging the instrument make sure the setting knob is fully withdrawn and rotate to confirm disengagement of the knob from the gyro assembly.

Try some turns. Notice the immediate response of the instrument and that it is unaffected by the errors of the magnetic compass.

c) Watch the turn and slip indicator. Notice that when a turn is commenced the turn needle indicates its direction and rate. As the angle of bank is increased so the rate of turn increases.

In a balanced turn the ball remains in the centre. Deliberately apply too much rudder in the direction of turn. The aircraft is now skidding and this is shown on the ball which is displaced away from the turn.

Now take off rudder and apply a little in the opposite direction to the turn. The aircraft is now slipping and the ball has moved towards the centre of the turn.

In either case the turn can be brought into balance by applying rudder in the direction indicated by the ball.

d) The airspeed indicator will show changes of airspeed as they occur. Note the considerable time lag between a change in pitch attitude and a corresponding increase (or decrease) in airspeed. This is because of the aircraft's inertia.

e) During level flight the vertical-speed indicator reads 'zero'. Raise the nose slightly and notice that a rate of climb is indicated. Confirm the climb with the altimeter which will show a gain of height. Note decrease in airspeed.

Now depress the nose when a rate of descent will be shown on the instrument. The altimeter will indicate a loss of height.

In either case the vertical-speed indicator will only give a steady reading when the aircraft has settled into the climb or descent.

f) The readings of the altimeter are self-explanatory. During take-off or landing the instrument may read incorrectly owing to ground effect and position error. When the aircraft has landed the altimeter will read zero or airfield level according to the setting on the barometric scale.

On Instruments (after suitable preparation using one of the methods explained on page 124)

a) Concentrate on the artificial horizon and keep the symbol in line with the horizon bar.

b) Now gently raise the symbol above the horizon bar. Note the airspeed is decreasing and the vertical-speed indicator is showing a rate of climb. Cross-check the information with the altimeter.

Now return the symbol to the level flight position on the horizon bar.

c) Gently lower the nose and place the symbol below the horizon bar. Notice the airspeed is increasing while a rate of descent is indicated by the vertical-speed indicator. The altimeter is showing a loss of height.

d) Lower a wing so that the symbol on the artificial horizon takes up a gentle bank. The direction indicator will show a change of heading while the turn indicator will give the rate of turn. Now gently bank in the other direction and return to the original heading.

Form the habit of relating one instrument with the other so that the complete flight panel presents a picture.

Toppling Limits (when applicable to the aircraft installation)

In the Open

a) Deliberately place the aircraft in an extreme nose-up attitude when the direction indicator and artificial horizon will topple.

b) Return to level flight. Both direction indicator and artificial horizon are now inoperative and in practice instrument flight would have to continue on the limited panel.

19

The direction indicator can be caged and re-set immediately but unless a caging knob is fitted the artificial horizon will require up to ten minutes to re-erect.

2. Straight and Level Flight: Power/Attitude Flight

Full Panel

a)   Apply power for cruising flight. With reference to the artificial horizon adopt the cruising attitude by placing the symbol in the correct position on the horizon bar. Cross-check fore and aft level with the airspeed indicator which should indicate normal cruising speed.

b)   Watch the altimeter and correct any loss or gain of height by adjusting power. The vertical-speed indicator will give an early warning of incorrect power setting provided the airspeed has settled. Re-trim at the new power setting.

c)   Check lateral level with the artificial horizon and direction on the direction indicator. Make any necessary corrections with aileron and rudder. Trim out all control loads when power has been correctly adjusted for level flight.

d)   Check the direction indicator with the magnetic compass every 10–15 minutes.

e)   Continue the selective radial scan to maintain straight and level flight.

Changing Airspeeds

a)   Decide upon an airspeed below normal cruising. Reduce power to a setting estimated for that speed.

b)   Maintaining lateral level on the artificial horizon and direction on the direction indicator, as the airspeed decreases gradually raise the symbol above the horizon bar. Watch the altimeter and prevent a gain in height by correct use of the elevator control while changing attitude. Hold the aircraft steady at the new attitude.

c)   Allow sufficient time for the airspeed to change at the new attitude and, when it has settled to the required figure, re-trim. Check the balance indicator (ball).

d)   Watch the altimeter and vertical-speed indicator and if necessary adjust power to maintain height. Note the new position of the symbol in relation to the horizon bar.

e)   Now select a high cruising speed and repeat the procedure by increasing power and placing the symbol slightly below the horizon bar.

Limited Panel

a)   Apply cruising power and hold the aircraft in the correct pitch attitude, with reference to the airspeed indicator. All pitch corrections should be small and time must be allowed for the aircraft to gain or lose speed when the attitude is changed.

b)   When the speed has settled to the correct figure re-trim. Watch the altimeter and make any power adjustments necessary. Again check the airspeed and re-trim.

c)   Maintain lateral level and direction with reference to the turn and slip indicator. Consider movement of the turn needle as an indication of bank and correct with aileron. Hold the ball in the central position with rudder. Ignore small turn needle fluctuations.

d)   At frequent intervals check the heading on the magnetic compass and correct when necessary making gentle turns. When reading the compass be sure that wings are level and the airspeed is steady.

3. Climbing

Full Panel

a)   Apply climbing power and raise the nose so that the approximate climbing attitude is indicated on the artificial horizon. Check the ball for balance.

b)   Maintain lateral level on the artificial horizon and check the heading on the direction indicator.

c)   Adjust the climbing attitude until the required climbing speed is attained. Re-trim the aircraft. The rate of climb is now shown on the vertical-speed indicator.

d)   Continue the radial scan to ensure a steady climb on the correct heading.

Resuming Level Flight

a)   Shortly before the required height progressively lower the nose to the cruising attitude with reference to the artificial horizon.

b)   Maintain lateral level on the artificial horizon and check the heading on the direction indicator. Refer to the altimeter and keep the

19

height constant during the transition from climbing to cruising speed.
c) When cruising speed is reached, reduce power accordingly.
Re-check both airspeed and height, making power and attitude
corrections as required. Re-trim when the aircraft has settled in
cruising flight.

Limited Panel

a) When climbing power has been set, watch the airspeed indicator
and gently ease back the stick so that the indication changes gradually
towards climbing speed.
b) Maintain lateral level and direction with reference to the turn and
slip indicator.
c) As climbing speed is approached, prevent a further decrease in
speed by very gently easing off a little of the backward pressure. Allow
the airspeed to settle and re-trim.
d) Check the heading on the magnetic compass and correct if
necessary.

Resuming Level Flight

a) Shortly before the required height, ease the stick gently forward
so that the airspeed indicator shows a very gradual increase towards
cruising speed.
b) Maintain lateral level and direction with reference to the turn and
slip indicator.
c) As cruising speed is reached, very gently bring back the stick to
prevent a further increase in airspeed. Reduce to cruising power and
re-trim.
d) Check both airspeed and height, adjusting power as required.
Check the heading with the magnetic compass and correct as
necessary.

4. Descending

Full Panel

a) Decide upon a rate of descent at an appropriate airspeed and
adjust the engine controls to give the power estimated for the
performance. Check the ball for balance.
b) Adjust the attitude of the aircraft with reference to the artificial
horizon, allowing the airspeed to settle. Adjust the attitude to give the
required airspeed for the descent. Re-trim for the new attitude.

c) Maintain lateral level on the artificial horizon and check the heading on the direction indicator.

d) When the aircraft has settled check the rate of descent on the vertical-speed indicator and should an alteration be necessary adjust power accordingly. Maintain a constant air-speed during power adjustments by slight changes of attitude. Re-trim when they are sufficient to affect balanced flight.

Resuming Level Flight

a)   As the new flight level is approached apply cruising power. Hold the descending attitude, thus allowing the airspeed to increase towards cruising speed.

b)   Check lateral level on the artificial horizon and heading on the direction indicator.

c)   At the required height resume the level flight attitude with reference to the artificial horizon.

d)   Make the usual adjustments to power, attitude and trim to achieve balanced cruising flight.

e)   Now gain height and practise the descent with varying amounts of power and flap.

Limited Panel

a)   Decide upon a rate of descent at an appropriate airspeed and adjust the engine controls to give the estimated power for the performance.

b)   Gradually adjust the attitude to arrive at the required airspeed. Make necessary trim adjustments throughout the procedure.

c)   Maintain lateral level and direction on the turn and slip indicator and check the heading on the magnetic compass.

d)   When the aircraft has settled, check the rate of descent on the vertical-speed indicator. (*Note*. When there is no VSI, rate of descent is obtained by timing the change of height indicated on the altimeter.) Should an alteration in power setting be necessary, adjust accordingly. Maintain a constant airspeed during power adjustments and re-trim when they are sufficient to affect balanced flight.

Resuming Level Flight

a)   As the new flight level is approached apply cruising power. Hold the descending attitude, so allowing the airspeed to increase towards cruising speed.

b)   Check lateral level and direction on the turn and slip indicator and heading on the magnetic compass.

19

c)   At the required height gradually ease back the stick to check the descent. Re-trim and allow the airspeed to settle at the new attitude.
d)   Make the usual adjustments to power attitude and trim to achieve balanced cruising flight.
e)   Now gain height and practise the descent on the limited panel with varying amounts of power and flap.

5. Turns and Compass Errors

Full Panel

a)   Watch the artificial horizon and adopt a bank suitable for a Rate 1 turn.
b)   Check the rate of turn with the turn needle and if necessary adjust the angle of bank accordingly. Maintain the ball in the centre with sufficient rudder to balance the turn.
c)   Watch the altimeter and prevent loss of height by gentle backward pressure on the stick.
d)   When the aircraft is turning at a steady Rate 1 without gain or loss of height, note the position of the symbol in relation to the horizon bar and memorize for future turns. Note the airspeed is slightly less than normal cruising.
e)   Maintain an accurate height and turn rate by using the radial scan.
f)   To stop the turn, roll out in the usual way until the artificial horizon indicates level flight. Check both height and airspeed.
g)   Now repeat the exercise, turning left and right at varying angles of bank, gradually increasing to Rate 4. Height must remain constant throughout. Should for any reason the aircraft's attitude cause concern level the wings immediately.

Limited Panel

a)   With reference to the turn and slip indicator establish a Rate 1 turn by applying bank in the required direction. Maintain the ball in the centre with sufficient rudder to balance the turn.
b)   Watch the altimeter and prevent loss of height by slight backward pressure on the stick.
c)   To stop the turn, roll out in the usual manner. Use sufficient opposite rudder to keep the ball in the centre. At the same time allow the stick to return to its trimmed position.
d)   Check both airspeed and height when the turn has stopped.
e)   Repeat the exercise, gradually increasing the bank to Rate 4.

Compass Errors

These are fully described in exercise 9, *Flight Briefing for Pilots*, Vol. 1.

6. Climbing and Descending Turns

Full Panel

a) From a steady climb apply sufficient bank for a Rate 1 turn using the rudder to prevent slip or skid. Do not allow the airspeed to decrease but add sufficient power to maintain the rate of climb. Be prepared for a marked tendency to overbank.

b) To stop the turn, take off bank and make the artificial horizon indicate the climbing attitude. Reduce to climbing power.

c) Now practise descending turns at various power settings with and without flap.

Limited Panel

Climbing and descending turns are made using a similar technique to the full-panel method with the exception that bank attitude is indicated on the turn needle.

7. Turns on to Headings and Timed Turns

Full Panel

a) Check the direction indicator with the magnetic compass, allowing for deviation.

b) Decide upon a new heading and turn the more direct way at Rate 1.

c) Shortly before the new heading appears on the direction indicator, gradually roll out of the turn. Re-check the direction indicator with the magnetic compass.

d) Now practise turns at more and less than Rate 1, becoming accustomed to the point at which to roll out so that the wings are levelled as the new heading appears against the Lubber Line on the direction indicator.

e) Practise climbing and descending turns on to a new heading.

19

Limited Panel (Two methods)

Timed Turns

a)   Translate the number of degrees between the present and new heading into seconds allowing 3° per second.

b)   Roll into the turn and start timing or counting. Maintain an accurate Rate 1 on the turn and slip indicator.

c)   When the calculated number of seconds has elapsed, roll out of the turn and resume straight and level flight. Allow the magnetic compass to settle and check its reading with wings level and airspeed constant. Corrections may be made with another timed turn. Avoid chasing the compass needle by allowing sufficient time for the instrument to settle after a change of heading.

Compass Turns

a)   Decide which is the more direct way to turn. Start the turn which must be limited to Rate 1.

b)   When the new heading is northerly, roll out of the turn before the reading coincides with the Lubber Line.

When the new heading is southerly, roll out of the turn after the reading coincides with the Lubber Line. (*Note.* The number of degrees in both cases is at its maximum on N or S when as a guide 20°–25° should be allowed.)

When the new heading is easterly or westerly allow sufficient time for the 'roll out' so that the wings level as the reading coincides with the Lubber Line.

c)   Watch the airspeed indicator and turn and slip indicator. Continue flying straight and level and allow the magnetic compass to settle. When the required heading fails to coincide with the Lubber Line make the usual corrections.

d)   Now practise climbing and descending turns on to a new heading, using the limited panel.

8. Taking Off

Full Panel

a)   While taxying to the holding position check the instruments for serviceability. Pitot heat must be 'on'.

b) Engine RPM while at the holding point must be sufficient to ensure vacuum to spin the instruments.

Go through the vital actions and when clear taxi on to the runway. Position the aircraft on the centre line and set the direction indicator to the QDM of the runway or, when more convenient, to the nearest 5° mark on the instrument.

Check the magnetic compass and finally scan the engine instruments (temperatures and pressures etc.).

c) Holding the stick in the neutral position open the throttle sufficiently to start taxying. Concentrate on the direction indicator correcting the slightest swing with rudder and if necessary brake. When the aircraft is running straight, progressively open the throttle maintaining direction on the DI. Should a swing develop, close the throttle(s) immediately, abandon the take-off, return to the holding point and start again.

d) As the aircraft gathers speed, ease the stick back slightly to remove weight from the nosewheel. Keep straight on the direction indicator. The ailerons must be neutral.

e) At a safe speed apply further back pressure on the stick and make the artificial horizon indicate a nose-up attitude. When the aircraft leaves the ground, check the turn and slip indicator and allow speed to increase naturally while holding direction and lateral level. At the correct speed adopt the climbing attitude on the artificial horizon. Re-trim.

f) At a safe height raise the undercarriage, raise the flaps (when applicable) and reduce to climbing power. At the correct climbing speed re-trim the aircraft.

9. Going Round Again

Full Panel

a) Imagine that during an instrument approach you are instructed to 'go round again'. Immediately open the throttle to take-off power. Tighten the throttle friction to prevent the throttle creeping back.

b) With reference to the artificial horizon adopt the 'flaps down' climbing attitude and trim the aircraft at this new performance.

c) Maintain lateral level on the artificial horizon and check the heading on the direction indicator. Cross-refer the information with the turn and slip indicator.

d) When the aircraft is steady at the correct airspeed for a climb with flaps down, raise the undercarriage and re-trim.

19

e)   At a safe height raise the flaps intermittently and re-trim at each new flap position. When the flaps are finally raised adjust power, airspeed and trim to give the normal climbing performance.

f)   Level out at the correct height for the procedure or as instructed.

Limited Panel

The procedure is as outlined for the full panel with the exception that pitch attitude is monitored on the ASI and lateral level and direction on the turn and slip indicator.

During the climb away and while the undercarriage and flaps are raised the magnetic compass will be subjected to acceleration errors when the over-shoot occurs on an easterly or westerly heading. Direction must be maintained on the turn needle which should be controlled as on page 109.

When the aircraft has settled in the climb with wheels and flaps 'up', the heading should be checked on the magnetic compass and any necessary corrections made accordingly.

10. Recovery from Stall

Full Panel

a)   Apply carburettor heat (when applicable) and close the throttle. Raise the nose until the artificial horizon indicates a 'nose up' attitude similar to the climb.

b)   Maintain lateral level and direction in the usual way and be prepared for the stall by watching the airspeed indicator.

c)   When the aircraft stalls apply full power and move the stick gently forward until the artificial horizon indicates a nose-low level flight position. Should a wing drop make no attempt to use the ailerons until the aircraft is unstalled, but prevent a yaw developing by application of rudder away from the lower wing.

d)   At the correct airspeed set the engine controls for cruising flight and re-trim.

e)   Now practise the stall and recovery with power and with flaps and undercarriage lowered.

Limited Panel

Proceed as before but maintain lateral level and direction with reference to the turn and slip indicator and obtain pitch information from the ASI.

11. Recovery from Unusual Attitudes

Note. It is assumed throughout that both artificial horizon and direction indicator have toppled during a manoeuvre beyond the limits of these instruments, which should be masked.

Limited Panel

Recovery from a Dive

a)   Dive the aircraft to a high airspeed and if necessary prevent the engine overspeeding by reducing power.
b)   Return to level flight by gently easing back the stick. Excessive loading during the recovery will produce a false turn indication from the turn needle.
Maintain lateral level and direction on the turn and slip indicator.
c)   When the airspeed indicator stops increasing and begins to decrease towards cruising speed the aircraft will be near the level flight attitude. Hold the level flight attitude by slight forward pressure on the stick.
d)   Apply cruising power. Allow the airspeed to settle and re-trim at cruising speed. Check the heading on the magnetic compass and correct if necessary.

Recovery from a Spin

a)   Go into a spin in the usual way by applying full rudder in the required direction just before stalling speed is reached. Hold the stick right back. Notice the turn needle is indicating a Rate 4 turn in the direction of spin, the ball shows a skid, the airspeed is low and rate of descent high.
b)   To recover apply full rudder away from the direction indicated on the turn needle and slowly ease the stick forward until the turn needle centralizes or flicks in the opposite direction. At this point spinning has ceased and the rudder must be centralized.
c)   Ignore the senses and gently ease back the stick recovering from the dive as explained in the previous exercise.
Note. The turn needle is controlled with rudder during the spin recovery only. Once autorotation has ceased the turn and slip indicator is used in the normal manner during the recovery from the dive.

19

Recovery from a Spiral Dive

a)   Begin a steep turn but allow the nose to drop. The aircraft is now in a spiral dive.

b)   Notice that the turn needle indicates a Rate 4 turn in the direction of the spiral but, unlike the spin, airspeed is high and rapidly increasing. The ball is in balance. Maintain engine RPM limits.

c)   To recover, centralize the turn needle by applying aileron in the opposite direction to the turn. Keep the ball in the centre with rudder.

d)   With the turn and slip indicator showing no bank or yaw, recover from the dive in the usual way and return to cruising flight.

12. Failure of One Engine (Multi-engined Types)

Note. To be demonstrated after Ex. 23 is fully understood.

Full Panel

a)   Imagine that an engine has failed during level flight on instruments. Notice the indication of the flight panel. A turn towards the dead engine is shown on the turn needle coupled with a change in heading on the direction indicator. A roll towards the dead engine is indicated by the artificial horizon while both altimeter and vertical-speed indicator show a loss of height. *When constant-speed propellers are fitted* RPM and in certain cases manifold pressure and oil pressure remain unchanged on the dead engine.

b)   To continue flight with the dead engine check the yaw by centralizing the turn needle with opposite rudder and correct the roll with aileron.

c)   Carry out the procedure outlined in Ex. 23 and trim out all rudder and stick loads at the correct speed for flight with a dead engine. Note the position of the symbol in the artificial horizon and maintain this indication throughout cruising flight.

d)   Check the instruments for the live engine, electric charge and the vacuum gauge.

e)   Now practise gentle turns always maintaining the ball in the central position.

Limited Panel

Carry out the procedure described for the full panel but maintain lateral level and direction on the turn and slip indicator and adopt the correct 'engine out' attitude with reference to the airspeed indicator.

7   Night Flying

The aim of this exercise is to teach the pilot the technique of flying at night.

The feel and handling characteristics of an aeroplane are unchanged at night from that experienced during normal day flying, the difference in the two flight environments being confined to the pilot's inability to recognize even familiar features in darkness. These limitations vary according to conditions, which may range from full moonlight, when flying is little removed from normal day conditions, to total darkness demanding more or less complete reliance on the instruments.

It follows that before contemplating instruction in night flying the pilot must attain a reasonable degree of proficiency, e.g. PPL standard, with his instrument flying of sufficient accuracy to enable a circuit to be flown without outside visual references. He must of course be thoroughly familiar with the aircraft, its equipment and the position of all switches and controls so that these can be used with confidence in the dark.

The Airfield at Night

The equipment available for night flying varies considerably at different classes of airfield. Most medium and large civil airports are well lighted with permanent electric installations which may include some or all of the items listed in the following description. (*See also* Fig. 58.)

1. Approach Lighting
This is used to guide the aircraft towards the runway threshold. It consists of white or sodium lights which may be of high intensity. The approach lighting may incorporate **Cross Bars**

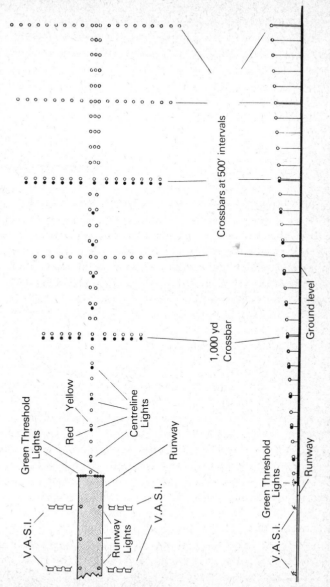

Fig. 57. Approach lighting.

Green Threshold Lights

Red Yellow

Centreline Lights

Runway

V.A.S.I.

Runway Lights

V.A.S.I.

Crossbars at 500' intervals

1,000 yd Crossbar

Ground level

Green Threshold Lights

V.A.S.I.

Runway

20

mounted on poles above ground level. The bars are represented by a line of lights running across the path of approach, those farthest from the runway being highest above ground level, the others descending step by step as the airfield boundary is neared so that an angle of descent indication is provided (Fig. 57).

2. Visual Approach Slope Indicators (VASI)

The purpose of this equipment is to assist the pilot in making a visual approach at the correct descent path angle.

The installation consists of two rows of three units either side of the runway. Two colours are projected, red and white although pink will be seen during the transition from one colour to another. During a correct approach the six units nearest the airfield boundary (downwind units) will show white, whereas the second row of upwind units are red, the two rows being set at slightly different angles (usually $\frac{1}{2}°$) to produce a beam. When the approach is high both rows show white while a low approach causes all units to turn red. The VASI units are normally adjusted to coincide with the ILS beam and their position in relation to the runway may be seen in Fig. 57.

The VASI system replaces an earlier one embracing three colour units which showed red when the aircraft was too low, green for a correct approach and amber if the pilot was above the glidepath. The main advantages of the VASI system is accuracy and ease of interpretation but even these improved angle of approach aids have their limitations. The transition from white to red or red to white goes through pink and it can be difficult under some weather conditions to determine the exact transition point between the colours. Furthermore over the runway threshold the VASI approach channel is some 9 to 12 metres deep (30 to 40 feet) and the system is generally regarded as being of limited value below an approach height of 200 feet.

A development of the VASI, one that has produced encouraging results, is known as the **Precision Approach Path Indicator (PAPI)**. It consists of a single row of four lights either side of the runway. The lights are set at $\frac{1}{2}°$ to $\frac{1}{3}°$ increases in

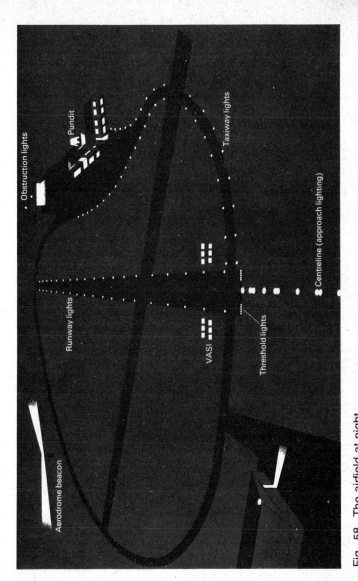

Fig. 58. The airfield at night.
The taxiways are lighted according to the runway in use.

angle, the outer units being lowest and the innermost at the steepest angle. During a correct approach the two outer lights of the four situated either side of the runway show white with the inner pairs at red. This represents a 3° approach. A slightly high situation (3·3°) causes the next light on each side of the runway to change from red to white leaving only the innermost lights at red. Should all lights turn white the aircraft is high on the approach (more than 3·5°). A slightly low condition (2·7°) shows three reds on each side of the runway with only the outer lights at white, while an all red display means the aircraft is low

LOW   SLIGHTLY LOW

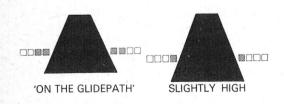

'ON THE GLIDEPATH'   SLIGHTLY HIGH

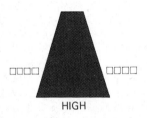

HIGH

20   Fig. 59. Precision Approach Path Indicator (PAPI).

(less than 2·5°). This is illustrated in Fig. 59.

Over the threshold the approach channel is only 2 metres (6 feet) deep and this accuracy, coupled with the elimination of a pink transition from one colour to the other, represents a considerable improvement on other systems. Its accuracy is such that a visual aiming point for touchdown is provided and since it may be used when close to the threshold PAPI will be of particular assistance in conditions of low cloud or wind sheer.

3. Runway Lights

Often of variable intensity these white lights are spaced at regular intervals along each side of the runway. The outline of the runway in use is completed by a bar of **Threshold Lights** across the beginning of the runway and a similar bar at the windward end denoting the extremity of the landing area.

On grass airfields, when permanent electric runway lights are not usually installed, paraffin flares of the **Gooseneck** type may be laid out in a single or double line when a night-flying programme is to occur. Such a system is referred to as a **Flarepath** but in the interest of simplicity the term 'runway lights' will be used throughout the chapter.

The appearance of the runway lights on the approach is a good indication of descent path.

4. Taxi Lights

Taxiways from the dispersal to the runway in use are lined with blue lights on the edge adjacent to the airfield proper and amber lights along the outer edge. Like the runway lights brightness may be adjusted from the control tower according to conditions. Some airfields may have all blue or amber lights.

5. Pundits

These lights are arranged to flash the airfield-identification letters in morse. Neon lights are commonly used, green for civil airports and red for RAF stations. In clear visibility these airfield beacons can be seen for some thirty miles and are of considerable value as a means of airfield identification.

20

6. Occults

These powerful lights rotate through 360°, their beams being visible for 60 miles under ideal conditions. Sometimes called **Aerial Lighthouses** these installations are in use at important civil airports flashing an alternate white and green beam. Major RAF airfields display white and red beams.

7. Obstruction Lights

On airfields and within their environs, obstructions such as tall chimneys, church steeples, cooling towers, etc., are marked with red obstruction lights at their highest points. Very tall structures such as television masts are lighted at 200 ft vertical intervals. Obstruction lights may be of the flashing variety.

Aircraft Night-flying Equipment

Aircraft equipment differs widely according to the type of aeroplane but the following description covers the night-flying equipment likely to be met.

1. Navigation Lights

This system of lights is so arranged that the aircraft displays a white light when approached from astern, a red light on the port side and a green to starboard (Fig. 60).

The angular spread of light is in each case limited by a suitable shield and, while it is usual to position the port and starboard navigation lights on the wing tips with the white light in the extreme rear of the aircraft, a single unit incorporating the three-sector is on occasions attached to the top of the fuselage. This system avoids the need for lengthy electric leads through the wings and fuselage although it is necessary to have an additional three-sector unit below the aircraft to ensure all round visibility of the navigation lights.

When the weight of the aircraft does not exceed 5,700 kg (12,500 lb), navigation lights may flash in unison alternating with a white light showing in all directions. Aircraft registered in some countries replace the white light with a flashing red light visible through 70° either side of dead astern.

20

Larger aircraft (weighing more than 5,700 kg) must carry non-flashing navigation lights and an anti-collision beacon.

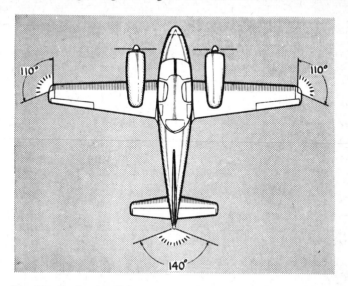

Fig. 60. Navigation lights.

2. Landing Lights

One or possibly two high-intensity landing lights are usually arranged, either in a transparent portion of the wing leading edge, in the fuselage nose cone or on the nosewheel undercarriage strut. Alternatively they may be placed under the port wing and retracted when not in use. It is sometimes possible to alter the beam angle on the approach. Landing lights make heavy demands on aircraft batteries and must therefore only be used for brief periods when the generator has cut out at low engine speeds.

3. Taxying Lamps

Some aircraft are fitted with additional lights of lower power than those used for landing. Their function is similar to the headlights on a car.

20

4. Anti-collision Beacon

A red rotating beacon may be fitted for use by day and night for the purpose of avoiding collision with other aircraft. It is mandatory equipment when the aircraft weighs more than 5,700 kg.

5. Strobe Lights

Similar to electronic flash units used in photography these powerful lights are positioned on the wingtips and are a valuable anti-collision aid for use by day and by night. Because of their power and the risk of excessive glare they should not be used when flying in cloud.

6. Cockpit Lights

These may comprise –

(*a*) White instrument lights or the ultra-violet type which activate the fluorescent instrument markings.

(*b*) Standby red lighting system to be used in the event of failure of the normal instrument lights.

The intensity of both main and standby systems is adjustable.

(*c*) Adjustable cockpit lights to be used for reading charts.

Night-flying Briefing

An essential part of any night-flying programme is the night-flying briefing. This is separate and additional to the usual instructional pre-flight briefing and is normally discussed in conjunction with ATC.

During the briefing the airfield lighting system will be explained with the aid of a model or drawings together with the position of obstructions. Radio frequencies will be confirmed.

The air-traffic controller will outline special points of importance, navigational warnings and expected air-traffic movements. It is always of great value for the pilot under training to be shown the airfield lighting installation in daylight.

The briefing will conclude with a visit to the met. officer for the following information –

(*a*) A general forecast followed by the local forecast for the
period.
(*b*) Icing index.
(*c*) Freezing level.
(*d*) Cloud base.
(*e*) Visibility.
(*f*) Wind velocity.

Preparation

The usual pre-flight inspection is carried out with the addition
of a check on the operation of the navigation, anti-collision
strobe, cockpit and landing lights.

It is essential to carry a torch to enable the final external
inspection to be completed. Furthermore a small torch must be
carried in the pocket as an added safeguard in the unlikely
event of instrument light failure. Throughout these explanations it is assumed that radio is fitted and the installation should
be thoroughly tested during the pre-flight inspection.

Night vision may be materially improved if time is allowed for
the eyes to become accustomed to the dark before flying begins.
Bright lights should then be avoided.

On entering the aircraft the flight panel lights should be
adjusted to the lowest level consistent with good illumination of
the instruments so that vision outside the aircraft is not pre-
judiced. Undercarriage and other warning lights should be
dimmed, when provision is made, either in the form of a dark
filter or an adjustable iris shutter.

The aircraft is then started and the engine(s) allowed to warm
up. By now the pilot under instruction will fully appreciate the
wisdom of knowing his cockpit well enough to find all controls
and switches in the dark.

Taxying

To guide aircraft into and out of the dispersal area groundcrew
may use a pair of blue torches, signals following daytime
pattern. Normally the airfield will be under air-traffic control,

20

taxying and other clearance instructions coming from the tower by R/T or Aldis Lamp when no radio is fitted. This does not absolve the pilot from exercising particular care while taxying since it is not easy to judge speed or distance at night. Slow and careful taxying allows time to see obstructions and the navigation lights of other aircraft on the ground.

While it should be possible to taxi to the holding point without difficulty using the airfield taxiway lights, these may be supplemented by the aircraft taxi lights when they are fitted. When any doubt exists the aircraft should be stopped and if there are no taxi lights the landing lamp may be switched on for a brief period to ascertain the aircraft's position on the aerodrome.

On reaching the holding point the usual power check is carried out clear of other aircraft. While the pre-take-off vital actions are completed the engine(s) must be left running fast enough to ensure electric charge from the generator(s) and adequate supply of vacuum to the flight panel. The instrument lighting should be checked and adjusted if required. Permission to line up on the runway is now requested on R/T.

The Take-off

On the runway the direction indicator may be turned to the nearest 5° mark as for an instrument take-off. After a final check of the instruments and when permission to take-off has been obtained the brakes are released and the take-off begins.

In the early stages direction is maintained on the runway lights.

Tailwheel Aircraft

During training on tailwheel types some pilots experience difficulty keeping straight at night and the process can be simplified by deliberately aiming the aircraft at the last runway light while looking along the left-hand side of the fuselage. In practice there is no danger of hitting this light and a straight take-off will result. There is a tendency to raise the tail too high in an effort to improve forward visibility. This is a common fault

20

which must be avoided. A nosewheel undercarriage simplifies the night take-off.

No attempt should be made to lift the aircraft off the ground until full take-off speed has been reached when a gentle climb should commence immediately with no attempt to hold down the aircraft in an effort to build up speed quickly. By following this procedure the aircraft will be prevented from sinking back on to the ground at a time when the runway cannot be seen.

After becoming airborne two references will be available –

1. The runway lights now receding below the aircraft.
2. The flight panel.

When no outside references are visible the attention must be transferred to the instruments without delay. In making this early transition the sudden change from a well-lighted runway to the darkness ahead is avoided and time is allowed to settle down on instruments.

The Climb and Circuit

By now the airspeed will be near that recommended for the climb. Before any attempt is made to raise the undercarriage or reduce to climbing power, a positive reading must show on the altimeter.

On a clear night the flight panel may be supplemented by using stars as a guide while maintaining direction during the climb, although too much reliance should not be placed on outside visual references which may suddenly become obscured.

The climb is continued with reference to the flight panel until the usual 500 ft when a 90° climbing turn is made to place the aircraft on the crosswind leg. It is however advisable to climb straight ahead to circuit height, level off and then turn when the wind is strong enough to shorten the downwind leg and so cramp the circuit.

The remainder of the circuit is similar to the usual daylight pattern for an engine-assisted approach with the runway lights providing an excellent guide for the downwind leg. At this stage the attention is divided between the instruments and such

20

outside visual references as exist.

It is very easy to mistake a star or lights on the ground for another aircraft at night, particularly when the changing angular relationship between say two or more lights and the aircraft gives an impression of movement, when in fact the lights are fixed objects on the ground.

The normal downwind vital actions are completed and the aircraft reported 'downwind' on R/T. When the sky is obscured and there is mist a risk of disorientation exists. Ground lights may be mistaken for stars, or vice versa, and it is imperative that the instruments are believed.

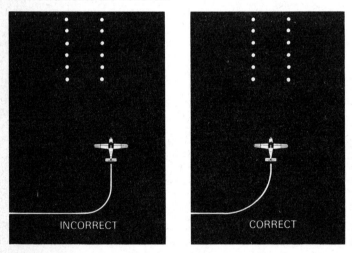

Fig. 61. Turning on to the approach.

A position on the approach-light pattern should be selected as a guide for the base leg turn or, when night-landing facilities are limited to a flare path, this should pass well behind the trailing edge of the wing to allow room for a good engine-assisted approach. The strength of the wind must obviously influence the length of the downwind leg. Handling of the undercarriage, flaps, propeller control, etc., represents no change from day-flying procedure.

20   With the aircraft settled on the base leg a gradual turn on to the approach should be planned rather than a late turn of small radius which usually causes the aircraft to line up on the far side of the runway (Fig. 61). The aircraft is then reported on 'finals' by R/T.

The Approach

It is essential to use an engine-assisted approach so that full adjustment of the descent path is available. This is judged predominantly by the appearance of the runway lights with the angle of approach indicator used as a supplementary source of information.

During the approach if the spacing between the runway lights appears to diminish, the aircraft is undershooting, while an

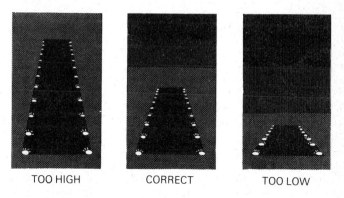

TOO HIGH   CORRECT   TOO LOW

Fig. 62. The runway lights used as the primary means of judging the angle of approach.

increase in apparent distance between the lights denotes an overshoot. During an ideal approach the VASI show white (near rows) and red (far rows) while the appearance of the runway lights remains constant. The use of the runway lights as a means of judging the approach angle is illustrated in Fig. 62.

Should at any time the near row of VASIs turn red, power must be increased to reduce the rate of descent and, if **20** necessary, full power must be applied so that white/red is regained without delay.

The descent path is adjusted with the throttle in the usual manner while a constant airspeed is maintained with the elevators.

The final stages of the approach must be planned to enable the first landing check to occur shortly after the runway threshold is passed.

Because they are inaccurate at low levels the Visual Approach Slope Indicators should be ignored when the aircraft has descended to 200 ft and the remainder of the approach completed with reference to the runway lights only.

The Landing

Except during conditions of bright moonlight the ground will not be seen at night so that the initial landing check and the subsequent hold-off must be judged by watching the runway lights.

When a landing light is installed this should be switched on during the final stages of the approach and to avoid dazzle the eyes should follow the illuminated ground rather than the beam itself. Many experienced pilots prefer to consider the landing light as an aid with the runway lights as the predominant source of landing information.

The landing light will throw its beam farther up the runway as the tail is lowered during the hold-off, but the illuminated portion of the runway ahead certainly assists the landing.

When a landing must be made with the aid of the runway lights only it is advisable to leave on a little power until the actual touchdown, so reducing the rate of sink and the possibility of a heavy landing.

With tailwheel aircraft some pilots prefer to use the wheel landing technique at night and here again a trace of power should be left on until contact is made. Whether a three-point or wheel landing is made, the throttle(s) must be closed to minimize landing run as soon as the aircraft has made normal contact.

Going Round Again

It may be necessary to overshoot for any of the following reasons –

1. Badly judged approach.
2. Following too closely behind another aircraft on the circuit.
3. In response to an instruction from control.
4. Because of a bad landing requiring more room for recovery than is available.

Whatever the reason for going round again a good lookout must be kept for other aircraft and, when the circuit is being flown during a night-flying training programme with other aircraft participating, care should be exercised that, in overshooting, spacing around the circuit is not crowded to the inconvenience of other pilots.

It is good practice to ease over to the right of the runway lights during an overshoot so that other aircraft taking off may be kept in view.

When the overshoot is occasioned by an ill-judged approach or a bad landing the decision to go round again should not be delayed.

Engine Failure, Asymmetric-powered Overshoot and Landing

The engine failure on take-off procedure as it applies to single-engined aircraft is little changed at night from normal daylight practice with the exception that while avoiding obstructions full use must be made of the landing lights. Flaps should be used when possible and the fuel and ignition must be 'off' for the landing.

The various considerations applicable to engine failure on multi-engined aircraft may be placed under the following headings –

1. The ability to control the aircraft with an engine out of

20

use. This is fully described in Ex. 23, Part II, 'Asymmetric Power Flight', the relevant text being –

11. Failure of an engine during take-off (page 245).
12. Landing with asymmetric power (page 249).
13. Asymmetric-powered overshoot (page 251).

2. When an engine fails at night the instruments play a prominent part while control is safeguarded supplemented by such outside visual references as are available at the time. The importance of instrument flying at night has been stressed throughout this chapter and the considerations applicable to the situation will be found in Ex. 19 'Instrument Flying' under the sections dealing with multi-engined aircraft on page 139.

3. Because of the cockpit and handling procedures associated with engine failure on a multi-engined aircraft the pilot must be able to find every control in the dark without hesitation.

Provided these three considerations are clearly understood an engine failure at night may be faced with confidence, particularly when the engine-out performance of the aircraft is known to be good. Should the aircraft be of a type incapable of climbing away with a dead engine, the emergency should be treated as engine failure on take-off with a single-engined type and the best possible landing made ahead taking all the usual precautions.

Flight Practice

COCKPIT CHECKS (Vital Actions)

T: Trim for take-off.
   Tighten throttle friction.
M: Mixture rich, carb. heat cold (carburettor engines).
P: Pitch fine.
F: Fuel on and sufficient for flight, electric pump 'on', fuel pressure checked.
F: Flaps up or take-off position.

20

Harness and hatches secure.
Instruments and radio set and checked.
Adjust the instrument lights.
Check Beacon/Strobes and Navigation Lights 'on'.

(Note. The engine(s) must be left running fast enough to ensure adequate vacuum supply to the flight panel and sufficient electric charge for the navigation lights, etc., while the vital actions are completed. Certain items such as 'pitch' and 'flaps' may not relate to some light aircraft. Nevertheless the pupil pilot should recite this list in full since it is a standard check suitable for more advanced aircraft which may be flown at a later date.)

OUTSIDE CHECKS

a) Position the aircraft so that the lights of aeroplanes taking off, flying around the circuit and landing can be seen.
b) Obtain clearance from the tower and ensure that no aircraft is on final approach before taxying on to the take-off area.

AIR EXERCISES

1. Circuits and Landings

Taking Off

a) When the vital actions have been completed and after permission has been given, taxi carefully on to the runway. Line up with the runway lights and check the direction indicator which may be set to the nearest 5° mark. Be sure all instruments read correctly.
b) When take-off clearance has been received look along the left of the nose and select the last runway light as a marker on which to keep straight. Open the throttle smoothly and fully and check full power is being obtained. As speed increases move the stick back slightly to take the weight off the nosewheel. Keep straight with the runway lights.
c) At a safe take-off speed lift the aircraft off the ground.

20

Climbing

a)   Immediately after take-off make full use of whatever outside visual references are available and confirm with the instruments. Make no attempt to gain climbing speed quickly by holding down the aircraft. Keep straight on the direction indicator and with reference to the instruments allow the aircraft to settle naturally into a climb.

b)   When the altimeter shows a gain in height retract the under-carriage. At a safe height throttle back to climbing power.

c)   At 500 ft start a climbing turn in the direction of circuit.

The Circuit

a)   Check the crosswind leg with the runway lights and if necessary compensate for drift. Look out for the lights of other aircraft.

b)   Level out at circuit height and at circuit speed reduce power accordingly.

c)   Turn downwind using both instruments and outside visual refer-ences. The wing tip should now be running along the runway lights. Report 'Downwind'.

Complete Vital Actions –
B: Brakes off.
U: Undercarriage down and locked.
M: Mixture rich, check carb. heat for ice (carburettor engines).
P: Pitch fine, or in pre-landing position.
F: Fuel sufficient for 'overshoot'. Electric pump on.

d)   When the runway lights are well behind the trailing edge of the wing (or, if applicable, when opposite the appropriate approach light) turn on to the base leg.

The Approach and Landing

a)   On the base leg reduce speed and apply part flap as required. Correct for drift in the usual way.

b)   Commence a wide descending turn towards the runway lights and look for the Visual Approach Slope Indicator. Aim to complete the turn in line with the runway at 500 ft. Advise 'Turning Finals'.

c)   Reduce to the correct engine-assisted approach speed and aim for the threshold lights. Apply full flap on short finals (crosswind conditions excepted). The runway lights must appear at the same angle throughout the approach. Help maintain this angle by keeping in

20

the red/white section of the VASIs. Reduce power for 'all white' and add power if 'all red' appears.

d) Maintain a constant approach speed and adjust for drift. Switch on the landing light. Towards the end of the approach ignore the VASIs and concentrate on the runway lights, aiming to check the descent just past the threshold.

e) Leave on a little power and hold off using the runway lights as a guide. Complete the landing and throttle right back. Keep straight on the runway lights.

f) Clear the runway without delay, switch off the landing light, raise the flaps and taxi away.

Going Round Again

a) To overshoot, apply take-off power and re-trim at the 'flaps down' climbing speed.

b) Position the aircraft to the right of the runway so that other aircraft can be seen taking off.

c) At a safe height raise the undercarriage and flaps taking the usual precautions to prevent sink.

d) Position the aircraft in relation to others on the circuit.

2. Engine Failure on Take-off

Single-engined Aircraft

a) Adopt gliding speed.

b) Switch landing light 'on'.

c) Use flaps as required and land ahead making gentle turns to avoid obstacles.

d) Turn ignition and fuel 'off' before landing. Operate the idle cut-off.

e) Before landing unlatch the door(s).

Multi-engined Aircraft

See Ex. 23, Part II, page 259.

8 Aerobatics

The aim of this exercise is to teach the pilot how to perform aerobatic manoeuvres without danger to himself, the aircraft or any third party.

The question is often asked 'what is the purpose of aerobatics?' It is perhaps easier to give a satisfactory answer when the query is referred to a military pilot since aerobatics have in the past formed the basis of the fighter pilot's evasive action, and even now have an application in Service flying.

In so far as the civil pilot is concerned no such claim can be made and it is freely admitted that benefit is confined to –

(*a*) The pilot's confidence in his handling ability.

(*b*) Practice in the control of the aircraft in extreme attitudes.

(*c*) Good aerobatics are a pleasure to watch and a source of enjoyment to the competent pilot.

(*d*) Aerobatic competitions, on an international scale, have become an important sport.

In the course of aerobatics, airframe, engine and pilot are subjected to loads in excess of and occasionally in the reverse direction to normal. Such inverted loads occur for example during a slow roll and, unless the engine has been designed or specially modified for this condition, the carburettor will cease to function and oil pressure will be lost. Precautions must be taken, and the correct engine handling is outlined later in the chapter.

Good aerobatics are the result of practice in the ability to make all control sequences merge smoothly into one another. Harsh movement of the controls must be avoided for the following reasons –

1. Unnecessary loading is caused on aircraft and occupant(s).

2. Sudden application of the controls can cause loss of speed and particularly on more advanced aircraft a high-speed stall may occur.

Not all aircraft are stressed for aerobatics and under no circumstances are they to be attempted unless the aeroplane has an aerobatic category. The likely result of disregarding this advice is structural failure by overloading the airframe.

While an aeroplane with an aerobatic category is designed to withstand loadings of plus 9 or 10 'g', the average pilot will 'black out' after being subjected to ten seconds at $4\frac{1}{2}$ 'g'. The 'black out' can be delayed by adopting a 'crouching' or 'hunching' posture while bracing the stomach muscles, but provided aerobatics are correctly performed loads need never exceed 4 'g' and a complete sequence of all basic manoeuvres need not entail more than $2\frac{1}{2}$ 'g'.

During the early stages of training it is not uncommon for a pilot to suffer from sickness but this will disappear as he becomes accustomed to and improves his aerobatics.

Some of the manoeuvres are associated with extra speed at one stage or another and it is important that engine limitations are not exceeded during these periods.

Civil aircraft with aerobatic capabilities are mostly of the elementary type with fixed-pitch propellers and the descriptions which follow are written with these in mind. Certain aerobatics are completed with surplus speed in hand and this should be used to regain height by climbing in a steeper than usual attitude.

The following aerobatic manoeuvres are in the Civil Aviation Authority approved syllabus –

1. **Loop.**
2. **Stall turn.**
3. **Slow roll.**
4. **Roll off the top of a loop.**
5. **Barrel roll.**

Additional variants will also be described although some of these represent a combination of several basic manoeuvres.

6. **Aileron turn.**

21

7. **Half roll.**
8. **Vertical figure of eight.**
9. **Cuban eight.**
10. **Four-leaf clover.**

There are other manoeuvres but these are not recommended unless the aircraft is approved for them. In some aircraft they might, in fact, prove dangerous. They are –

Flick Roll. This is in effect a spin in the horizontal plane and, unless the aircraft is designed or modified for the purpose, structural damage can be caused.

Outside Loop. Throughout this routine both aircraft and pilot are subjected to prolonged inverted loading, since the aircraft goes around the loop with the pilot on the outside. Excessive negative 'g' will cause a 'red out', an unpleasant experience to be avoided. Bearing in mind that few aeroplanes are designed to withstand heavy inverted loads, here again structural damage or even failure may result. Unless the engine has an inverted lubrication system oil starvation could cause a seizure.

Tail Slides. During these the aeroplane behaves as the title implies and damage to the ailerons in particular may result from the reversed airflow.

Although these remarks are intended as words of warning against indulging in dangerous practices negative 'g' manoeuvres are quite feasible in aircraft designed for the purpose. The ten variants listed as suitable are well within the limits of any aeroplane with an aerobatic category and their practice can be rewarding and a great source of pleasure.

Airmanship Checks

Particularly during the early stages considerable height may be lost and the pilot is advised to commence each practice at 4,000 ft or above so that the routine can be completed not below 3,000 ft. These figures allow sufficient margin for lack of skill in a light aeroplane.

Practice should be conducted away from towns or airfields and outside Controlled Airspace. It is usual for the flying school to designate a special **Aerobatic Area** for the purpose.

There must be no loose equipment in the aircraft and the occupant(s) will be provided with an aerobatic harness which must be tight. Many aerobatic aircraft are fitted with 5-strap harnesses giving negative 'g' support.

It is easy to become engrossed in aerobatics and care must be exercised so that a known landmark remains in sight otherwise there is a risk of becoming lost.

From the ground aerobatics look best when carried out into or down wind but other considerations such as the position of the sun and the availability of a good horizon must influence

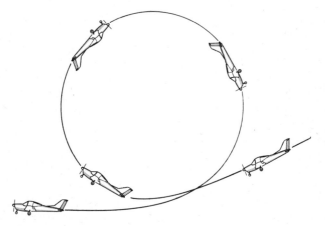

Fig. 63. The loop

choice of direction. It is often advantageous to use a ground feature such as a railway line on which to keep straight during, for instance, a loop or a barrel roll.

When gyro instruments are fitted the direction indicator and, when it is possible, the artificial horizon must be 'caged' during aerobatics unless they have complete freedom of movement and do not in consequence topple.

It is of course most important to ensure that no manoeuvre is started above or in close proximity to another aircraft and clearing turns in either direction must precede any aerobatics. The importance of a good lookout cannot be over-stressed.

21

Loop

The loop is a complete circle flown in the pitching plane (Fig. 63) and is perhaps the simplest aerobatic manoeuvre.

The first half amounts to an ever-steepening climb to past the vertical while the airspeed decreases so that, should the manoeuvre be started with too little speed, insufficient energy will be present to carry the aeroplane over the top. For this reason in a light aeroplane it is usually necessary to increase the airspeed by some 25–30% above cruising and a moderate dive serves this purpose. As the aeroplane accelerates a glance at the engine-speed indicator will show if maximum permissible RPM are being approached; the throttle is reduced accordingly. When the recommended speed has been reached the aeroplane should be eased into the loop. Speed can be dissipated by coarse use of the elevators – a common fault prompted by a desire to get around the loop while the airspeed is high. When this is attempted by harsh backward movement of the stick, due to inertia, the aeroplane continues on its original path at a high angle of attack and speed is lost.

The stick should be eased back smoothly but sufficiently to produce a comfortable feeling of being pressed into the seat. There is no need to increase the loading to the point of discomfort. As the nose comes up above the horizon the throttle should be opened fully to assist the aeroplane around the climbing sector of the loop. At this stage a check should be made on lateral level using the horizon and adjustments are made on the ailerons.

During the first half of the loop the elevators will become progressively less and less effective as the speed decreases so that the backward movement must be increased; otherwise the radius of the loop will increase to the detriment of the loading which is vital to the function of the carburettor.

When the aircraft reaches the vertical stage it is possible to check if the loop is perpendicular to the horizon and should there be any tendency to lean left or right the fault can be corrected with rudder.

The critical point occurs at the top of the loop when speed is at its lowest. It is essential to maintain positive loading or 'g' at this stage; otherwise the engine will stop firing and the occupants will tend to leave their seats. Indeed but for their safety harness they would fall out of the aircraft should the loading cease while the aircraft is inverted.

Conversely too much backward pressure on the stick will cause some aeroplanes to 'flick out' of the top of the loop in what amounts to a horizontal spin. In practice the correct degree of control pressure is gauged by the feel of the aeroplane and the amount of 'g' experienced. Provided loading is maintained throughout there will be no tendency for the occupants to fall out or the engine to cease firing while upside down at the top of the loop.

It is interesting to note that, since the loading is less than normal during the top sector of the loop, stalling speed is likewise less than normal and this aerodynamic consideration is of assistance when performing a roll off the top of a loop, described later in the chapter.

Over the top of the loop speed will begin to increase and the throttle must be brought back to prevent the engine from exceeding its limitations. The loop is completed by easing the

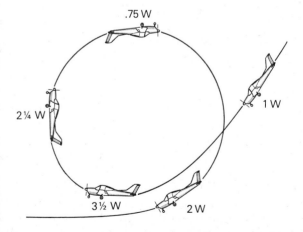

Fig. 64. Loading during a loop expressed in terms of aircraft weight. **21**

aeroplane out of the dive without increasing loading beyond the point of comfort, and when level the surplus speed can be used to regain height.

When two occupants are in a looping aircraft the 'piloted' will always 'black out' at a lower 'g' than the pilot; the pilot controlling the aircraft is able to withstand the higher 'g' possibly because he anticipates the increased loading and instinctively braces his muscles as he moves the stick.

In a properly executed loop neither occupant should 'black out' and Fig. 64 shows typical loadings at each stage of the loop. The highest 'g' occurs while entering the loop and the loading is less than 1 (normal) at the top.

Stall Turns

There are several variants of this manoeuvre which originated during the First World War as a 'dog fight' method of changing direction through 180° while shaking off a following enemy aircraft.

It is perhaps most effective and certainly smoother when performed without stalling, with the engine running through-out. All the movements should be merged into one another to

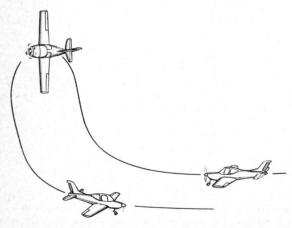

Fig. 65. The stall turn.

preserve continuity and positive loading must be maintained or the engine will cut.

In a stall turn the aircraft is made to climb in a near-vertical attitude when rudder is applied to make the nose yaw towards the left or right horizon. This movement continues until the aircraft is in a near-vertical dive when a pull-out will bring the aeroplane into level flight in the opposite direction to the original heading (Fig. 65).

This is a pleasant aerobatic and the detailed handling is quite simple. It can be initiated from cruising flight, although a little additional speed will help during the early stage of practice. It is of assistance to line up with a prominent ground feature such as a main road or railway line.

The stall turn is commenced with a smooth backward pressure on the stick and, as the nose comes up above the horizon, full power is applied to help maintain the airspeed. As the near-vertical attitude is approached, a little of the backward pressure must be released to prevent the aeroplane from attempting to loop and going over on its back. The forward movement on the stick must be just sufficient to hold the desired attitude; the pilot must avoid a deliberate push forward which will produce negative 'g' and may even stop rotation of the propeller. At this stage the airspeed will be decreasing rapidly and rudder must be applied in the required direction without too much delay. As the nose begins to yaw towards the left or right horizon, there may be a tendency for a roll to develop; this is more pronounced on some types than others but in any case a little aileron applied in a corrective direction will stop the unwanted roll.

As the nose comes down and begins to go below the horizon the throttle should be brought back a little to prevent over-speeding of the engine during the dive which follows. The stick should be brought back slowly so that, as the nose falls through the last 45° or so of yaw, recovery from the dive will have commenced. By anticipating recovery from the dive in this way, positive loading is ensured and the engine will continue to run without any suggestion of a 'cut'.

Excellent co-ordination practice can be gained by going from

21

one stall turn to another in a continuous series, particularly when they alternate left and right, although the importance of maintaining a good lookout must once again be mentioned.

Some instructors advise raising the nose to a steep attitude, a deliberate forward movement of the stick to hold the aircraft in the correct attitude, followed by a pause while the speed decreases to near the stall when rudder is applied to cause a sudden yaw, rather similar to the action of the nose when it drops during a stall.

Although this variant more closely follows the impression conveyed by the term 'Stall Turn', the method described in the preceding paragraphs is more pleasant to watch, certainly more comfortable to experience and there is less risk of stopping the engine.

Slow Roll

This aerobatic entails a roll through 360° about the fore and aft axis of the aeroplane. The ailerons cause the roll, rudder and elevators being used to maintain direction and level in the pitching plane (Fig. 66).

The manoeuvre is more difficult to accomplish in a relatively slow light aeroplane than in a higher-powered Service type, and it calls for more handling skill than the loop or stall turn. All controls are involved, sometimes co-ordinated in the same direction but at various stages moved in opposition to one another, and as with any complex operation, explanation is simplified by breaking down the sequences into smaller parts.

It is possible to slow roll during a glide or climb. The steepness of a **Climbing Roll** is largely a question of engine power most light aircraft being unable to achieve more than a steep climbing attitude, as opposed to the repeated vertical upward rolls which are within the scope of a modern fighter aircraft. Therefore this description is confined to the most usual slow roll – one that conforms so far as is possible to level flight.

Before commencing the roll it is advisable to find a point on the horizon for use as a reference while keeping straight.

Stage 1

Because most engines will cease to provide power when the aircraft is inverted and subjected to negative 'g', extra speed is required to convey the aircraft through the 'thrustless' section of the roll without too much loss of height.

The extra speed is gained in a shallow dive with the engine just below its maximum permissible RPM. The speed recommended for a slow roll will vary according to the type of aircraft but a 20–25% increase above normal cruising speed would be typical.

At the correct speed the nose is raised gently and smoothly above the reference point on the horizon. A 'nose-up' attitude is necessary to maintain height throughout the roll, particularly during the inverted stage when a large angle of attack is needed to compensate for the inefficiency of the wing under these conditions.

Before the roll is started, the nose should be firmly established above the point on the horizon by relaxing a little of the backward pressure which placed the aeroplane in this attitude after the dive. At the same time the throttle is opened fully to help maintain height and airspeed.

The roll is initiated by moving the stick in the direction required, the amount of aileron applied being dependent upon the desired rate of roll. The effects of aileron drag (page 23) must be combated at this stage by using a little rudder in the same direction, although as the bank steepens aileron drag will be of benefit.

Assuming a roll to the left, the manoeuvre begins with left aileron supplemented with a little left rudder. With the controls in this position the aeroplane will tend to turn to the left. This is prevented by easing the stick forward very slightly as the roll continues so that, when a 90° bank has been reached, the stick will be in the neutral position. It will be realized that any backward pressure at this stage would cause a steep turn. Additionally, as the roll proceeds and the bank approaches 90°, weathercock action will pull the nose down below the horizon and this must be corrected by changing the rudder direction – in this case to the right which will be towards the wing which is

21

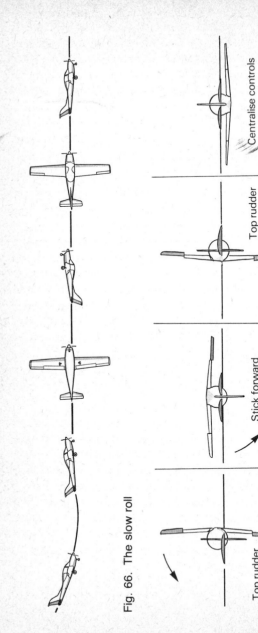

Fig. 66. The slow roll

Fig. 67. Stage 1

Top rudder

Fig. 68. Stage 2
(The throttle is closed while inverted.)

Stick forward

Fig. 69. Stage 3

Top rudder

Fig. 70. Stage 4

Centralise controls

above the horizon. The effect of **Top Rudder** is assisted by aileron drag from the depressed aileron which is on the right wing. At this point the weight of the aeroplane cannot be supported by the wings and it is important to maintain the nose above the horizon with top rudder so that with the aid of lift from the side of the fuselage and the upward inclined thrust line little height is lost. These forces are aided by the momentum of the aircraft (Fig. 67).

Stage 2

It will of course be necessary to hold on aileron throughout the roll which by now will have proceeded past the 90° bank attitude and this stage ends in the inverted position.

As the aeroplane begins to roll over on to its back it will be necessary to move the stick forward progressively to prevent the nose from dropping below the horizon. By the time the fully inverted position has been reached the wings will be required to provide a decreased pressure from what is normally the under-surface together with an increased pressure from the more cambered top-surface which is now underneath, and the stick will be well forward to maintain the large angle of attack necessary while the wing is in this inefficient position. In fact the stick is moved progressively forward during the first half of the roll.

As the aircraft rolls from the vertical to the inverted position aileron drag will become reversed since what was originally the depressed aileron (most aileron drag) will now be raised because its related wing is lower surface uppermost. The transfer of aileron drag from one wing to the other is entirely the result of inverted flight and it will be necessary to hold top rudder – in this case right rudder – so that direction is maintained on the reference point while inverted.

As the inverted position is approached, negative 'g' will become more pronounced and the weight of the occupant(s) will be transferred from seat to safety harness.

After the early practice stage, no difficulty should be experienced in keeping the feet on the rudder pedals when inverted.

At this stage carburettor engines will cut and the throttle

21

must be fully closed to prevent the sudden burst of engine power without oil pressure which would occur at a later stage were the throttle left open. Closing the throttle while inverted assumes still greater importance with certain types of constant-speed propellers. With these the loss of power causes the propeller to go into fine pitch and a power surge can result in an **Overspeed** when maximum permissible RPM are exceeded. When this occurs some types of propeller will prove reluctant to change from fully fine pitch. Fuel injected engines will normally run while inverted, provided the fuel supply from the tanks can be assured (Fig. 68). For prolonged inverted flight the oil system must be modified.

Stage 3

From the inverted attitude the third quarter of the roll continues towards a vertical or 90° bank position for the second time. On this occasion the depressed aileron is on the lower wing, so that, unlike the previous 90° bank, aileron drag will assist the weathercock tendency to pull the nose down below the horizon, which must be resisted with top rudder (in this case to the left). Because the airspeed will have decreased through-out the roll, fairly coarse use of rudder will be needed to hold up the nose and maintain height.

The beginning of this stage saw the aircraft inverted with the stick well forward; were it to be left in this position an outside steep turn with negative 'g' would result as the wings approached the vertical attitude and this must be prevented by gradually easing back the stick so that it is in the neutral position when the 90° bank has been reached (Fig. 69).

Stage 4

During this final stage rudder which was applied in the direction of roll (Stage 3) and lateral stability of the aircraft may tend to speed up the rate of roll and it will be necessary to decrease the amount of aileron which has been held on throughout the manoeuvre. As the wings become level the ailerons are central-ized. At the same time the stick must be brought back from its neutral position so that the nose is held up as the roll is completed.

The control of the elevators amounts to a continuous backward pressure as the aircraft rolls from the inverted to the level position during the second half of the roll.

Throughout the last 45° or so of roll top rudder is progressively decreased so that direction is maintained. Simultaneously the throttle is gradually opened to cruising power as the wings become level (Fig. 70).

Faults During a Slow Roll

(a) Control of Direction

During the four quarters of the roll directional control passes from rudder to elevators as the first 90° bank is reached, elevators to rudder as inverted flight is attained, rudder to elevators once more as the 90° bank is arrived at during the second half of the roll, and finally from the elevators back to the rudder during the last phase. During their periods of directional control the successful function of the elevators is confined to attaining a neutral position at each of the two vertical bank positions, while the 'rudder phases' are complicated by the changing conditions of aileron drag.

Once this theory is understood it is perhaps simplest to learn the control sequences which are put concisely in the Air Exercise section of this chapter.

(b) Control when Inverted

The transition from steep bank to inverted flight is without doubt the most difficult part of the manoeuvre. The most common faults are –

1. Failure to get the stick far enough forward to prevent the nose from dropping below the horizon thus causing the aeroplane to fall out of the roll in a half loop. When this fault persists during practice the aircraft should be trimmed 'nose heavy' before the roll is attempted. This is of particular assistance when the controls are inclined to be heavy, or alternatively when the pilot has a short reach and finds difficulty in easing the stick well forward when it is over to one side of the cockpit (as it would be during a roll).

21

2. Failure to hold on aileron while inverted. Naturally when this happens the roll ceases and it is usually not long before indecision causes the inexperienced aerobatic pilot to let the nose drop with the results that have already been explained under fault No. 1.

3. Nose held too high while inverted. This fault may develop when a pilot tries to prevent the nose from dropping following on a number of attempts at a slow roll which have been spoiled by fault No. 1. When too much forward pressure is applied the airspeed decreases as would be the case when the stick is eased back during normal level flight. The lower airspeed reduces the effectiveness of the ailerons so that the rate of roll becomes erratic. On some aircraft it may prove impossible to complete the roll until the airspeed is increased by moving the stick back (remember the aircraft is inverted). It is of course always possible to regain level flight by easing the stick back and putting the aircraft into a half loop, although the airspeed will build up rapidly and considerable height loss may result.

4. Failure to close the throttle. For reasons already explained this omission can cause damage to carburettor-type engines which may be aggravated when a constant-speed propeller is fitted. There is, however, this exception: some engines are designed to function when inverted and various standard engines can be modified to make inverted power possible. In either case it is clearly advantageous to leave the throttle open throughout the manoeuvre, so maintaining power and height.

When the pupil pilot begins his training he is told during 'Effects of Controls' that the ailerons, elevators and rudder act in the same direction relative to the pilot irrespective of the attitude of the aircraft. This principle should be applied throughout a slow roll to make the aircraft maintain direction and fore and aft level. To ensure firm support of the pilot while the aircraft is inverted the safety harness must be tighter than usual.

A fairly brisk rate of roll will be found easier during the early practice stage. A really slow roll is certainly better to watch but it is more difficult to accomplish, and this can be perfected later.

The loop, stall turn and slow roll represent maximum changes of direction in the pitching, yawing and rolling planes respectively and all other aerobatics are evolved from these three basic manoeuvres. It will be noted that, whereas the loop and roll rotate a full 360° around their associated axes, the stall turn is limited to 180° or so of yaw. It has been proved possible to complete a 360° yaw in a high-powered twin-engined turbojet by using maximum thrust from one engine only at the top of a stall turn, but this could not be effected on rudder alone and a complete circle in the yawing plane is outside the scope of this book.

Roll off the Top of a Loop

This is a combination of two basic aerobatics – the loop and the roll. It entails the first half of a loop followed by a roll through 180°, bringing the aircraft from the inverted to the level flight condition in the opposite direction to the original heading. The manoeuvre is usually referred to as a 'roll off the top' (Fig. 71).

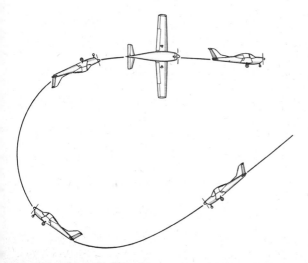

Fig. 71. The roll off the top.

The roll occurs when the airspeed is at its lowest (at the top of the loop) and an entry speed some 40 per cent above cruising will be required. This is rather higher than that required for a loop and the initial dive will in consequence be steeper. The engine must be kept below maximum permissible RPM as the aircraft accelerates.

At the recommended speed for a roll off the top the aircraft is eased into a loop. The throttle is opened fully as the nose comes up above the horizon and the first part of the manoeuvre is identical to the loop except that the airspeed is higher and on most aircraft of limited power rather more loading is required to complete the sequence.

The 'roll out' takes place shortly before the nose comes down on to the horizon in the inverted attitude. This is completed without actually stopping the loop so that some positive 'g' remains, thus enabling the engine to continue running – one of the features of a well-performed roll off the top.

In the case of a 'roll off' to the right, aileron is applied in that direction while the nose is just above the horizon. At the same time the rate of loop is decreased by easing the stick forward a little so that the actual control movement is a diagonal one, forward to the right with emphasis on the movement to the right. The stick movement is co-ordinated with a little rudder pressure in the same direction. The roll is a little different to a slow roll (which is around the longitudinal axis of the aeroplane) because in this case the aircraft is rolling while a loop is in progress so maintaining positive loading. These implications are discussed more fully under 'Barrel Roll'.

The roll off the top is completed by throttling back to cruising power as the wings become level with the horizon.

Faults during a Roll off the Top of a Loop

Three main faults can be observed in the carrying out of this manoeuvre:

1. Engine cutting during the roll out. This is usually caused by the pilot's failure to maintain positive loading during the roll

which in turn can result from –

(*a*) Attempting to stop the loop before commencing the roll

(*b*) Moving the stick too far forward during the roll out.

2. Stalling at the top of the loop when attempting to roll out. There are several possible causes of this fault which may culminate in a flick roll on some occasions –

(*a*) speed too low at the start of the manoeuvre

(*b*) speed correct but insufficient loading during the looping phase

(*c*) attempting to roll out prematurely with the nose too high above the horizon.

In practice it is possible to complete the roll out at a surprisingly low airspeed. This is because loading is less than normal at the top of the manoeuvre thus decreasing the stalling speed.

3. Failure to roll out with the aircraft flying at 180° to the original heading. This may be caused by –

(*a*) poor directional control during the roll out

(*b*) not checking lateral level and direction during the first part of the manoeuvre (page 180).

Like most aerobatics a ground feature is of assistance during a roll off the top and, when only one section of the horizon is clearly defined, the aircraft should begin by diving in the opposite direction to it. The roll out can then be completed with reference to the good horizon.

Barrel Roll

Whereas the aircraft is made to roll about its longitudinal axis in a slow roll, a spiral path is described during a barrel roll (Fig. 72).

Viewed from the aircraft the nose describes a circle, half of which is above the horizon with the other and second half

21

21

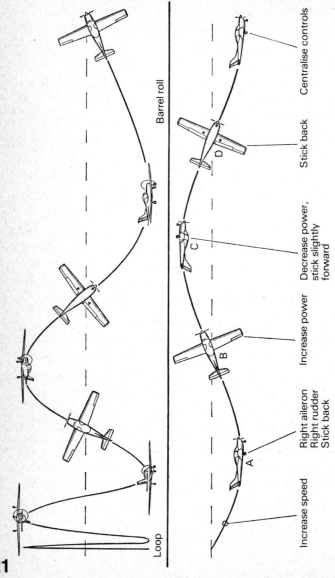

Loop

Barrel roll

| Increase speed | Right aileron
Right rudder
Stick back | Increase power | Decrease power,
stick slightly
forward | Stick back | Centralise controls |

Fig. 72. The barrel roll.
Upper drawing shows the relationship between loop and barrel roll, while lower drawing indicates the control sequence.

below. The manoeuvre is in fact part roll and part loop and its configuration may be modified to conform more to one than the other so that a 'tight' barrel may result which is akin to a slow roll, a spiral loop representing the other extreme. In practice the barrel roll looks at its best when it is more of a roll than a loop. When done correctly positive loading is maintained throughout, so that engine power remains during the inverted phase, and it is possible to execute a number of barrel rolls, one after the other, without loss of height.

With practice the manoeuvre can be started at cruising speed although before proficiency has been gained speed recommended for a loop will be found more suitable. At the correct airspeed the nose is eased up until the wings are parallel to and level with the horizon.

The control sequences which follow are very simple and in the case of a barrel roll to the right entail moving the stick to the right while maintaining the backward pressure. A little right rudder is applied at the same time to overcome the effects of aileron drag. The aircraft will now be on the rising side of the spiral and the throttle should be opened to at least climbing power during this phase. The nose is made to describe a large arc well above the horizon, the wings appearing to be vertical at the highest point of the arc (Fig. 73). When the aircraft is inverted with the wings level the top of the barrel will have been reached; the aircraft will enter the descending side of the spiral, and power should be reduced a little so preventing the engine from exceeding maximum RPM. Aileron and rudder are held on throughout the manoeuvre, but a little of the backward pressure must be relaxed on the descending side of the spiral to prevent its path steepening since this would place the second half of the barrel too far below the horizon.

The descending section of the spiral continues below the horizon as the nose describes the other half of the circle with the wings appearing vertical as the aircraft reaches the bottom of the arc. The last quarter brings the aeroplane on a climbing spiral path until the horizon is reached with the wings level once more. The controls are then centralized for level flight or another barrel roll can follow.

21

The complete manoeuvre as it appears to the pilot is shown in Fig. 73. What actually occurs during the roll is illustrated in Fig. 72 and the two figures should be compared.

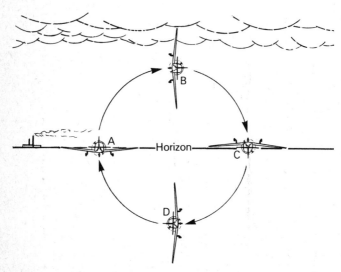

Fig. 73. Phases of a barrel roll as seen by the pilot, an illusion created by the position of the nose relative to the horizon. Compare the lettered aircraft with those in the previous illustration.

Faults in a Barrel Roll

1. *Engine cuts while inverted*. This is caused by excessively moving the stick forward as the aircraft approaches the inverted position so removing the positive loading which is needed to keep the engine running.

2. *The manoeuvre ends in a spiral dive*. This can result from –

(*a*) holding on too much backward pressure on the stick after the aircraft has gone over the top of the barrel so that it is below the horizon by the time the wings are horizontal;

(*b*) failing to bring the nose sufficiently high above the horizon at the top of the circle;

21

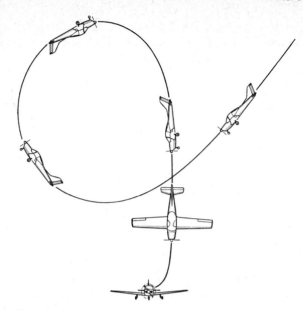

Fig. 74. The aileron turn (in this case through 90°).

(c) too much backward pressure throughout and not enough roll, so that the manoeuvre resembles an out-of-true loop.

Aileron Turns

In this manoeuvre the aircraft is made to roll while in a vertical dive. The pull out is usually on a different heading to that at the start of the aileron turn, and will depend upon the number of degrees of roll (Fig. 74).

Because of the vertical dive, speed will build up very rapidly and care must be taken not to exceed maximum diving speed for the type. With these thoughts in mind it is clearly advantageous to begin the aileron turn at a low airspeed and this is to some extent bound up with the method of entering the dive. The alternatives are –

1. *From a loop*. Over the top the loop is discontinued when the aircraft is pointing vertically downwards.

21

2. *From a roll*. The stick is brought back when the inverted position is reached. Because half a roll only is required cruising speed will be sufficient. In this way the dive will begin at a moderate airspeed. A half barrel roll will be found preferable to a slow roll because of the rather lower speed when inverted, and the advantages of continuous positive loading, although the slow roll technique may be used.

3. *From a stall turn*. The aileron turn can commence as soon as the aircraft has reached the vertical dive which follows the yaw during a stall turn.

4. *From straight and level flight*. This method is not recommended since, if negative loading is to be minimized, the transition from level flight to vertical dive must be made by very gradually easing forward the stick with the airspeed increasing rapidly in the process.

In endeavouring to keep the airspeed low, possibly the loop represents the best method of entry for an aileron turn.

Once the vertical dive is attained, the roll is made with reference to a ground feature using aileron supplemented by a little rudder in the same direction to overcome aileron drag. The roll can be made in either direction through whatever number of degrees is required provided the airspeed remains within the aircraft's limits. During the diving roll engine RPM must be kept below maximum permissible.

The roll is stopped by centralizing both aileron and rudder as the aircraft lines up with the ground feature. To complete the aileron turn the aeroplane is eased out of the dive on to its new heading when the surplus speed can be used to regain height.

Half Roll

This is half a roll followed by a half loop which brings the aircraft on to a reciprocal heading. From the illustration it will be seen to be a 'roll off the top' executed roll first (Fig. 75).

Airspeed is high at the beginning and low at the end of a roll off the top, whereas the reverse is the case in a half roll and, to prevent speed building up unduly with great loss of height, the manoeuvre must be started as slowly as possible.

After selecting a ground feature for reference while keeping straight the aircraft is rolled until inverted when the stick is brought back and the looping phase begun. The wings must be kept level and the engine RPM checked during the descending

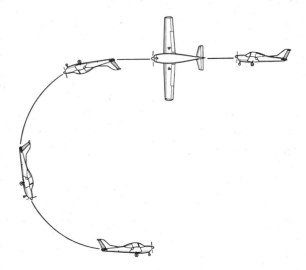

Fig. 75. The half roll.

loop which is completed by easing the aircraft out of the dive on its new heading at 180° to direction of entry to the half roll. The surplus speed is available for gaining height.

Vertical Figure of Eight

By combining a loop, a half roll and a roll off the top in continuous sequence the aircraft can be made to describe a vertical figure of eight. The manoeuvre is of considerable vertical extent and, although it starts and finishes at the middle of the '8', ample height must be allowed for the lower half of the sequence (Fig. 76).

After selecting the usual ground feature a loop is completed. As level flight is regained there follows a half roll which is

21

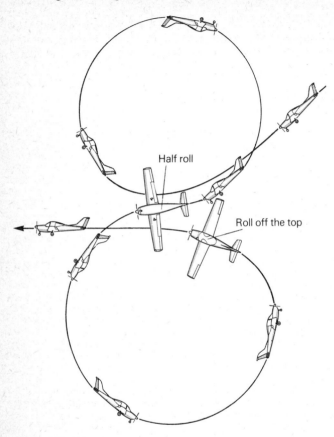

Fig. 76. Vertical figure of eight.

continued into a roll off the top when the aircraft will once more be in level flight on its original heading.

When experience has been gained in the basic manoeuvres no difficulty will be experienced in this or any other continuity aerobatics.

The initial loop should be continued, past the level flight attitude so that the half roll can be started in a nose-up attitude so reducing airspeed before the second part of the half roll. It

21

will be remembered that speed can build up very rapidly during a half roll and a low starting speed is to be preferred. Notwithstanding this precaution, plenty of speed will be available for the final roll off the top.

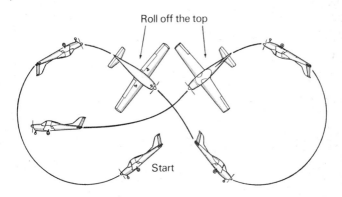

Fig. 77. Cuban eight.
(Horizontal figure of eight).

Cuban Eight

Sometimes called a **Horizontal Figure of Eight**, this manoeuvre describes an '8' on its side which is made up of two loops and two descending rolls. The complete pattern is illustrated in Fig. 77.

Because the rolls are made while descending, commencing speed need not exceed that required for a normal loop. The sequence for a Cuban eight begins with a loop which is allowed to continue until the aircraft is over the top and at an angle of approximately 45°. At this point a roll is effected using the same technique as that applied in a roll off the top so that the engine is kept running. The roll takes the aircraft from the inverted attitude to a 45° dive, pilot uppermost, when the second loop can be started and the procedure repeated to complete the 'eight'.

21

The Cuban eight can be repeated without loss of height.

An alternative to the Cuban eight is called the **Continuous Half Roll** and, although the aircraft describes the same horizontal eight, the method employed is different and is shown in Fig. 78.

The continuous half roll starts at looping speed when the

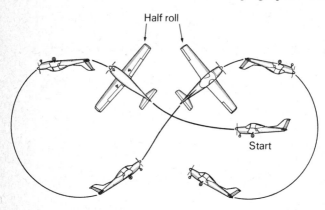

Half roll

Start

Fig. 78. Continuous half roll.

aircraft is eased into a 45° climb. As the speed decreases a half roll is started which is continued into another 45° climb, pilot uppermost, when a further half roll completes the sequence. From this explanation it will be seen that in a Cuban eight the rolls occur while descending, whereas climbing rolls make up the continuous half roll. Like the closely related Cuban eight, continuous half rolls may be repeated without loss of height.

Four-leaf Clover

This is a combination of four loops and four 90° aileron turns. Two roads crossing at right angles or a similar road-rail crossing make a good ground feature for this manoeuvre which is illustrated in Fig. 79.

The sequence commences with a normal loop which is

continued over the top until the aircraft is in a vertical dive, when an aileron turn is made through 90° in preparation for the next loop. This is repeated four times and on completion of the four-leaf clover the aircraft will be on its original heading.

Four 90° Aileron Turns

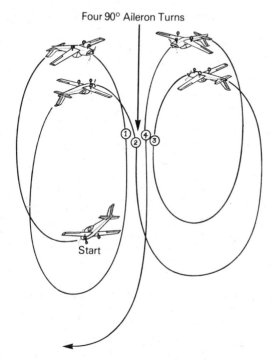

Fig. 79. The four-leaf clover.
A combination of four loops and four 90° aileron turns.

To compensate for height lost during each aileron turn, the loop should be elongated slightly by relaxing a little of the backward pressure on the stick when the vertical climbing attitude is reached. Backward pressure must be resumed after a few seconds; otherwise speed will decrease below that needed to complete the loop.

21

Restarting the Engine in Flight

With certain aerobatic manoeuvres there exists the risk of stopping the engine, the possibility being greatest when the throttle has been closed at a low-speed phase of the sequence. Although most modern aircraft have electric starters some aerobatic designs are without such equipment, making it necessary to start the engine by other means.

Before this procedure can be demonstrated it will be necessary deliberately to *stop* the engine and whereas it is not unknown for this to occur when least expected (e.g. during a stall turn) it can nevertheless prove surprisingly difficult to stop rotation intentionally unless the correct technique is applied.

Turning off the fuel and ignition will prevent the engine from running under its own power but the airflow at normal gliding speed will be sufficient to **Windmill** the propeller so that rotation will continue until an engine compression can overcome the force exerted on each blade by the airflow. Since a cool engine will stop more readily than one at running temperature a glide descending 500 ft or so will assist during practice, although it should be remembered that without an engine starter considerable height may be required to restart the engine. Therefore the glide should leave ample height in hand for the remainder of the exercise and a figure of 3,500 ft would be typical for most light training aircraft.

To stop the engine operate the idle cut-off and raise the nose to a steep climbing attitude above the horizon. Should the propeller continue to windmill depress the nose and gain a little speed so that another attempt can be made, this time with the nose somewhat higher above the horizon. Some instructors advise a one-turn spin in the case of an engine reluctant to stop, but this will lose precious height needed for the re-start and the procedure is therefore not recommended.

Without a starter it will be necessary to gain speed in a steep dive so that the airflow will overcome the compression of the engine and windmill the propeller. Before commencing the dive which is likely to be near vertical, the mixture control must be moved from 'idle cut-off' to 'rich' and the throttle half opened.

21

The dive is continued until the engine starts but not below a height which is likely to make a forced landing difficult in the event of failure to start. The actual 'pull out' from the dive will usually produce the additional force needed to rotate a stubborn engine. An engine which shows no sign of going over compression during the dive can often be coaxed by 'fish tailing', i.e. yawing from left to right at roughly one-second intervals.

The foregoing must only be practised with a qualified flying instructor and it is restricted to suitable aircraft types only.

Flight Practice

Note. A fixed-pitch propeller is assumed throughout.

Pre-aerobatic HASEL checks

H.	Height:	sufficient for manoeuvre
A.	Airframe:	flaps up, brakes off, gyro instruments 'caged' where possible
S.	Security:	harness and hatches secure. No insecure articles in cockpit
E.	Engine:	temperatures and pressure normal, carburettor heat control cold, fuel pump on
L.	Location and Lookout:	clear of airfields, towns, other aircraft and controlled airspaces.

AIR EXERCISE

Loop

a) After a thorough search for other aircraft and when sure the area is clear for aerobatics, depress the nose to a shallow dive and gain speed, keeping straight along a line feature. Keep the RPM below maximum permissible.

b) At the correct speed gently raise the nose and, as it comes up above the horizon, open the throttle fully. Check lateral level and, if necessary, correct with aileron.

21

c) As the speed decreases maintain loading by progressively increasing the backward pressure on the stick. As the vertical attitude is reached check that the loop is straight and, if necessary, correct with rudder.

d) Continue bringing back the stick and look out for the horizon as the aircraft approaches the inverted attitude. Check lateral level and, if necessary, adjust with aileron.

e) Throttle back slightly and allow the aircraft to continue the second half of the loop. Relax some of the backward pressure on the stick as the speed increases, so preventing excessive loading. Check the RPM during the dive.

f) Ease the aircraft out of the dive and either resume level flight or use the surplus speed to gain height.

Stall Turns

a) When sure that the area is clear for aerobatics position the aircraft on a line feature.

b) From a fast cruising speed ease back the stick and, as the nose of the aircraft comes up above the horizon, open the throttle fully.

c) As the vertical attitude is approached, apply rudder firmly in the required direction, at the same time relaxing a little of the backwards pressure on the stick, so maintaining the vertical attitude. Prevent any tendency to roll with opposite aileron. The nose will now yaw towards the horizon.

d) Hold on rudder and allow the yaw to continue below the horizon. Reduce power slightly and gently ease back the stick as the nose drops.

e) When the diving attitude is reached, centralize the rudder. Gently ease the aircraft out of the dive and either resume level flight, go into another stall turn, or use the surplus speed to gain height.

f) Now try a stall turn in the other direction.

Slow Roll

(In this exercise the air instruction is intentionally brief so that it may be synchronized with the control movements during a slow roll. To convey the correct timing the sequences are illustrated.)

a) Make sure the area is clear for aerobatics. Choose a point on the horizon on which to keep straight. Go into a gentle dive and keep the engine below maximum RPM.

b) At the correct airspeed raise the nose above the horizon keeping the reference point in sight. Hold the attitude by relaxing a little of the backward pressure on the stick and open the throttle.

(The instructions and accompanying diagrams are for a roll to the left.)

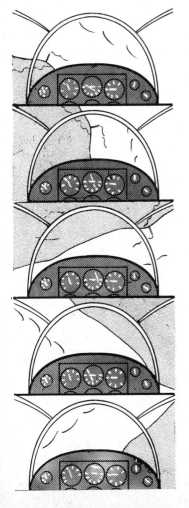

c) Stick to the left with left rudder.

d) Top rudder.

e) Stick forward. Keep straight.

f) Close throttle (carburettor engines) with stick well forward.

g) Change to top rudder. Stick back to neutral.

h) Stick back. Reduce bank. Open throttle.

21

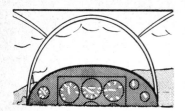

i)   Centralize stick and rudder.

j)   Now try a roll in the opposite direction.

Roll off the Top of a Loop

a)   When sure the area is clear for aerobatics, position the aircraft on a line feature so that the horizon behind the aircraft is clearly defined.

b)   Depress the nose into a fairly steep dive and increase speed. Prevent the engine from exceeding maximum RPM.

c)   At the correct airspeed, gently ease the aircraft into a loop.

d)   As the nose comes up on the horizon check lateral level and open the throttle fully.

e)   Maintain loading by continued backward pressure and check the attitude when the aircraft reaches the vertical position, making correction with rudder.

f)   Look backwards and as the nose approaches the horizon apply left (or right) aileron and rudder. Slow down the loop with gentle forward pressure on the stick.

g)   As the wings become level, centralize the controls and reduce power to cruising RPM. The aircraft should be on a reciprocal heading on the line feature.

h)   Now repeat the exercise with a roll in the opposite direction.

Barrel Roll

a)   When sure the area is clear for aerobatics, choose a point on the horizon and gain speed in a shallow dive. For a barrel roll to the right the reference point should be to starboard during the dive.

b)   At the correct airspeed move the stick back and, when the wings become level with the horizon, open the throttle to approximately climbing power and apply aileron and rudder in the direction of roll.

c)   Maintain the backward pressure on the stick and make the nose describe a half circle well above the horizon with the reference point in the centre.

21   *d)*   As the aircraft becomes inverted with the wings on the horizon relax a little of the backward pressure on the stick and reduce power slightly.

e)   Make the nose describe another half circle below the horizon with the reference point in the centre.

f)   As the nose comes up on the horizon with the wings level, either resume straight and level flight, go into another barrel roll, or use the surplus speed to gain height.

g)   Now try a barrel roll in the opposite direction.

Aileron Turn

a)   When sure the area is clear for aerobatics, position the aircraft above a line feature.

b)   Start a loop and continue until the aircraft is over the top and into the second half.

c)   When the aircraft is in a vertical dive, apply aileron and rudder in the intended direction of roll.

d)   Allow the roll to continue for 180° with reference to the line feature, then stop the roll and ease the aircraft gently out of the dive.

e)   Use the surplus speed to gain height then check the reciprocal heading with the line feature.

f)   Now try an aileron turn in the opposite direction.

Half Roll

a)   When sure the area is clear for aerobatics, position the aircraft on a line feature.

b)   From cruising speed commence a barrel roll with the nose well above the horizon.

c)   As the aircraft becomes inverted check the roll with the wings level and centralize the rudder.

d)   Gently ease the stick back and, as the aircraft performs a half loop, throttle back to keep the engine below maximum RPM.

e)   Ease the aircraft out of the dive and use the surplus speed to gain height.

Vertical Figure of Eight

a)   Make a thorough pre-aerobatic search above and below the aircraft and select a line feature on which to position the aircraft so that it leads towards a clearly defined horizon.

21

b)   Go into a shallow dive and while gaining speed for a loop prevent the engine from exceeding maximum permissible RPM.

c)   At the correct speed note the height and execute a loop.

d)   At the end of the loop allow the nose to come up above the horizon and proceed into a half roll.

e)   When the half roll is completed maintain backward pressure on the stick and continue the loop into a roll off the top.

f)   Complete the roll out and note the height which should be similar to that at the beginning of the first loop. The aircraft should still be on the line feature and on its original heading.

Cuban Eight (Horizontal Figure of Eight)

a)   When sure the area is clear for aerobatics, position the aircraft above a line feature.

b)   Go into a loop and continue until the aircraft is over the top.

c)   When the aircraft is in a 45° inverted dive move the stick diagonally forward and sideways in the direction of the roll. Apply a little rudder in the same direction.

d)   When the wings become level stop the roll and proceed into another loop followed by a 180° roll as before.

e)   When the wings become level again ease the aircraft out of the dive, resume level flight or go into another Cuban eight. Alternatively use the surplus speed to regain height. The aircraft should still be on the line feature.

Continuous Half Rolls

a)   When sure the area is clear for aerobatics, position the aircraft on a line feature.

b)   Gain speed for a barrel roll, then ease the aircraft into a 45° climb, opening the throttle as the nose comes up above the horizon.

c)   Hold this attitude and, as the speed decreases, roll the aircraft into the inverted position, then ease the stick back and complete the half roll restricting the engine speed in the usual way.

d)   At the bottom of the loop continue into another 45° climb, allow the speed to decrease and repeat the half roll.

e)   At the bottom of the loop, resume level flight or go into another continuous half roll. Alternatively use the surplus speed to regain height. The aircraft should still be on the line feature.

Four-leaf Clover

a) When sure the area is clear for aerobatics, position the aircraft above two line features crossing one another at 90°.

b) Increase speed in a dive along one arm of the line feature, starting at the intersection, and go into a loop.

c) Continue over the top of the loop until a vertical dive is reached. With reference to the ground feature execute an aileron turn through 90° and ease the aircraft out of the dive.

d) Go into another loop and, when the vertical climbing attitude is reached, relax the backward pressure on the stick, so gaining height. After a brief pause resume backward pressure on the stick and continue over the top of the loop into another 90° aileron turn.

e) Complete two more loops, gaining height as before, followed in each case by a 90° aileron turn.

f) Ease the aircraft out of the final dive and resume straight and level flight on the original heading.

Emergency Exercise (Ex. 21E): Re-starting the Engine (aircraft without electric starters)

Note: It will be necessary to stop the engine before demonstrating this exercise. This procedure was explained on page 204. To re-start the engine

a) Petrol **On**.

b) Mixture **Rich**.

c) Throttle set half open.

d) Ignition **Contact**.

e) Go into a steep dive.

f) If the engine fails to rotate try 'fish-tailing'.

g) Recover from the dive when the height demands and if this fails to re-start the engine prepare for a Forced Landing Without Power.

21E

9 Formation Flying

The aim of this exercise is to teach accuracy and co-ordination in aircraft handling and to relate these skills to aircraft positioning within a formation.

Any number of aircraft flying closely together and controlled by a designated leader is known as a formation. For the purpose of explanation throughout this chapter a formation of three aircraft is considered.

Formation flying found its origins during World War I when, for tactical purposes, fire power could be concentrated and mutual defence strengthened since one aircraft could protect others while itself receiving cover from the remainder of the formation of flight, squadron or wing strength. This in turn promoted confidence and efficiency. Although in civil flying there is no similar need for such tactical benefits the same skills apply as are needed in military formation flying and these skills have their value as a development of basic flying techniques. Formation flying demands accuracy of a high order combined with good airmanship and excellent co-ordination, the end products providing a great deal of enjoyment to participants and spectators alike.

Flight Formations

For the purpose of positioning it is the practice to number each aircraft in a formation. By convention the leader is always No. 1 with odd numbers on the left and even numbers on the right. Formations form the basis of the more complex patterns executed by the relatively large teams of service aircraft that have become an integral part of most flying displays throughout the world.

Fig. 80. 'V' or Vic formation.

'V' or Vic (Fig. 80). When the formating aircraft are of straight-wing design (i.e. unswept), aircraft at positions 2 and 3 will place themselves with wingtips some half-span distance

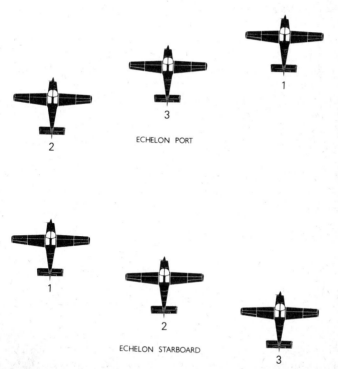

Fig. 81. Echelon formation.

Fig. 82. Line abreast formation.

away from the leader. Their wingtips should be in line with the leader's tailplane.

Echelon (Fig. 81). This formation may be flown either as **Echelon Port** or **Echelon Starboard**. Positioning relative to the leader is similar to the Vic formation.

Line Abreast (Fig. 82). In this formation all aircraft fly in line with wing tips at approximately half-span intervals.

Line Astern (Fig. 83). Aircraft fly behind the leader at intervals of approximately half a length. This formation introduces the problem of slipstream effect, which must be avoided by 'stepping down' below the aircraft ahead as shown in the

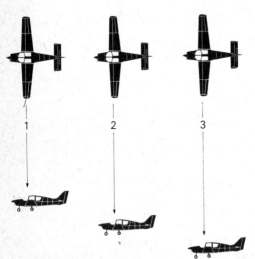

Fig. 83. Line astern formation.
Showing method of avoiding slipstream from the aircraft ahead.

Fig. 84. Box formation.

illustration. Flying within the slipsteam of another aircraft can present severe control difficulties.

Box (Fig. 84). A minimum of four aircraft is required for this formation which is virtually an elongated Vic with the introduction of an aircraft in 'box position' stepped down to avoid slipstream from the leading aircraft.

General Considerations

Of the various factors involved, an ability to judge distance while flying in formation is of prime importance. In everyday life the motorist must indulge in formation driving, maintaining his distance from the car in front while on occasions keeping a safe distance from vehicles in adjoining traffic lanes. When closing with other traffic on the road his assessment of speed and distance is aided by such fixed objects as trees, buildings and of course the road surface itself, to such an extent that the experienced driver will often determine his speed fairly accurately without reference to the speedometer.

In the air no such fixed references exist (other than cloud

22

when this is the vicinity of the formation) so that relative speed between aircraft assumes great importance. Furthermore in addition to **Longitudinal Station Keeping** (i.e. position forward or behind the leader) and **Lateral Station Keeping** (spacing of the aircraft) is the third variable of level relative to the lead aircraft or **Vertical Station Keeping,** an example being the 'step down' position already mentioned in the description of Line Astern and Box formations. Appreciation of closing speed will be enlarged upon under the sub-heading 'Joining Formation in the Air'.

Flying Technique

The main problems associated with formation flying may be considered under the following headings –

Leadership.
Joining formation in the air.
Maintaining station in formation.
Formation manoeuvres –
   (*a*) Formation take-off.
   (*b*) Formation climb.
   (*c*) Formation turns.
   (*d*) Formation descent.
   (*e*) Formation landing.
Formation changes.

Bad-weather formations and formation aerobatics are an advanced development of the art and outside the scope of this book.

Leadership

The success or otherwise of a formation is to a great extent dependent upon good leadership. The leader must observe the following basic rules –

1. He must at all times make his intentions clear to the others in the formation, either over the radio or by the standard hand signals described later in the chapter.

2. He must never lead his formation into a position where the formating aircraft are dangerously close to structures or objects on the ground and he must avoid running his formation into poor weather.

3. He must avoid all sudden movements of the controls, including the throttle.

4. For the formation to be able to maintain station he must choose a cruising speed in the lower range, thus allowing the other aircraft a reasonable excess of power for use in making up lost ground if for any reason they have dropped behind the leader.

5. As a guiding principle the leader must never use full power or fully close the throttle (except in an emergency). The significance of this rule will be apparent later in the text.

Joining Formation in the Air

Although the formation take-off is an essential part of formation flying there are occasions when it is more convenient to form up in the air. The following explanation is intended to assist the student in joining the lead and other aircraft both quickly and safely.

Assuming that the leader has taken off and settled at the agreed cruising speed and height the other aircraft will be some distance behind, flying at a higher speed in order to join formation. For the purpose of simple explanation imagine the leader is flying straight and level with the **Wing** aircraft closing from behind. The sequence of events is similar for each wing aircraft and this explanation is therefore confined to the left or No. 3 position.

As previously mentioned an appreciation of closing speed must be developed. At a distance the only reference available to the formating pilots will be the changing size of the lead aircraft. At ranges in excess of two miles little difference in size will be apparent but, as the closing distance decreases from one mile to say half a mile, the leader will rapidly become larger. Further decreases in separation between the two aircraft will appear as a steadily increasing closing speed. There is a tendency to under-

22

estimate closing speed, particularly during training, and care must be exercised not to over-shoot the leader.

In practice the better method of joining formation is for the lead aircraft to fly in a wide circle while the wing aircraft fly along the radius of the leader's turn (Fig. 85). Since this radius is constantly moving it follows that the wing aircraft must alter heading so that the leader appears on or near the nose of his aircraft. Should the leader move ahead of the nose the joining aircraft will increase its rate of turn and vice versa.

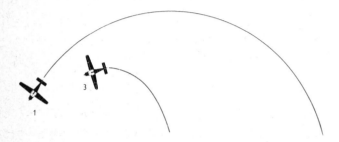

Fig. 85. Joining formation in the air.
No. 3 aircraft approaches along the radius of the leader's turn.

Maintaining Station in Formation

It will be necessary from time to time to make the following corrective adjustments –

1. *An acceleration or deceleration to maintain Longitudinal Station*. This is achieved by fine adjustment of the throttle, taking care not to overcorrect. In practice it is necessary for the formating aircraft to adjust power constantly but all throttle movements must be smooth and as small as possible. Only when the leader has been allowed to move some distance ahead should the wing aircraft apply a larger increase in power and since this will have the side effect of causing a climb above the leader, appropriate elevator adjustments will have to be made. With practice, relative movement between lead and formating aircraft can be anticipated by the latter and corrected on the throttle accordingly.

2. *A gentle turn towards or away from the leader to maintain Lateral Station*. This adjustment is made with aileron and rudder the angle of bank being limited to avoid large changes of heading and, of equal importance, losing sight of the leader. Since this correction may disturb both Longitudinal and Vertical Station Keeping the pilot must be prepared to make appropriate adjustments on the throttle and elevators.

3. *A minor change in height, up or down in relation to the leader to maintain Vertical Station*. Unless the correction is a large one elevator alone is sufficient, larger adjustments requiring an increase or decrease in power.

Since the foregoing corrections involve changes of position in terms of feet or at the most yards it follows that all control movements must be smooth, gradual and just sufficient to achieve the re-positioning. Smoothness is of particular importance when the wing aircraft is itself being formated upon (e.g. in echelon port or starboard or in large formations) there being a tendency for erratic corrections to magnify towards the outer aircraft causing a 'whiplash effect' in the Longitudinal and Vertical planes. This may be avoided by all aircraft using the leader as a reference for Longitudinal and Vertical station keeping while Lateral separation is attained by judging distance from the adjacent aircraft.

All aircraft in the formation must avoid violent over-corrections since for reasons already explained these are likely to cause a chain reaction which in extreme cases may result in some of the aircraft having to take evasive action.

Formation Manoeuvres

(*a*) *Formation Take-off*. After power checks and pre-take-off vital actions have been completed the leader should position his aircraft on the centre of the runway, the wing aircraft (Nos. 2 and 3) taking up their appropriate positions for a Vic formation. Brake will be applied and the engine opened up to 1,200–2,000 RPM. After ascertaining that the other aircraft are ready (by radio or hand signal) the leader will release his brakes and begin the take-off. At no time should full power be used, otherwise, the formating aircraft will find it impossible to keep station.

22

With most light aircraft some 50–60 per cent throttle opening should be adequate for take-off, thus leaving plenty of power in hand for the wing aircraft to maintain position.

While the leader is concentrating on the take-off the formating aircraft must confine their attention to the leader, maintaining direction on him and lifting off as the leader becomes airborne. Any attempt to look ahead in the normal way during take-off may create a risk of collision.

When a box formation is taking-off the aircraft in box position must delay lift-off until the other aircraft are at a sufficient height to allow avoidance of the leader's slipstream.

(*b*) *Formation Climb*. When flaps have been used during take-off the leader will delay raising them until the formation has settled into the climb and then only after prior warning. The climb presents no special problem but the leader must *not* use full throttle.

Fig. 86. Formation turn seen from ahead.
Note that although the inner aircraft has dropped below No. 1 while the outer aircraft has climbed above, the relative positions of the lead aircraft and Nos. 2 and 3 remain as for straight and level flight.

(*c*) *Formation Turns*. During turns the formation must bank as a unit. A little thought will reveal that, other than in line astern, were aircraft to bank individually the pilot on the inside of the turn would lose sight of the leader and the leader would lose sight of the aircraft on the outside of the turn. Therefore as the turn is initiated the aircraft on the inside will drop below leader while the outside aircraft will raise above, all aircraft maintaining position relative to one another (Fig. 86). During the turn the outer aircraft will fly on a larger radius than the leader while the inner aircraft will fly on a smaller radius. Although the differences in airspeed between the three aircraft are small they are nevertheless significant, making it necessary for the outside aircraft to increase power while the inside aircraft reduces power. Fig. 87 shows that when the lead aircraft is settled in a rate 1 turn at 100 MPH the corresponding speeds for the inner and outer aircraft are 98·2 MPH and 101·8 MPH respectively (assuming 50 ft separation between flight paths).

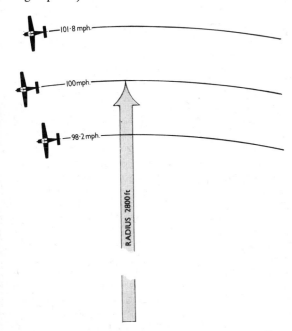

Fig. 87. Difference in speed of aircraft in a formation.
Rate 1 turn (flight paths at a spacing of approximately 50 ft).

Although the difference in speed between aircraft remains constant irrespective of the speed of the leader, spacing has a direct effect and is the main factor limiting large formations

22

turning in Vic or Line abreast. For example in a formation made up of seven light aircraft the approximate difference in airspeed between the inner and outer positions, during a rate 1 turn would be in the region of 9·6 kt (11 MPH).

In Line Astern the stepped down aircraft turn on a larger radius than the leader (Fig. 88).

Fig. 88. Turning in line astern (seen from ahead).
Note that No. 2 must turn on a slightly greater radius than the leader while No. 3, the rearmost aircraft, will turn on a still larger radius.

In the early stages of training, pilots flying on the outside of a turn may gain the impression on occasions that there exists a danger of slipping in towards the leader. This cannot occur if horizontal station keeping is maintained with aileron and rudder in the normal manner.

(d) *Formation Descent*. Provided the leader executes all power and configuration changes (e.g. flaps, undercarriage) smoothly and only after the appropriate signal the descent presents no particular problems. Here again at no time should the leader completely close his throttle, since to do so would cause the formating aircraft to overrun. In practice this means that all descents must be powered descents.

(e) *Formation Landing*. In common with all formation man-oeuvres the success or otherwise of a formation landing is very largely in the hands of the leader. He must plan his circuit well ahead, allowing ample time for the formation to settle into the landing configuration at the correct approach speed.

During the approach he must ensure that he is lined up with the centre of the runway so ensuring maximum room either side for the wing aircraft in No. 2 and No. 3 positions. He must constantly bear in mind that to either side of him may lie tall trees or other obstructions which although not in *his* path of descent, could nevertheless be a hazard to another aircraft in his formation. Safety of the formation is at all times the responsibility of the leader.

Power must be left on throughout the approach. Only minor adjustments that are essential to maintain a satisfactory glide path should be made.

At the hold-off the leader will reduce power sufficiently to allow the aircraft to sink to the ground and even after touchdown a little power must be left, or otherwise aircraft 2 and 3 will most likely run past the leader. Only when the formation is finally on the ground may the leader close his throttle.

For the formating aircraft the approach is identical to a formation powered descent. They must concentrate attention on the lead aircraft and ignore the runway ahead. During the pre-hold-off descent check the ground will enter the picture thus enabling the formating pilots to judge the proximity of the ground by watching the lead aircraft. No attempt should be made to complete the landing with normal references to the ground but formation flying should continue until the wheels are felt to have made contact. Usually it is then possible to close the throttle completely (while the leader leaves on a trace of power). As the formation decelerates the landing run may be completed making whatever adjustments are necessary with brake and throttle.

The foregoing exercise may sound both difficult and hazardous. In practice, average pilots require little time to become reasonably proficient. Polish can then be attained with further practice.

Formation Changes

One of the most impressive displays of precision flying is that of well-executed changes in formation. On the other hand, nothing looks more ragged and untidy than aircraft struggling to maintain some semblance of order in the air. The various changes from one formation to another are numerous and it is not the

22

intention in this chapter to list every possible move. In all cases the same considerations apply and may be summarized thus –

1. The leader must make his instructions clear, either by radio or using the standard hand signals listed on page 225.

2. During changes the pilots involved must have all the other aircraft in view since loss of visual contact can be extremely dangerous.

3. All position changes must be gradual, smooth and without violent manoeuvres on any axis.

4. When moving from one side of a formation to the other it will be necessary to avoid slipstream by dropping below the aircraft ahead.

Fig. 89 shows a three-aircraft formation changing from Vic to Echelon Starboard. The leader will give the radio command 'YELLOW FORMATION (or whatever call sign has been agreed) ECHELON STARBOARD, ECHELON STARBOARD—GO' when the No. 3 aircraft will gently reduce power to slowly drift one length behind No. 2 on the other side of the leader. At the same time he will drop below the other aircraft so avoiding their slipstream during the cross over. He will then apply a little bank and rudder to the right and *slowly* drift across behind the leader and No. 2 keeping them in view all the time, until he is a safe distance to starboard of No. 2, when, with the aid of a little power he will raise his aircraft to the same level as the formation and pull forward to the correct position, i.e. wingtip opposite the elevator of No. 2.

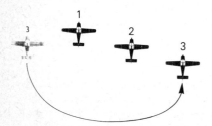

Fig. 89. Formation change from Vic to Echelon Starboard.

Standard Signals

By Radio

In principle the leader will repeat his instructions twice followed by the command 'Go' when the formation will take action accordingly. It is usual to have an agreed call sign for the formation although this need not be used except after long periods of silence. When the instruction applies to a particular aircraft in the formation the message will commence with the words 'number three aircraft' or 'number two' as the case may be.

By Hand

A comprehensive list of hand signals has been evolved by the RAF but only those applicable to civil formation flying have been included in the following table. Action is taken by the formation at the end of the signal, usually when the leader's hand is lowered.

GENERAL	
COMMAND	LEADER'S SIGNAL
1. Run up engine	Forefinger held upwards above head and rotated in the horizontal plane.
2. Ready for take-off	Thumb up to each pilot in the formation.
3. Commence take-off	Chopping action towards windscreen with edge of hand held flat with fingers together.
4. Increase power	Forward nod of head.
5. Decrease power	Backward movement of head.
6. Turning	Start with forearms vertical and palm of hand in line of flight then move slowly in direction of intended turn.
7. Straight ahead	As for command 3.

22

8. Flaps	Hand held in view, fingers and thumb together then opened several times followed by hand up for 'up' or hand down for 'down'.
9. Undercarriage	Forearm vertical, fist clenched and moved up for 'up' and down for 'down'.
10. Climbing	Point forefinger upwards.
11. Descending	Point forefinger downwards.
12. Levelling out	Side-to-side movement of hand held palm down at face level.
13. Break formation	Rapid side-to-side movement of hand held fingers apart, palm forward and at face level.
14. I am returning/ you are to return to base	Point at self (or aircraft which is to return) then point downwards.
15. What is your fuel state?	Clenched fist with thumb in mouth, head back in drinking attitude. OTHER AIRCRAFT ANSWER – My fuel is low – as for command 15. Fuel sufficient – thumb up. Fuel gauge u/s – as for command 15 followed by thumb down.
	FORMATION CHANGES
16. Take over as leader	Point to new leader then indicate No. 1 position by raising forefinger above head.
17. Line abreast	Hold forearm level with hand extended and line up with wing span.
18. Echelon	Point to aircraft concerned then move hand across face towards the new position (i.e. port or starboard).
19. Line astern	Clenched fist, thumb extended moved rearwards, 'hitch hike' fashion.
20. Reform Vic (or basic formation as briefed)	Rock wings of aircraft.

22

	EMERGENCY SIGNALS
21. Your aircraft is on fire	Fly alongside burning aircraft, rock wings to attract pilot's attention then simulate throat-cutting action with fingers until pilot acknowledges (thumb-up signal).
22. My electrics have failed	Map, Flight Plan or piece of paper held against the canopy.
23. My transmitter has failed	Hold up or tap microphones then give thumb-down signal.
24. My receiver has failed (or total failure of R/T equipment)	Tap earphone then give thumb-down signal.

Flight Practice

OUTSIDE CHECKS

a) Altitude: Sufficient for the exercise.
b) Location: Clear of cloud and outside controlled airspace.
c) Position: Check in relation to a known landmark.

AIR EXERCISE

Joining Formation in the Air

Leader
a) Fly in a wide circle and at a low cruising speed.
b) Allow the formating aircraft to take up position.
c) Shortly before the required heading is attained signal 'straight ahead' then gently roll out of the turn.

Formating Pilots
a) Locate the lead aircraft and fly towards him on the inside of his turn. Keep a lookout for other aircraft.
b) As the lead aircraft begins to move backwards relative to you be prepared to reduce power. Avoid over-shooting the leader.

22

c)   Make fine adjustments to power as necessary and position the aircraft some two to three wing-spans away from the leader and approximately one length behind.

d)   Be prepared for the 'straight ahead' signal, then roll the wings level in unison with the leader.

Maintaining Station in Formation

Leader

a)   Concentrate on maintaining an accurate height and heading.

b)   All corrections for height, heading and turbulence must be gentle and progressive.

Formating Pilots

(Assumed to be in the position described under 'Joining Formation').

Longitudinal Station Keeping

a)   Using the throttle ease the aircraft forward until the wingtip is opposite the tailplane of the lead aircraft. Maintain longitudinal station by constant throttle adjustment as required, if necessary over the whole range of movement.

b)   Be prepared for a gain in height with large applications of power and a loss in height when the throttle is closed.

c)   Practice anticipating minor adjustments to power so that throttle movements are reduced to a minimum.

Lateral Station Keeping

a)   Using very light aileron pressure, drift in until the wingtip is approximately one span from the tailplane of the lead aircraft.

b)   Maintain lateral station with gentle use of aileron coordinated with rudder. Never apply steep bank.

c)   If at any time aircraft appears to be drifting too close to the leader turn away without delay.

d)   Avoid flying with crossed controls by keeping the wings level.

e)   Now practice maintaining lateral station at half span from the leader's tailplane.

Vertical Station Keeping

a)   With gentle use of elevator hold the aircraft at the same level as the leader.

b)   Check that aircraft is correctly trimmed.

c) Avoid all harsh movement, particularly when there is a danger of climbing above the leader.

d) When large changes of power are required maintain vertical station with the elevators.

e) If for any reason the lead aircraft cannot be seen turn away immediately.

f) Practice maintaining station so that all corrections are minimal.

Formation Climb

Leader

a) Make the appropriate radio or visual signal prior to the climb. Check that it is safe to climb.

b) Open the throttle leaving a power margin for the following aircraft.

c) Ease into the climbing attitude.

d) To resume level flight make the appropriate radio or visual signal. Check that it is clear to level out.

e) Gradually lower the nose to the level flight attitude.

f) As speed approaches the required formation cruising speed reduce power to the correct setting.

Formating Pilots

a) On receiving the radio or visual signal to climb be prepared to open the throttle.

b) As the leader goes into the climb maintain station in the usual way using all controls.

c) On receiving the signal for the return to level flight follow the leader, easing forward on the stick and adjusting power as required to maintain longitudinal station.

Formation Descent

Leader

a) Make the appropriate radio or visual signal prior to the descent. Check that it is safe to descend.

b) Reduce power to achieve the required rate of descent but on no account must the throttle be fully closed.

c) Changes in airspeed must be gradual and if flap is required to steepen the descent the 'flaps down' signal must first be given.

d) When resuming level flight give the appropriate signal well in advance before attaining the required height. Check that it is clear to level out then gradually increase to cruising power.

22

Formating Pilots

a)   After receiving the signal to descend be prepared to reduce power.

b)   Maintain station in the usual way using all controls.

c)   When lowering or raising flap be prepared for a displacement from station and a change in trim.

d)   On receiving the signal to level out maintain station by opening the throttle and raising the nose in unison with the leader.

Formation Turns

Leader

a)   Give the appropriate radio or visual signal for a turn in the required direction. Check that it is safe to turn.

b)   Gently roll into a medium turn. Check for balance and correct height.

c)   Throughout the turn keep looking out and ensure that the formation remains clear of cloud, other aircraft and high ground.

d)   Well before the required heading is reached signal 'straight ahead'. Check that it is safe to stop the turn.

e)   Gently roll out of the turn. Check for balance and height.

Formating Pilots

a)   Watch the leader for a signal to turn.

Pilot Inside the Turn

b)   Roll into the turn holding the wings at the same angle as the leader at the same time dropping below his aircraft to maintain vertical station.

c)   Be prepared to reduce power slightly and maintain station as if flying straight and level.

d)   Look for the signal to fly straight ahead.

e)   Roll out of the turn in unison with the leader at the same time raising the aircraft to maintain vertical station.

f)   Be prepared to increase power slightly.

Pilot Outside the Turn

b)   Roll into the turn holding the wings at the same angle as the leader, at the same time raising above his aircraft to maintain vertical station.

c) Be prepared to increase power slightly and maintain station as if flying straight and level.

d) Look for the signal to fly straight ahead.

e) Roll out of the turn in unison with the leader, at the same time lowering the aircraft to maintain vertical station.

f) Be prepared to reduce power slightly.

Formation Take-off

Leader

a) Give the signal to run up. Complete vital actions then, when clear, taxi to the centre of the take-off area.

b) Allow the aircraft to run forward a few yards to ensure that the nosewheel/tailwheel is straight.

c) Apply brake and allow the formation to take up position.

d) By radio or visual signal obtain confirmation that the formation is ready for take-off, open the throttle slightly, give the take-off signal then release the brakes.

e) Check that the formation is maintaining station then slowly move the throttle to the half-open position.

f) Concentrate on keeping straight then, at the correct speed, gently lift the aircraft off the ground.

g) Allow the speed to build up naturally, then climb away.

h) Except in emergency the throttle should never be more than two-thirds open.

Formating Pilots

a) Look for the signal to run up. Complete the vital actions then follow the leader onto the take-off area and take up the pre-arranged position.

b) Apply brake then open up to approximately 1,200 RPM.

c) Watch the leader for the signal to take-off then release the brakes.

d) Maintain longitudinal station by progressively opening the throttle and lateral station with use of rudder. Concentrate on the leader and make no attempt to watch the airfield boundary.

e) Rotate the aircraft in unison with the leader and when the aircraft leaves the ground maintain station in the normal manner.

Formation Landing

Leader

a) Position the formation on the downwind leg which should be

22

further away from the airfield than usual.

b) Complete the normal downwind vital actions (BUMPF) and after giving the appropriate signal, lower the first stage of flap.

c) Fly far enough downwind to ensure a long straight-in approach then turn on to base leg. Reduce speed gradually to that required for an engine assisted approach.

d) At no time should the throttle be completely closed.

e) When clear to land, turn the formation on to finals. If conditions require more flap give the signal early in the approach.

f) Adjust the approach with throttle in the usual way, making sure that some power is left on at all times. Look out for obstructions likely to affect others in the formation.

g) At the correct height above the ground progressively check the descent and reduce power sufficiently to allow the aircraft to sink to the ground.

h) Concentrate on keeping straight and leave on a little power until it is safe to use the brakes, then throttle back completely.

i) Ensure that the formating aircraft are maintaining station then gently apply brake, bringing the formation to a halt.

j) Taxi off the landing area, complete the post-landing checks then lead the formation back to the parking area.

Formating Pilots

a) When on the downwind leg complete the normal vital actions (BUMPF) without diverting too much attention from the leader.

b) Look out for the 'flaps down' signal and be prepared to lower first stage.

c) Follow the leader around the circuit and when on the base leg be prepared to reduce power, if necessary completely closing the throttle.

d) Maintain station and be prepared to turn on to the approach.

e) Look out for the signal to lower full flap (if required).

f) During the approach concentrate on the lead aircraft and resist the temptation to watch the airfield.

g) As the landing area comes into view be prepared for the lead aircraft to raise the nose and check the descent. Make no attempt to look along the left of the nose but watch the lead aircraft and the ground beneath its wheels. Maintain station so that contact with the ground is felt as the leader touches down.

h) During the landing run be prepared to close the throttle completely and use brake as required to maintain station.

i) On no account overrun the leader but bring the aircraft to a halt in formation with the other aircraft.

j) Follow the lead aircraft off the landing area, complete the post-landing checks then taxi in formation to the parking area.

Formation Changes

Note: A member of a formation may be instructed to change to any position or to take over the leadership of the formation. In all changes the same basic principles apply and the following air instruction is confined to the change from No. 3 position in a Vic formation to Echelon Starboard. Other than giving the correct visual or radio signal the leader takes no action throughout this procedure.

Formating Pilot (in No. 3 position)

a) Look out for the Echelon Starboard signal from the leader.
b) Reduce power slightly and drop below the leader to avoid slipstream from the other aircraft.
c) Move approximately one length behind the other formating aircraft in No. 2 position.
d) Apply very gentle bank to the right, no more than a few degrees, then drift across and behind the other aircraft.
e) Keep the formation in sight at all times.
f) When approximately one span to the right of No. 2 aircraft level the wings, open the throttle and move up into position with the wingtip aligned with the tailplane of No. 2.
g) Maintain vertical station on the leader and longitudinal and lateral station with reference to No. 2.

Important

To achieve the high degree of airmanship and sense of awareness that are required in practising these exercises it is essential that all formation flying is preceded by a thorough pre-flight briefing. This will include –
  (a) The exercises to be practised.
  (b) Weather (visibility, turbulence, cloudbase, etc.).
  (c) Duration.
  (d) Area.
  (e) Call sign and RT frequencies approved by ATC.
  (f) Signals to be used.
  (g) Actions in event of emergencies.

10　Multi-engine Conversion

Part I of this exercise is a conversion on to multi-engine aircraft using applicable sections of the single-engine syllabus. Part II, Asymmetric Power Flight, is intended to demonstrate the immediate and subsequent actions required to retain control of a multi-engined aircraft when one or more engines fail.

Part I

The first section of the two-part conversion course is confined to normal flight with all engines operating, using the following exercises from the CAA approved single-engine syllabus–

1, 1E, 2, 4, 5, 5E, 6, 7, 8, 9, 10, 12, 13, 13E, 15 and 19

A multi-engine aircraft may possibly provide the pilot with his first experience of constant-speed propellers (page 48) and the retractable undercarriage. These, together with the importance of correct loading (weight and balance, Chapter 3, Vol. 4), a more detailed understanding of take-off and landing performance, limiting speeds and all matters relating to the operation of multi-engine aircraft form part of the ground course.

Part II　Asymmetric Power Flight

Notwithstanding the improved reliability of the modern power plant, flying with one or more engines failed must be fully understood and practised by the pilot during visual and instrument flight. Since for practical purposes an engine failure on a 'twin' presents a similar situation to loss of two engines on the same side of a 'four', in the interest of simplicity a twin-engine aircraft is referred to throughout the following text.

In normal flight, thrust on a twin-engine aircraft is divided equally port and starboard of the centre line. Failure of one engine confines all thrust to the live motor side and this, together with drag from the windmilling propeller, will initiate a yaw towards the dead engine. The yaw will induce a roll and this will be further assisted by slipstream from the live engine which is situated on the up-going wing. If this sequence of events (illustrated in Fig. 90) remains unchecked a steep spiral dive will develop.

From the foregoing it follows that when an engine fails the resultant yaw must be checked immediately by firm application of rudder towards the live engine. In some aircraft considerable physical effort is required and full use should be made of the rudder trim. An aircraft flying with off-set thrust is said to be on **Asymmetric Power**. Modern multi-engine aircraft may be trimmed to fly 'hands off' in asymmetric flight – however a small bank angle of up to 15° towards the live engine can be beneficial when rudder trim proves inadequate, otherwise it is probably best to maintain lateral level.

Engine failure will be accompanied by a loss of height unless the angle of attack is increased. However to maintain height on half the normal cruising power would require an angle of attack considerably greater than best lift/drag angle, an inefficient mode of flight which must engender still lower airspeed. This in turn will pose another problem; reduced airflow over the rudder at a time when it is required to oppose the asymmetric thrust from the live engine. Therefore during asymmetric flight it is the practice to select an airspeed somewhere between normal cruising and the inefficient low speed mentioned. This is known as **Best Single-engine Speed** and it is chosen for the best performance (air miles/gallon, cruising speed and controllability) while flying with an engine inoperative. Any attempt to fly faster or slower than this speed will cause a deterioration in performance.

To maintain height at best single-engine speed it will be necessary to increase power on the live engine.

23

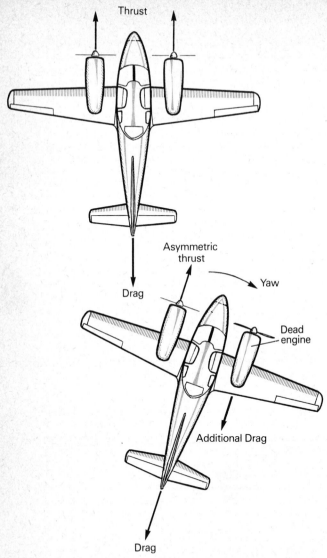

Fig. 90. Power failure on a twin-engined aircraft.
The top picture shows the aircraft in normal flight. Failure of the
starboard engine (lower illustration) causes a yaw to the right,
accentuated by additional drag from the windmilling propeller.

Aerodynamic Considerations

Minimum Control Speed

When an engine fails the yaw which occurs must be controlled and mention has already been made of the important function of the rudder for the purpose. In common with all aerodynamic surfaces, the rudder is dependent upon airflow for its function so that under single-engine conditions full rudder may be needed to hold the aircraft straight when the airspeed is low. For any particular power setting on the live engine, the amount of rudder needed to hold the aircraft straight will increase as the airspeed is decreased until full rudder is reached when any further decrease in airspeed will cause a yaw towards the dead engine. This is called the **Minimum Control Speed** and it represents the lowest speed at which the aircraft can be flown on one engine while keeping straight. Obviously minimum control speed will alter according to the amount of power on the live engine; the higher the power, the more yaw caused by the live engine and therefore the higher the speed required by the rudder to keep straight, or in other words the higher the minimum control speed. While power is the main factor determining the minimum control speed there are others and these are listed below.

1. *Altitude*. The effect of power on the minimum control speed was explained in the previous paragraph. It therefore follows that, at full-throttle altitude where maximum power can be developed, the minimum control speed will be highest when the engine is set for maximum power.

2. *Load*. The more weight an aircraft carries the greater will be its wing loading. This in turn means that for any speed a heavily loaded aircraft must fly at a greater angle of attack than its lightly loaded counterpart. The larger angle of attack induces more drag which must be overcome by greater thrust and, since it has been established that higher power causes a higher minimum control speed, it follows that the more heavily loaded the aircraft the higher will be its minimum control speed.

3. *Critical Engine*. On twin-engined aircraft both propellers usually rotate in the same direction although there are excep-

23

tions to this arrangement. The effects of slipstream and engine torque on the directional stability of the aircraft are explained on page 55. Additionally when an engine fails the airspeed must be reduced and this is associated with a more nose-up attitude when asymmetric blade effect will occur (page 56). If, when seen from behind, the propellers turn clockwise the centre of thrust will shift to the right bringing thrust from the port engine closer to the aireraft's centre line and moving starboard thrust further away. The resultant greater leverage of starboard thrust will produce more yawing effect so that minimum control speed will be higher when the port engine fails. This is known as the **Critical Engine**. When propeller rotation is anti-clockwise the starboard engine is critical.

4. *Drag*. Since drag must be overcome by thrust it follows that higher drag necessitates more power which will increase the tendency to yaw and the chain of effects results in a higher minimum control speed. Drag must be kept to a minimum by all the means at the disposal of the pilot; undercarriage up, flaps up and even windows or hatches closed.

5. *Flaps*. The effect of flaps on minimum control speed is difficult to define, their effect being dependent upon aircraft design, type of flap and the circumstances at the time of engine failure. As a general principle it is better to consider flaps under the heading of drag and keep them 'up' unless there are special recommendations for the aircraft type.

6. *Windmilling*. 'Fixed-pitch' propellers cause drag while windmilling on a dead engine and so contribute to the undesirable yaw. A variable-pitch propeller causes most drag when windmilling in 'fine' pitch so that by selecting 'coarse' pitch the minimum control speed can be lowered. When the propeller can be 'feathered', drag will be still less and the minimum control speed will decrease accordingly.

7. *Pilot Limitations*. Determined by the strength and skill of the pilot.

The implications of minimum control speed should be fully understood. It is not intended that the aircraft should be flown at this speed when an engine has failed; rather, it represents the **23** minimum for fully controlled flight at any particular power setting. Airspeed must be maintained above this critical speed when an engine fails even if in so doing a loss of height is entailed. This is bound to happen when the emergency occurs above the aircraft's single-engine ceiling.

A gentle dive will increase the airspeed when it has decreased below minimum control speed but when there is insufficient height for this procedure power will have to be reduced on the live engine in order to keep straight. Alternatively a combination of both methods can be advantageous to regain minimum control speed.

Under normal flight conditions the aircraft's performance is limited at the lower end by the stalling speed which tends to decrease with the addition of power. Under asymmetric power conditions the lower limit is determined by the minimum control speed and this increases with the addition of power from the live engine.

Engine Considerations

With the reduction in total power which follows the failure of an engine, rate of climb, cruising speed and ceiling deteriorate. Additionally the aircraft's range will be less on one engine than two. This less obvious fact will perhaps surprise many students so that an explanation is warranted. When flying for maximum range with both engines the aircraft will be at its best lift/drag ratio angle of attack with the engines at a setting which provides the most economical speed/horse-power ratio. At this power setting it will be possible to select 'weak' mixture without fear of overheating the engines and the RPM will be relatively low so further increasing fuel economy. When an engine fails the live engine will be called upon to produce extra power to maintain best single-engine speed and 'rich' mixture will have to be selected before the throttle can be opened beyond the 'weak' mixture range. Furthermore in order to obtain the extra power, RPM must be increased by selecting a finer pitch on the propeller control and a descent may have to be made from the best altitude for range. This adds up to a higher fuel consumption in gallons per hour compared with usual cruising consump-

23

tion, coupled with a considerable decrease in cruising speed so that as the 'gallons per hour' increase, the 'miles per hour' decrease and the net result is a shorter range. In fact while there are a number of alternative economical speeds for an aircraft under normal conditions, the choice is greatly reduced when flying on one engine.

Although best single-engine speed will demand higher than usual cruising power from the live engine this must not exceed 'maximum continuous power setting' except in emergencies, and a careful watch should be maintained on oil pressure, oil temperature and cylinder-head temperature. However, some modern aero engines are cleared for continuous operation at maximum power and this will be stated in the Owner's/Flight/Operating Manual. Other factors affecting the amount of power required from the live engine are –

1. *Load*. At any speed the increased angle of attack resulting from a heavy load in an aircraft induces more drag which in consequence demands more power to maintain flight. The amount of power required from the live engine can be reduced by jettisoning all removable and unnecessary load (if the aircraft type allows), although the single-engine performance of modern aircraft should ensure that these steps are only necessary under the most unfavourable conditions.

2. *Altitude*. When flying at low altitudes it is easier to maintain height without overtaxing the live engine because the air is denser than that at height so a gradual descent at best single-engine speed (topography permitting) will ensure that the live engine is not being forced to maintain an unnecessarily high altitude. Remember that on one engine the aircraft's ceiling is bound to be lower than when flying on two.

3. *Outside Air Temperature*. At any particular height the air will be denser when the temperature is low. Temperature changes affect the single-engine ceiling of an aircraft and it has been calculated that a 10° C increase in outside air temperature will produce an effect similar to a 3% increase in all-up weight.

The principles governing single-engine flight having been explained, it now remains to apply them to engine failure during differing flight conditions.

23

Failure of an Engine during Cruising Flight

In principle the various corrective actions to be taken when an engine fails can be divided into two categories –

1. *Immediate Actions:* those necessary to maintain control while an attempt is made to find the cause of engine failure and if possible effect a remedy.

2. *Subsequent Actions:* these are taken to make the aircraft fly as efficiently as possible when it is found necessary to continue the flight on one engine.

When an engine fails during cruising flight both the immediate and subsequent actions are usually straightforward enough and it is largely a question of applying these in sequence. There are of course many types of aircraft and their single-engine characteristics may differ to a marked degree so that slight variation in procedure may be necessary from one design to another. Since this is a training manual, reference is made to twin-engined aircraft throughout the explanations which follow.

Imagine the starboard engine has failed without warning during cruising flight –

Immediate Actions

1. Prevent yaw with rudder and if necessary maintain lateral level with aileron towards the live engine, in this case to the left. The yaw must on no account be allowed to develop.

2. Attain recommended best single-engine speed.

3. Identify the failed engine. The leg applying rudder is adjacent to the live engine so identify the failed one by saying out loud 'dead leg – dead engine'. Experience has shown that in a real emergency it is not unknown that the live engine has been stopped as a result of haste.

4. Decide whether or not to feather according to circumstances. Fire or a serious mechanical fault accompanied by excess vibration and noise or oil and/or smoke coming from the engine nacelle is usually apparent. In these cases the propeller must be feathered immediately to stop rotation of the engine which would, if allowed to continue, cause further damage. When loss of power is not accompanied by any of these

23

symptoms it may be possible to re-start the engine therefore –

5. Open up power on the live engine to prevent loss of height.

6. Find the cause of engine failure, check –

> Ignition switches
> Fuel contents
> Fuel pressure
> Carburettor heat
> Mixture control

If necessary select another fuel tank and in case failure has resulted from a faulty mechanical pump switch on the electric fuel pump. Fully close the throttle to the failed engine and slowly re-open to ascertain if power is available. Should the engine fail to re-start close the throttle again, move the mixture control to idle cut-off, switch off fuel and ignition and –

7. Feather. The procedure so far described will have taken a matter of seconds and it now only remains to ensure that the aircraft is safeguarded by adopting correct post-failure procedures. Before a landing can be made it may be necessary to continue the flight for several hundred miles with an engine inoperative so that the following subsequent actions are of prime importance.

Subsequent Actions

1. Safeguard the instrument and electric supply. In some aircraft it may be necessary to select an alternative vacuum source. When the generator/alternator on the live engine is unable to support the aircraft's demands, every possible economy should be made in the use of electrical equipment since the battery will be the only other source of supply.

2. Tanks may be selected for asymmetric flight. By now fuel will have been cut off from the failed engine and the pilot may cross-feed this to the live engine as required. To prevent air locks in the system management of the fuel cocks must be fully understood.

3. Airframe clean-up. It is important to reduce drag to a minimum and although flaps and undercarriage will be up

23

during cruising flight their position must be checked in case 'creep' has allowed them to move from the fully retracted position. Cooling flaps or gills must, if possible, be closed and since open cabin windows can incur a noticeable drag penalty these too must be shut. Accurate trim is important.

4. Revise the flight plan and notify air traffic control accordingly. Choose a suitable cruising altitude. As a guiding principle a low height consistent with safety is best suited to asymmetric flight.

If the aircraft is above its single-engined ceiling no attempt should be made to keep it there by overtaxing the live engine or holding up the nose but a gradual descent to a lower level and denser air should follow. When for reasons of terrain clearance a descent must be delayed it may be necessary to jettison any removable and unnecessary load, assuming a window can be opened. This is of particular importance in hot climates (page 240). Temperatures and oil pressure on the live engine must be watched.

Actions following an engine failure during cruising flight may be remembered by the mnemonic –

PAID OFF STAR (*see* air exercise)

This exercise can readily be practised but care should be taken not to allow the stopped engine to go completely cold, although a drop in temperature cannot be avoided. The exercise should be practised with each engine stopped in turn. In the case of most light twins an engine should not be feathered below 3,000 ft AGL. Below that height zero thrust should be used (page 252). When an aeroplane is flying on one engine the actual flight path is out of line with its fore and aft axis although no slip or skid will be indicated on the turn and slip indicator. The amount of 'crab' is negligible unless accurate navigation over featureless country is involved; but when even limited radio facilities exist this aspect is of academic interest only.

When failure is the result of fire or mechanical fault no attempt should be made to re-start the engine.

23

Instrument Indications

Should an engine fail while cruising on instruments the same actions are involved as for visual flight. The following indications are given –

1. *Artificial Horizon:* a roll towards the dead engine coupled with a nose-down pitch.
2. *Turn and Slip Indicator:* the ball will indicate a skid towards the live engine while the turn needle will show a yaw towards the dead engine.
3. *Direction Indicator:* turn towards the dead engine.

After the initial failure but before the application of additional power on the live engine both the vertical-speed indicator and the altimeter will show a loss of height.

Engine Fire Drill in the Air

The considerations governing fire in the air were explained in Vol. 1, Chapter 1. The same procedure is applicable to twin- and multi-engined aircraft except that there is often a fire warning system as well as a more comprehensive fire-extinguisher system or spray ring. On those aircraft fitted with feathering propellers it is a simple matter to stop rotation of the burning engine.

Asymmetric-powered Medium and Steep Turns

On modern twins turns both with and against the live engine are accomplished without difficulty provided (*a*) the aircraft is trimmed so that no rudder loads exist and (*b*) the airspeed is sufficient for the angle of bank. The ball of the turn and slip indicator will reveal a slip if the speed is too low for the amount of bank. Remember that no more rudder may be available to correct this so that bank will have to be reduced. Turns can be made in either direction and the roll-out is quite normal when the aircraft is correctly trimmed, but it is important to keep the ball of the turn and slip indicator in the centre throughout all turns.

When the aircraft cannot be trimmed to fly 'feet off' it is preferable to make turns towards the live engine since the return to straight flight will be easier although the turn may require a little more effort to initiate. As in straight flight on one engine, alterations in speed and/or power will affect rudder response and the addition of power in a steep turn will of course raise the critical speed. The angle of bank during turns on one engine should be kept below that which is normal for the manoeuvre when flying on both engines.

Engine Failure during Turns

Should an engine fail during a turn the behaviour of the aircraft is largely a question of which engine fails and the direction of turn. When the engine on the inside of the turn fails, all of the remaining power is concentrated on the outside and there will be a tendency for the bank to increase. The turn will tighten up and unless the situation is checked a spiral dive will result. In the extreme case it may be necessary to throttle back the live engine before straight and level flight can be regained.

Conversely when the live engine is on the inside of the turn, as it will be should the engine on the outside fail, the aeroplane will have a tendency to roll out of the turn and the pilot must be prepared to apply coarse rudder and on occasions aileron towards the live engine, because a yaw will develop in the opposite direction to the turn as soon as the wings become level (Fig. 91).

Whether the engine failure is inside or on the outside of the turn the sequence of events which follows is as outlined under 'Failure of an Engine during Cruising Flight'.

Failure of an Engine during Take-off

The single-engine performance of modern twins is so improved that on some types it is possible to take-off from a standstill on one engine although such a procedure is usually reserved for

23

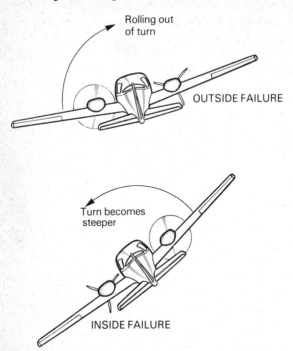

Fig. 91. Engine failure during turns.

demonstration pilots whose task it is to impress others with the capabilities of the aircraft. Nevertheless an unexpected engine failure during take-off is a very different proposition from a deliberate demonstration where the controls are properly set in advance, and it represents the most serious form of engine failure because two important factors are working against one another – the airspeed is low and the power from the live engine is at its maximum.

Minimum control speed applicable to the take-off configuration (i.e. undercarriage down, take-off flap, maximum power on the critical engine and a windmilling propeller on the failed engine) is known as **Minimum Control Speed, Airborne.** Since it represents the minimum speed *under ideal conditions* below which it will not be possible to maintain direction an engine failure below minimum control speed must entail abandoning the take-off because the live engine will have to be throttled back if the runway is not to be departed. As a target safety speed during take-off, minimum control speed is therefore of marginal value and although the speed will be quoted in the aircraft flight manual a safety margin is added to minimum control speed which is then called **Safety Speed.** For aircraft of up to 12,500 lb maximum weight, minimum control or, ideally, safety speed should be attained before lift-off.

Safety speed assumes the following conditions –

(*a*) Aircraft at its maximum authorized all-up weight.

(*b*) The live engine is at its maximum take-off power.

(*c*) The pilot is of average physique and ability.

(*d*) The undercarriage and flaps are not yet retracted.

(*e*) Sudden and complete failure of the engine which produces the most yaw (critical engine).

(*f*) The propeller on the dead engine still in 'fine' pitch.

(*g*) It must be possible for pilot of average ability to maintain control under the foregoing conditions without re-trimming and with the application of rudder and aileron only.

Although conditions for safety speed assume that initially the pilot will be called upon to maintain direction before he has time to retract the undercarriage, feather the propeller on the dead engine or re-trim, rudder control must be sufficient to avoid having to reduce the power on the live engine all of which will usually be needed to keep the aircraft in the air immediately after take-off.

The actions which follow the immediate correction after engine failure are dependent upon the phase of the take-off, but the significance of safety speed is quite simple: once the aircraft has left the ground safety speed must be maintained and exceeded before any attempt is made to climb away.

On take-off the engine may fail during one of these stages –

1. While accelerating on the ground.
2. Airborne above minimum control but below safety speed.
3. Airborne above safety speed.

23

Engine Failure while still on the Ground

The risk of damage to the aircraft under these circumstances is negligible provided the resultant swing can be checked and the aircraft brought to a halt before it runs off the airfield. Both throttles should be closed immediately and the swing corrected with coarse use of rudder assisted with brake. When collision with an obstruction seems unavoidable both fuel and ignition should be turned off and the mixture moved to idle cut-off. If necessary violent avoiding action must be taken.

Engine Failure after Take-off before Safety Speed has been Reached

Runway length permitting safety speed should be attained before take-off although an engine failure above minimum control speed should be containable. Below minimum control speed, a potentially dangerous situation, it will be impossible to maintain directional control without reducing power on the live engine. Unless the aircraft is lightly loaded height will then be lost when the situation must be treated as power failure after take-off on a single-engine aircraft. This means that the best possible forced landing must be made ahead, avoiding obstacles with gentle turns. While some assistance may be forthcoming from the live engine it should never be opened up to the point where directional control is lost. In most cases it is better to land with the undercarriage down and both throttles should be closed and fuel and ignition turned off before the actual touchdown. Experience has shown that a nosewheel undercarriage will protect the occupants from quite major impact. However, tailwheel aircraft can 'nose-over' and these undercarriages should be retracted.

Engine Failure after Take-off when Safety Speed has been Reached

23 It is assumed that the aircraft is capable of climbing on one engine although certain earlier twin-engined designs were unable to gain height unless they were only partially loaded.

The immediate actions are as always when an engine fails – check the yaw with the rudder and aileron. The safety speed must be maintained, holding the level altitude, so that the full power from the live engine can be used. This entails a deliberate forward movement on the elevator control to prevent rapid loss of airspeed. The undercarriage should be retracted after the dead propeller has been identified and feathered and the aircraft retrimmed. Asymmetric drag must be reduced without delay. When there is sufficient height any flap used during the take-off should be raised although there may be contrary recommendations for some types (see aircraft Flight Manual).

The temperatures and oil pressures on the live engine should be monitored although the events which have been outlined take little time and the maximum power limitations on the engine should rarely be exceeded.

While some of the early twin-engine aircraft had a marginal asymmetric climb performance this aspect has been improved on modern types. However it should be remembered that with an engine failed the speed range is greatly reduced, particularly so during the climb. The best single-engine climb speed is now required to be marked on the airspeed indicator as a blue line and when an engine fails it should be climbed at **Blue Line Speed**.

Landing with Asymmetric Power

The pilot should become accustomed to both left- and right-hand circuits with either the port or starboard engine out of action. An asymmetric landing in a modern aircraft is usually quite straightforward. It should be remembered, however, that use of the available power is limited by minimum control speed which, other things being equal, rises as the power is increased.

Because of the burden on the live engine caused by additional drag when the undercarriage is lowered, it may be left retracted until a later than usual stage of the circuit. The time needed to

23

lower and lock the undercarriage will to a large extent dictate when 'wheels down' should be selected, but the base leg is ideal. On the downwind leg the flaps may be lowered to the maximum lift position which for most types means a depression of 15° or so. They are left at this setting until the pilot is sure he can reach the airfield.

With the greatly improved handling characteristics of modern aircraft, a normal engine-assisted approach should be planned. Older types may not be possessed of such excellent asymmetric flight performance when a slightly steeper than usual engine-assisted approach will prove more satisfactory. It will then be possible to reduce power progressively as the airfield boundary draws near, thus avoiding the possibility of an undershoot with little chance of reaching the airfield.

Whatever the asymmetric performance of the aircraft safety speed must be maintained during the approach. Flap should be used according to circumstances but as a guiding principle full application must be left until there is no doubt that the airfield can be reached. A landing should be considered as mandatory once the flaps are fully lowered. With the reduction in power from single-engine cruising conditions, rudder trim will be too much for a 'feet off' approach but it is good practice to leave it in its 'cruising' position so that, should full power be required during an overshoot, directional control will be assisted.

During an approach the decision to land or overshoot will have to be made at a height dependent upon the asymmetric performance of the aircraft. This is known as **Decision Height** or **Committal Height** and it will be listed in the Aircraft Owner's/Flight/Operating Manual.

The actual landing is no different from normal with the exception that the hold-off may, on certain types, be noticeably longer because of the decreased drag from the feathered propeller on the dead engine. On the ground any tendency to swing can only be controlled by use of rudder (nosewheel steering) assisted with brake, but when the swing is towards the live engine power can be added in extreme cases. Some aircraft may prove difficult or impossible to taxi on one engine, but if possible, the runway should be cleared after landing.

23

Asymmetric-powered Overshoot (Flaps and Wheels Down)

With the undercarriage down and locked and the flaps fully extended, drag will be at a very high level so that the decision to overshoot must be taken as early as possible. The minimum height permissible for an overshoot will differ from type to type, and is to a certain extent a question of the pilot's ability. On some aircraft it may be 300 ft and on others 500 ft, while an overshoot once the flaps are fully depressed may be impossible on earlier designs. It is good practice to delay application of full flap until after committal height has been passed. With wheels and flaps down and the live engine at maximum power, minimum speed at which direction can be maintained is referred to as **Minimum Control Speed, Landing.** This will be quoted in the flight manual, but when the aircraft is flown commercially it is usual for the operating company to compile their own operating notes. At no time during the approach may the speed be allowed to fall below minimum control speed.

While the decision is best made on the base leg when there is plenty of height and the flaps are not fully depressed, when the aircraft is badly positioned for a landing or if the runway or landing area is not clear, it may be imperative to break off the approach and go around again. Whenever it is decided to overshoot it should be in the certain knowledge that there is sufficient height for the procedure. Power on the live engine should be increased and as the throttle is opened the nose must be depressed so that safety speed is maintained, thus ensuring that full use can be made of the power available from the live engine. Height may be lost during this stage; this is one of the reasons for the decision or committal height mentioned earlier in the exercise.

Obviously drag must be reduced and when the flaps are raised to achieve this aim a further loss of height may occur. The undercarriage must also be retracted and the decision as to which should be operated first is dependent upon which action will give the quickest decrease in drag. When the flaps are at their 'max. lift' setting, retraction of the undercarriage will give

23

the bigger reduction in drag whereas most aircraft would obtain more benefit from raising the fully depressed flaps before the undercarriage, although the resultant loss of height must then be considered. No fixed procedure can be laid down for all aircraft and the Owner's/Flight/Operating manual for the type should be consulted.

With the live engine at maximum power and the flaps and undercarriage up the aircraft should now be re-trimmed at its best single-engine climbing speed (blue-line speed) and power reduced on the live engine as soon as possible to the recommended setting for single-engine climbing.

Practising Asymmetric Landing and Overshoot Procedures

As a safety precaution during training it has become the practice **not** to stop and feather one engine below a safe height (3,000 AGL is typical for a light trim), similar conditions being achieved by setting the 'dead' engine to produce **Zero Thrust**. Realistic handling characteristics result from this procedure which has the advantage that power remains available should it be required for any reason during training. Zero thrust power setting is shown in the Owner's/Flight/Operating manual but it may be found as follows –

1. At a safe height stop the required engine, feather and trim out all rudder load.

2. Re-start the engine, set cruising pitch and with the wings level and feet off the rudder adjust the throttle on the 'dead' engine so that the aircraft maintains heading on the previously set rudder trim. The engine is now at zero thrust.

Asymmetric-power Stalls

At the stall certain twin-engined aircraft are sensitive to yaw, and the ensuing recovery, often from an extreme attitude, may involve considerable loss of height and subject the aircraft to stresses beyond the designed limits for the type. It is therefore **23** recommended that the stall with asymmetric power should not be practised by the student or demonstrated by the flying instructor.

Conclusions

With the considerable progress made in the asymmetric-power performance of modern twin and multi-engined aircraft, much of the hazard associated with engine failure has disappeared. Turbojets have still further improved the situation because, not only is slipstream effect removed and torque reaction reduced by the absence of propellers, but their non-existence makes it possible to install the engines so that their thrust lines are close to the fore and aft axis of the aircraft, so minimizing the yaw produced by asymmetric power when an engine fails.

These improvements do not detract from the importance of knowing the limitations of the aircraft and keeping in practice with different engines out of action under various conditions of flight.

The pilot who is sure of this aspect of flying – and it is a very interesting one – will be able to act coolly in an emergency and take the correct actions which will safeguard his passengers and prevent damage to the aircraft.

Handling of Large Multi-engined Aircraft and the 'V' Code

Flown by the pilot only, or fully loaded, the handling characteristics of light twin-engined aircraft remain little changed. There are, however, additional considerations applicable to medium and large transport aircraft which because of their payload/range potential and the wide variety of operating conditions they are likely to encounter can handle very differently from one flight to another, particularly in so far as take-off performance is concerned.

For example a multi-jet aircraft may take-off partly loaded from London Airport and have the benefit of a 3,600-metre runway. London Airport is on average only 77 ft AMSL and in, for example, April, the mean daily temperature would not usually exceed +13°C. At a later stage of the flight the same aircraft may have to take-off with a full load from an African airport, 7,000 ft AMSL at a time when the outside air temperature is +43°C.

To cater for these widely differing requirements a section of the aircraft flight manual is devoted to take-off performance. Taking into account runway length, airfield height AMSL outside air temperature gradient and the loaded weight of the aircraft, from a series of graphs are found three speeds of vital importance to the safe operation of the aircraft during take-off –

1. The speed at which it must be decided whether or not to continue the take-off (beyond this speed the aircraft cannot be stopped without over-running the runway).
2. The speed at which to **Rotate** (Lift off).
3. The safety speed for the initial climb out.

It is the practice to write these speeds on an *aide memoire* affixed in a prominent position on the instrument panel or they may be set with 'bugs' (markers) provided for the purpose on the ASI. So that the Captain may concentrate on controlling the aircraft during take-off the First Officer assists by calling out when each pre-calculated airspeed is attained.

For convenience these and other significant velocities have been incorporated into the 'V' code. The complete code is given in CAA Airworthiness Division, British Civil Airworthiness Regulations and while many of the velocities quoted refer to design requirements some are of importance to the pilot. The three examples already explained are known as V_1, V_R, and V_2. Some other examples are as follows –

V_{MCG}	The Minimum Control Speed, Ground.
V_{MCA}	The Minimum Control Speed, Airborne.
V_{MCL}	The Minimum Control Speed, Landing.
V_{NE}	The Never Exceed Speed.
V_{NO}	The Normal Operating Speed.
V_F	The Design Flap Limiting Speed

Flight Practice

COCKPIT CHECKS

As applicable for the exercise being demonstrated. A check list is normally used for multi-engine aircraft.

OUTSIDE CHECKS

Altitude: sufficient for the demonstration.
Location: not over other aircraft or towns or in controlled airspace.
Position: check in relation to a known landmark.

Air Exercise, Part I

The following exercises from the single-engine syllabus should be demonstrated, stressing handling differences as they apply to a multi-engine aircraft –

1, 1E, 2, 4, 5, 5E, 6, 7, 8, 9, 10, 12, 13, 13E, 15 and 19

Taxying (twin-engined aircraft) is explained in Chapter 5, page 87 of this volume.

Air Exercise, Part II

Applicable to aircraft not certified in Performance Group 'A', i.e. light multi-piston-engine aircraft under 5,700 kg (or 12,500 lb).

1. Flying on Asymmetric Power

a) The aircraft is now flying with an engine inoperative and the correct flight deck procedures have been completed. Notice that the aircraft is maintaining height although the cruising speed is lower than usual.
b) Now try some turns in both directions. The aircraft behaves normally during straight and level flight and throughout all gentle manoeuvres.

23

2. Effects and Recognition of Engine Failure in Level Flight

a)   The aircraft is now cruising on all engines. Trim the aircraft so that hands and feet may be removed from the controls.

b)   Close one throttle and make no attempt to correct the aircraft. A yaw will develop followed by bank towards the dead engine and the nose will drop, as though harsh rudder had been applied.

c)   Now close the other throttle and the yaw and roll will stop. Return to cruising flight.

d)   Repeat the exercise this time by closing the opposite throttle so that a yaw and roll occurs in the other direction.

3. Method of Control and Identifying the Failed Engine

a)   With the aircraft correctly trimmed in straight and level flight, close one throttle. Prevent the yaw by applying rudder towards the live engine.

b)   The aircraft will now maintain direction and lateral level. Additional power from the live engine may be required to maintain height.

c)   Confirm which engine has failed. 'Dead leg – dead engine'.

4. Engine Failure during Turns. Methods of Control

a)   With the aircraft trimmed for straight and level flight on all engines commence a medium turn.

b)   Without attempting to correct the aircraft close the throttle for the engine on the outside. The aircraft will attempt to roll out and go into a turn in the opposite direction.

c)   Return to a normal medium turn on all engines and again simulate failure of the engine on the outside. Prevent the aircraft rolling out of the turn by applying rudder towards the live engine.

d)   Now try failing the engine on the inside of a turn. Prevent the turn from tightening by applying rudder towards the live engine. Maintain the bank at the correct angle with aileron.

e)   If at any time during turns the aircraft becomes difficult to control, reduce power on the live engine.

23

5. Correct Use of Controls at Varying Speed and Power Conditions

a)   The aircraft is now cruising with an engine throttled back. Trim the aircraft so that to correct yaw no pressure is required on the rudder.

b)   Now increase power on the live engine. Notice that more rudder is required to correct yaw. Should the rudder trim be insufficient to remove all foot loads, bank the aircraft gently towards the live engine. Too much bank will cause a sideslip, and loss of height.

c)   Reduce power on the live engine. Notice that less rudder is required to counteract yaw.

d)   Now increase the airspeed in a gentle dive, when the rudder will become more effective. Reduce power as for a high-speed descent and note that engine failure is difficult to recognize.

6. Establishing Minimum Control Speed

a)   Close one throttle and keep straight with rudder. Now open up to full power on the live engine correcting the yaw with further rudder pressure.

b)   Gradually raise the nose while holding neutral the ailerons and as the airspeed decreases more rudder will be needed to prevent yaw. Continue raising the nose until, in an effort to keep straight, full rudder has been applied. The aircraft is now at minimum control speed for these conditions.

c)   Now raise the nose still further when even full rudder will fail to maintain direction. A yaw and a roll will result followed by a spiral dive.

d)   To recover, either reduce power on the live engine or increase speed until the rudder becomes more effective.

e)   Now find the minimum control speed while flying with a different failed engine. The speed will alter because of slipstream and torque effect.

f)   Note the effect of feathering (at a safe height, otherwise use zero thrust) on minimum control speed.

7. 'In Flight' Engine Failure Procedure

Close the throttle on one engine to simulate engine failure. Carry out the immediate actions – PAID OFF.

a)   **Prevent** yaw with rudder and if necessary maintain lateral level with aileron.

23

b)   **Attain** recommended engine-out-speed.

c)   **Identify** the failed engine. 'Dead leg – dead engine'.

d)   **Decide** whether or not to feather. If mechanical failure is obvious feather without delay. If not –

e)   **Open** up power on the live engine as required for engine-out flight.

f)   **Find** the cause of engine failure.

       Check – ignition
              fuel contents
              fuel pressure
              carburettor heat
              mixture control 'rich'.

Try another tank and switch on the electric fuel pump. Close the throttle and slowly re-open. If the engine will not re-start, turn off ignition and fuel, operate the idle cut off and –

g)   **Feather** the propeller on the failed engine.

Now complete the subsequent actions – STAR.

h)   **Safeguard** instruments and electrics. Select another vacuum source (if applicable). If the generator on the live engine is unable to meet demands switch off all unnecessary electric load.

i)   **Tanks** selected for asymmetric flight (as required).

j)   **Airframe.** Clean up and reduce drag. Check: Undercarriage and flaps up. Gills closed, windows closed. Retrim.

k)   **Revise** the flight plan. Choose a suitable cruising altitude according to circumstances. Watch the temperature and oil pressure on the live engine. Inform Air Traffic Control of the changed flight condition.

Engine Fire Drill in the Air

a)   Imagine a fire has occurred in the air. Close the throttle of the affected engine.

b)   Turn off the fuel to the burning engine.

c)   Feather the propeller (select minimum RPM when the propeller is of the non-feathering type).

d)   When the engine has stopped turning (or nearly stopped in the case of non-feathering propellers) switch the ignition off.

e)   Operate the fire extinguisher.

f)   Do not attempt to restart the engine when the fire has stopped.

g)   Complete the Subsequent Actions.

23   *h*)   Revise the flight plan and advise Air Traffic Control.

8. Effects on Performance

a) With one engine throttled back and the live engine adjusted to maintain height, trim the aircraft in straight and level flight.

b) Lower the undercarriage. Notice that as the airspeed decreases more rudder is required to keep straight. The aircraft is now sinking and additional power is required from the live engine to maintain height. As the throttle is opened keep straight by applying still more rudder.

c) Lower part flap. As the airspeed decreases still further more rudder must be applied to prevent yaw. Continue lowering flap in stages and prevent a loss of height by adding more power. Repeat the exercise at maximum power with full flap and undercarriage down. This is minimum control speed, landing.

d) Feather the dead engine (at a safe height) and the minimum control speed for any condition will be lower than before because of reduced asymmetric drag.

9. Engine Failure During and After Take-off

Below Minimum Control Speed

a) Climb to a safe height, lower the undercarriage, select take-off flap and continue climbing below minimum control speed.

b) At full take-off power fail one engine. Direction cannot be maintained.

c) Reduce power on the live engine until rudder control is regained. The aircraft now loses height.

This demonstration illustrates the importance of accelerating past minimum control speed before take-off.

Above Safety Speed

(*Note. Provided the aircraft is of a type known to climb well on asymmetric power the following sequence may be demonstrated after take-off when safety speed has been attained. When the 'engine out' performance is marginal the demonstration should be conducted at a safe height.*)

a) Take-off in the usual way, accelerate above safety speed then fail one engine. (Simulate by closing the throttle.)

b) Check the yaw with rudder and lower the nose to maintain speed.

c) Raise the undercarriage.

d) Feather the dead engine (zero thrust).

23

e) Apply rudder trim.

f) Adopt the 'blue line' speed and re-trim.

g) If the performance of the aircraft allows, reduce power on the live engine.

h) Position the aircraft for a landing with asymmetric power. While flying around the circuit try to establish the cause of failure and remedy if possible. Check temperatures and pressures on the live engine.

10. Circuit, Approach and Landing (Asymmetric)

a) Aim to complete a normal circuit. When the asymmetric performance of the aircraft is marginal, delay lowering the undercarriage to a later than usual stage of the circuit.

b) Keep above 'blue line' speed throughout the circuit.

c) On the downwind leg complete the usual vital actions. Check temperatures on the live engine.

d) Turn on to the base leg and plan a rather steeper than usual engine-assisted approach.

e) Turn on to the approach and after decision height lower more flap as required. Control the rate of descent on the live engine maintaining a slightly higher than usual approach speed during the early stages.

f) As the airfield boundary is approached gradually reduce power and speed. Lower full flap and carry out a normal landing.

11. Going Round Again on Asymmetric Power (Missed Approach)

(*Note. This exercise should be demonstrated at a safe height in the first instance when repeat demonstrations can occur on the approach. The minimum height for these subsequent demonstrations will be dependent upon the asymmetric performance of the aircraft type.*)

a) The aircraft is now descending with flaps and undercarriage down and one engine feathered (zero thrust).

b) Before decision height overshoot. Maintain safety speed, if necessary by depressing the nose.

c) Apply full power on the live engine. Use the rudder trim to assist in preventing yaw.

d) Raise the undercarriage and flaps (the order will depend upon the type of aircraft).

23

e) Concentrate upon maintaining 'blue line' speed even if this entails some loss of height.

f) If the climbing performance allows reduce power on the live engine.

12. Asymmetric-powered Medium and Steep Turns

a) With an engine stopped and feathered, trim the aircraft to fly at best asymmetric speed so that no control load exists on the rudder pedals.

b) The slip needle is now in the centre and turns in either direction may be made and completed in the usual manner.

Aircraft with Inadequate Rudder Trim

c) When it is not possible to trim out all loads on the rudder pedals additional pressure is needed to turn with the live engine inside. Notice that the aircraft tends to roll out of the turn and both aileron and rudder pressure must be maintained.

d) To come out of the turn relax both rudder and aileron pressure which must be re-applied to maintain straight and level flight when the turn is completed.

e) Now turn with the live engine on the outside. Maintain the rudder pressure towards the live engine but allow the aircraft to take up the correct angle of bank for the turn. Notice the tendency for the bank to increase. Prevent the nose dropping below the horizon and maintain the slip needle in the centre.

f) To come out of the turn apply firm aileron and rudder pressure until the wings are level when control pressure may be relaxed sufficiently to continue asymmetric flight.

g) Now practise turning, progressively increasing the angle of bank until height can no longer be maintained.

11 Flying Instructors' Ratings

The art of teaching others to fly must rank high amongst the many branches of aviation. The requirements which go to make a successful flying instructor are exacting and varied, but before delving into these qualification it is of benefit to know a little of the history of flying instruction since this has a very considerable influence on present-day procedure.

Since pre-World War I days, when flying training was on an *ad hoc* basis, the development of flying instruction has often been spearheaded by the air forces of the world. For example, the Central Flying School at Upavon was founded by the British Navy and Army as early as May 1912, but effective flying training did not really start until 1916 when, as a result of his letter complaining about the young ill-trained pilots that were sent to him on the Western Front, Lt. Smith-Barry was brought back to form No. 1 Reserve Squadron at Gosport. Here was developed the first 'patter' system of instruction using speaking tubes (known as Gosport Tubes to this day). Modern flying instruction throughout the world is based upon the Smith-Barry concept. In those days the various flying exercises and demonstrations were to a large extent handed down by word of mouth from one flying instructor to another, or at best passed on by typewritten sheets. At a later stage an Instructor's Manual was produced.

During the 1939–45 war pilot-training demands were such that many flying instructors had to be provided in excess of peace-time requirements. Realizing the necessity for standardization it was decided to call together a body of senior flying instructors from countries within the British Commonwealth and the various Allied Air Forces. Around this wealth of experience was formed at RAF Station, Hullavington, the Empire Central Flying School. This unit proceeded to re-write the existing flying instructor's manual in a form which would give guidance to the flying instructor yet allow scope for his own personality – a factor of great importance in instructor/pupil relationship. The work emerged in two parts, AP 1732a, *Elementary Flying Training* and AP 1732b, *Advanced Flying Training*. Both books were to become world-famous and could be found as the standard work of reference in many foreign Air Forces. These works continued in RAF use until 1949, when the Empire Central Flying School completed their last work before disbanding. This volume, AP 3225, replaced both 1732a and 1732b in so far as the RAF is concerned.

Civil Flying Instruction

Throughout the period traced in the foregoing paragraphs, Civil Flying Schools and Clubs were largely staffed by ex-RAF or other Service pilots so it is not surprising to find that Service methods have prevailed almost exclusively.

Until recent times both Service and Civil pilots received their *ab initio* training in similar or identical light aircraft so that AP 1732a was an ideal training manual for the guidance of Civil flying instruction. This book is now out of print and the replacement AP 3225 has been written with the Service pilot very much in mind. Modern RAF training is jet orientated and in consequence there has existed an urgent need for a Civil training manual. *Flight Briefing for Pilots*, Vols. 1, 2, 3 and 4, were written to meet this need. These books differ from the RAF works in that they are designed for pupil reading in addition to their function as an instructor's work of reference.

Unless his licence carries a valid instructor's rating, no pilot however experienced may give flying lessons, or courses for the purpose of gaining a pilot's licence or rating of any kind. As licensing authority the UK Civil Aviation Authority will only endorse a pilot's licence provided proof of competency to instruct is forthcoming. Following what is common practice amongst professions, the qualifying authority is vested in a body representative of the particular profession. Candidates for the flying instructor's rating are examined by the Panel of Examiners, a body appointed by the UK Civil Aviation Authority. It is in fact a committee of very experienced flying instructors with instructional experience covering helicopters, light aircraft and all types of piston and gas-turbine multi-engined types. The Panel of Examiners meets at regular intervals under its Chairman and frames recommendations governing all aspects of flying instruction. A senior officer from the RAF Central Flying School is included in the committee and representatives from the Civil Aviation Authority attend the meetings. The members of the Panel are situated geographically so that tests can be arranged within reasonable flying distance from the home airfield.

Aimed at making full use of the comprehensive accident statistics filed by the Civil Aviation Authority a small working party of the Panel known as the Flying Training Safety Committee meets at intervals to study in depth those categories of accidents that may be the result of poor training. Safety Directives are produced for the guidance of panel members and those instructors approved for the training of future flying instructors.

Two qualifications exist and these are known as the **Assistant Instructor's Rating** and the **Instructor's Rating**. Broadly speaking a pilot without previous Service instructional experience is required to undergo a flying instructor's course which consists of a minimum of twenty-five hours flying of which twenty hours are with the instructor and five are flown with another pupil instructor in mutual practice. The candidate for an assistant rating must have a minimum flying experience of 150 hours in command of an aircraft and usually a total of ten hours night flying (dual and solo) is required. Course requirements are listed at the end of this chapter.

A flying instructor's course may only be given by certain approved instructors at designated schools and candidates are advised to ensure that they are in the hands of one so approved.

The assistant instructor must teach under the supervision of a fully rated instructor and he may not send a pupil on his first solo flight or first solo cross-country. After he has completed a minimum of 200 instructional hours the assistant instructor may apply for upgrading to the instructor's rating provided he has been instructing for at least six months and subject to a minimum of 400 hours as pilot in command of an aircraft. There are separate night, instrument, multi-engine and aerobatic endorsements.

The standards for the instructor's rating are naturally higher than those expected for an assistant rating, both in flying and knowledge of ground subjects. In each case the test is carried out by a member of the Panel of Examiners and takes the form of an oral examination and a flying test. During the oral examination the candidate is expected to demonstrate his knowledge of all ground subjects. At the same time his ability to explain clearly is assessed. The air test usually occupies one hour or a little more. The candidate must be able to demonstrate the various exercises and adhere to a standard procedure in his instruction which may be based upon the 'air exercise' sections in this book and Vol. 1. It is not intended that the 'patter' should be learned and repeated parrot fashion to the pupil. Rather the wording of the various demonstrations is meant to provide a basis upon which the flying instructor may develop his own descriptions.

The Flying Instructor

Not all pilots are able to instruct with success and it is perhaps opportune at this stage to mention some of the factors which contribute to the making of a flying instructor. His flying must be above average and, for the full rating, rather exceptional. Furthermore he must be able to maintain these standards while his attention is focused upon the pupil. Student pilots are often mystified by their instructor's ability to land perfectly while engaged in conversation. The flying instructor must be able to synchronize his 'patter' with the behaviour of the aeroplane so that, for example, when he tells the pupil that the aircraft 'sinks to the ground on the main wheels' touchdown occurs on the word 'wheels'. There are some who may argue that such perfect timing is not essential but it cannot be denied that from the pupil's point of view a demonstration accompanied by well-synchronized patter is very convincing.

The instructor must be prepared to allow his pupil to make mistakes and his own corrections. Only experience will teach the instructor how far he may allow the pupil to go before he must intervene. This in itself is insufficient and a flying instructor must be able to analyse his pupil's faults and make his explanations both clear and simple. It is important that the various ground subjects are fully understood. Nothing is more calculated to destroy confidence than the instructor who repeatedly fails to answer his pupil's questions on the ground.

Patience must be high on the list of attributes for a flying instructor. Not all pupils respond to instruction in the same manner and since rate of learning may be related to various indirect influences such as apprehension, over-confidence, degree of intelligence, etc., the flying instructor must be something of a psychologist or at least have an enlightened approach to the problem of human relations. The instructor's personality can have a very considerable influence on this very important aspect of flying training and clearly a sense of humour is an advantage.

The average light aeroplane is anything but an ideal classroom. The noise level is often high and standards of comfort may be low so that the pupil experiences difficulty in hearing what is said and his inability to relax may make concentration difficult. Both these shortcomings have been considerably improved in some modern aircraft and they are the subject of constant attention by designers and manufacturers on both sides of the Atlantic.

The value of Pre-Flight Briefing cannot be overstressed. The pupil who is aware of the object of each lesson before flight together with a clear explanation of the principles behind each exercise will most certainly learn more quickly than the student who is rushed into the air without preamble. The descriptive part of each chapter, which precedes the flight practice sections in this book and Vol. 1 is intended to provide a basis for the 'Long Briefing', the Pre-Flight Briefing being confined to 'what we are about to do and how we shall do it'.

The detailed requirements for Flying Instructors' Ratings

may be obtained from the Panel Secretary.

Ground and Flying Instruction required for the various Instructor's Courses

	GROUND		FLYING		TOTALS	
	Technical	Briefings	Dual	Mutual	Ground	Flying
Assistant Instructor	20	30	20	5	50	25
Instrument Flying (basic)	9	5	7	nil	14	7
Night Flying	nil	5	3	nil	5	3
Aerobatics	3	5	5	nil	8	5
Multi-engine Conversion	5	10	7*	nil	15	7

* 3 hrs normal flight and 4 hrs asymmetric.

(Figures are minimum and may be exceeded at the discretion of the FIC Instructor)

Civil pilots without a professional licence are required to pass a pre-entry examination to assess if their present standard will allow them to take advantage of FIC training. Training hours for the technical subjects and briefings may be varied according to the knowledge of the student instructor. The details given herewith apply to the UK only, each country having its own arrangements for the training and testing of flying instructors.

12 The IMC Rating

Prior to 1970 private pilots were permitted to fly in IMC (Instrument Meteorological Conditions) without formal instrument flying training and were granted Special VER clearances to fly in controlled airspace, although the air traffic services had no knowledge of the ability of the pilot to fly in weather conditions which often demanded above average instrument and navigational proficiency.

It became clear that some form of basic instrument flying skill was necessary not only to meet the Special VER case but, more particularly, to safeguard the pilot flying in marginal weather conditions, or in the event of his being committed to fly solely by reference to instruments. Too often the inability to maintain control in these circumstances was reflected in weather-related accident statistics.

The rapid development of aviation and considerable extensions of controlled airspace, matched by larger numbers of light aircraft equipped with full instrument flying facilities, created a situation where the limiting factor was the pilot's ability to use the aircraft and its equipment in a way that did not endanger other pilots and their passengers or other users of airspace.

From these considerations the IMC rating was formulated in its original form. It was a qualification quite distinct from the acquisition of a private pilot's licence and it required some basic instrument flying training and also the flying of a VDF let-down procedure, not always readily available at many airfields and requiring more skill than many other procedures. Moreover the original rating had little relevance as a stepping stone to the full instrument rating.

Over a number of years it became apparent that instrument flying must be an integral part of the syllabus for obtaining a PPL and that the standards of experience, skill and technical knowledge should be more closely related to flight under instrument meteorological conditions.

In 1981 new comprehensive regulations were introduced for a revised IMC rating and these are described in detail in *Flight Briefing for Pilots*, Volume 7 (*The IMC Rating Manual*), together with the subject matter necessary to qualify for the rating.

In its new form the regulation requires the applicant –

(*a*) to have the relevant flying experience;
(*b*) to demonstrate his/her competence assessed by a flying test;
(*c*) to pass a written technical examination.

The IMC rating is relevant only within the UK. Other countries have no such qualification at present.

Qualifying Experience

The requirements for obtaining an IMC rating are listed in CAP.53 but before an applicant may qualify he/she must –

(*a*) have completed 25 hours as pilot subsequent to qualifying for a PPL;
(*b*) have completed 10 hours as pilot in command, 5 of which must be point to point navigation;
(*c*) have completed a course of 15 hours dual instrument flying training to a CAA approved syllabus;
(*d*) be in possession of an R/T licence.

Certain variations may be permitted, including applicants holding night ratings, and some part (normally 5 hours) of the instrument flying instruction may be undertaken in a simulator.

Flying Training Syllabus for the IMC Rating (Basic and Applied) *Full Panel*

1. *Instrument Flight – Attitude*
    (*a*) Pitch Indications
    (*b*) Bank and Direction Indications
    (*c*) Effect of Power Variations and Aircraft Configuration
    (*d*) Instrument Limitations
    (*e*) Selective Radial Scan

2. *Basic Flight Manoeuvres*
    (*a*) Straight and Level Flight in Various Configurations
    (*b*) Climbing and Descending
    (*c*) Turns Level, Climbing and Descending, Compass Timed
    (*d*) Transfer to Instruments after Take-off
    (*e*) Recovery from Unusual Attitudes

3. *Limited Panel*
    (*a*) Simulated loss of Pitot/Static Pressures
    (*b*) Maintaining Altitude and Airspeed
    (*c*) Straight and Level Flight
    (*d*) Turns

4. *Pre-flight Planning*
    (*a*) Published Procedures (*UK Air Pilot*)
    (*b*) Aerodrome Operating Minima

5. *Departure and En-route*
    (*a*) Aircraft Equipment and Serviceability Checks
    (*b*) Communications and Liaison with ATC
    (*c*) Selection Operation and Use of Radio Navigational Aids
        (i) VOR
        (ii) ADF
        (iii) VHF (QDM, QDR, QTE)
    (*d*) Use of Radar Services
    (*e*) Interception, Maintaining Track and use of Bearings/Radials for Tracking and Establishing Position
    (*f*) Holding Procedures

6. *Approach and Let-down*
   (a) Use of Approach Charts
   (b) Calculation of Decision Height (Related to IMC Rated Pilots)
   (c) Holding Procedures
   (d) Flying the Vertical and Horizontal Procedures
   (e) Overshoot and Missed Approach Procedures
   (f) Training on at least two of the following aids, one of which must be pilot interpreted:
   VOR, ADF, ILS, VDF, QGH, Radar
   (the last two being considered ATC interpreted)

7. *Bad Weather Circuits and Landings*
   (a) Low Cloud – Good Visibility
   (b) Low Cloud – Poor Visibility

The Flight Test

The flight test will normally take approximately 1 hour 30 minutes and the candidate will be briefed by the examiner as to the form and scope of the test, selection of navigational let-down aid(s) and will be given adequate time for the briefing (met. flight planning) and the essential pre-flight inspection of the aircraft.

The candidate will be tested on his/her instrument flying proficiency including position finding by use of VOR or ADF and will be required to maintain track for at least 10 minutes using a pilot interpreted aid.

The test will conclude with a let-down procedure using one of the following pilot interpreted aids –

VOR, ADF, ILS, VDF

during which the candidate will be required to descend to the Calculated Decision Height before initiating the missed approach procedure and then fly a bad weather circuit and landing as directed by the examiner. The candidate will be expected to fly to the following tolerances, due allowance being made for turbulent conditions:

	Normal Flight	Limited Panel Flight	Asymmetric Flight
Height:			
1. In level flight	±100 ft	±200 ft	±200 ft
2. For initiating overshoot procedure from Decision Height	−0 ft +50 ft	N/A	N/A
Tracking on Radio Aids	±5 degrees on VOR ±10 degrees on ADF	N/A	N/A
Heading	±10 degrees	±15 degrees	±10 degrees
Speed	±10 knots	+20 −10 knots	±10 knots
	BUT NOT BELOW THRESHOLD SPEED		
ILS Approach	½-scale deflection on localizer and glidepath		

Ground Training Syllabus

The applicant for an IMC rating must be aware of the special considerations that apply to instrument flying once outside visual references are removed. Apart from the ability to control the aircraft solely by reference to instruments, other factors assume a new importance. These include –

(i) The safeguard of aircraft instruments, airframe and engine from the effects of icing.

(ii) Knowledge of radio aids and their practical appreciation for navigation and let-down.

(iii) Terrain clearance and the altimeter setting procedures.

(iv) Aerodrome operating minima and calculation of decision heights.
(v) Flight planning, selection of aids and alternates.
(vi) Meteorological considerations.

The course of training is designed to provide a greater depth of knowledge than is required for the acquisition of a PPL and to interrelate the considerations listed above. Candidates will be examined in the following subjects –

1. *Physiological Factors*
   (*a*) The Senses
   (*b*) Spatial Disorientation
   (*c*) Sensory Illusions

2. *Flight Instruments*
   (*a*) ASI, Altimeter, Compass, Directional Indicator, Turn and Slip Indicator
   (*b*) Principles of Operation
   (*c*) Pre-flight and In-flight Serviceability Checks
   (*d*) Errors and Limitations
   (*e*) System Failures

3. *Aeronautical Information Publications*
   (*a*) The *UK Air Pilot*
   (*b*) NOTAMs Class 1 and 2

4. *Rules of the Air and Air Traffic Services* (RAC Section of *The Air Pilot*)
   (*a*) Visual and Instrument Flight Rules
   (*b*) Flight Plans and Air Traffic Service Messages
   (*c*) Use of Radar and Air Traffic Services
   (*d*) Radio Failure
   (*e*) Special Rules Zones and Special Rules Areas and Special VFR
   (*f*) Controlled and Advisory Airspace
   (*g*) Holding and Approach to Land and Missed Approach Procedures

Communications
> Types of Services
> Use of Data

Aeronautical Charts
(*a*) Availability, Amendments
(*b*) Topographical, Instrument Approach and Landing

Flight Planning
> Preparation of the Flight Plan
> Selection of Routes, Levels and Radio Aids and alternates
> Factors affecting Aircraft and Engine Performance

Meteorological Information
> Services Available
> Weather Forecasts, Route Forecasts, TAFs, METARs, SIGMET

Altimeter
(*a*) Transition Altitude, Transition Level, Flight Level, QNH, QFE Standard Setting, Regional QNH
(*b*) Altimeter Setting Procedures

Terrain Clearance
> Selection of Minimum Safe Altitude
> Aerodrome Minimum Sector Altitude
> Obstacle Clearance Limitations
> Calculation of Decision Heights

Selection and Use of Radio Aids
(*a*) VOR, ADF, VDF, DME, ILS, Radar, Transponder
(*b*) Principles of Operation
(*c*) Range, Accuracy and Limitations
(*d*) Identification, Selection, Operation and Use of Navigational Aids
(*e*) Radar Approach Procedures

Privileges of the IMC Rating

The IMC Rating is an instrument qualification giving certain privileges not available to the holder of the PPL alone. The privileges relate to solo and passenger-carrying flights outside controlled airspace and to special VFR flights within Control Zones. Under the following flight conditions the privileges may be summarized and compared:

Flight Condition (*a*) – When flying solo outside controlled airspace.

Flight Condition (*b*) – When carrying passengers outside controlled airspace.

Flight Condition (*c*) – When flying within Control Zones.

IMC Pilots	*Non-IMC Pilots*
(*a*) No limits	Min. Flight Visibility 1½ n.m.
(*b*) No limits	Above 3000 ft in VMC only Below 3000 ft min. flight visibility 3 n.m.
(*c*) Special VFR clearance with min. flight visibility 1½ n.m.	Special VFR clearance, min. flight visibility of 5 n.m. except certain entry/exit routes to certain airfields

Recommended Aerodrome Operating Minima

No minimum cloud base is imposed by the regulations; pilots are expected to observe the Aerodrome Operating Minima for non-public transport aircraft detailed in the *UK Air Pilot* which relates primarily to pilots holding a full Instrument Rating. Consequently, proper allowance should be made by IMC rated pilots to *ensure that safety margins are increased*.

Exemptions

Private pilots who have held a civil or military instrument rating in the past 10 years and whose licence is current and contains a valid certificate of test or experience will be exempt from the examination, and pilots with 500 hours experience including 10 hours dual instrument flying and in current flying practice will also be exempt from the examination. Certain other exemptions are admissible, e.g. pilots holding a night rating may be granted a reduction in the amount of dual instrument flying; further details are listed in CAP.53.

From time to time amendments to the requirements for the IMC rating may be made, these will be notified through the Aeronautical Information Circular and/or NOTAMs.

Recommended Reading

Flight Briefing for Pilots Volume 7 – *The IMC Rating*.
Flight Briefing for Pilots Volume 8 – *The Instrument Rating*.
Radio Aids for Pilots (Airtour International).
Aeromedicine for Aviators (Read).
IMC Rating Syllabus (BLS Aviation, Elstree Aerodrome).
UK Air Pilot.
Aeronautical Information Circulars.
NOTAMs
CAP Publications 53, 85, 413.